BY THE MOTH

50 True Stories

All These Wonders

Occasional Magic

How to Tell a Story

HOW
TO TELL
A STORY

THE ESSENTIAL GUIDE

TO MEMORABLE STORYTELLING

FROM THE MOTH

HOW

TO TELL

A STORY

MEG BOWLES, CATHERINE BURNS,
JENIFER HIXSON, SARAH AUSTIN JENNESS,
AND KATE TELLERS

CROWN

NEW YORK

Published in the United States by Crown, an imprint of Random House,
a division of Penguin Random House LLC, New York.

CROWN and the CROWN colophon are registered trademarks of
Penguin Random House LLC.

LIBRARY OF CONGRESS CATALOGING-IN-PUBLICATION DATA
Names: Bowles, Meg, author. | Burns, Catherine, author. |
Hixson, Jenifer, author.
Title: How to tell a story / Meg Bowles, Catherine Burns, Jenifer Hixson,
Sarah Austin Jenness, and Kate Tellers ; foreword by Padma Lakshmi ;
introduction by Chenjerai Kumanyika.
Other titles: Moth radio hour (Radio program)
Description: New York : Crown, [2022] | Includes index.
Identifiers: LCCN 2021060351 (print) | LCCN 2021060352 (ebook) |
ISBN 9780593139004 (hardcover) | ISBN 9780593139011 (ebook)
Subjects: LCSH: Storytelling.
Classification: LCC PN4193.I5 H69 2022 (print) | LCC PN4193.I5 (ebook) |
DDC 808.5/43—dc23/eng/20220210
LC record available at https://lccn.loc.gov/2021060351
LC ebook record available at https://lccn.loc.gov/2021060352

PRINTED IN THE UNITED STATES OF AMERICA ON ACID-FREE PAPER

crownpublishing.com

2 4 6 8 9 7 5 3

Title-page and opening art for parts 1–3: Thomas Horsfield and Frederic Moore,
catalogue of the lepidopterous insects in Museum of Natural History
at the East-India House (caterpillar and chrysalis); C. Schach, from
Lorenz Oken's Universal Natural History/Florilegius (Alamy) (moth)
Opening art for part 4: Adobe Stock, including images by novac, Zbyszek Nowak,
Pakhnyushchyy, Alexey Protasov, Roman, Marco Uliana, and yod67

TO THE UNDISCOVERED STORIES
IN ALL OF US

CONTRIBUTORS, IN WORD AND SPIRIT

Suzie Afridi, Peter Aguero, Ali Al Abdullatif, Jenny Allen, Jay Allison, Maureen Amakabane, Jonathan Ames, Jackie Andrews, Maurice Ashley, Neema Avashia, Dr. Kodi Azari, Luna Azcurrain, Alistair Bane, Carl Banks, Erin Barker, Sara Barron, Tim Bartlett, Janice Bartley, Ishmael Beah, Kiri Bear, Jon Bennett, Amy Biancolli, Mike Birbiglia, Jennifer Birmingham, Hector Black, Micaela Blei, Nadia Bolz-Weber, Dori Samadzai Bonner, Phyllis Bowdwin, Barbara Collins Bowie, Kate Braestrup, James Braly, Phill Branch, Josh Broder, Bliss Broyard, Joan Juliet Buck, Wanda Bullard, Tricia Rose Burt, Sheila Calloway, Rosanne Cash, Shannon Cason, Moran Cerf, Ray Christian, Andy Christie, Maggie Cino, Tara Clancy, François Clemmons, Trisha Mitchell Coburn, Jacoby Cochran, Andrea King Collier, Max García Conover, Ruby Cooper, Emily Couch, Travis Coxson, June Cross, Jeni De La O, Mike DeStefano, Matthew Dicks, Mary Domo, Simon Doonan, Hannah Drake, Karen Duffin, Damien Echols, Ophira Eisenberg, Nathan Englander, Melvin Estrella, Jamie F., Quratulain Fatima, Lynn Ferguson, Brian Finkelstein, Michael Fischer, Dion Flynn, Terrance Flynn, Neshama Franklin, Neil Gaiman, Ed Gavagan, Marvin Gelfand, Elizabeth Gilbert, Morgan Givens, Frimet Goldberger, Nestor Gomez, Jon Goode, Adam Gopnik, George Dawes Green, Anthony

Griffith, Dr. Sybil Jordan Hampton, Ari Handel, Rick Hauck, Jerald Hayes, Flora Hogman, CJ Hunt, Dante Jackson, Michelle Jalowski, Samuel James, Journey Jamison, Mmaki Jantjies, Jeremy Jennings, Sivad Johnson, Carly Johnstone, Mark Katz, Cole Kazdin, Aleeza Kazmi, Dan Kennedy, Dr. Mary-Claire King, Tim King, Marina Klutse, Ed Koch, Alexandra Krotinger, Abeny Kucha, Chenjerai Kumanyika, Alfonso Lacayo, Padma Lakshmi, Faye Lane, Ellie Lee, Jen Lee, Shaun Leonardo, David Lepelstat, Victor Levenstein, David Litt, Dr. George Lombardi, Nancy Mahl, Cheech Marin, Jay Martel, Bina Maseno, Michael Massimino, Christian McBride, Catherine McCarthy, Darryl "DMC" McDaniels, Megan McNally, Leland Melvin, Hasan Minhaj, Monte Montepare, David Montgomery, Talaya Moore, Hannah Morris, Abbas Mousa, Sisonke Msimang, Aimee Mullins, Michaela Murphy, Michelle Murphy, Sarah Lee Nakintu, Sister Mary Navarre, Taylor Negron, Esther Ngumbi, Tig Notaro, Kendi Ntwiga, Edgar Oliver, Adelle Onyango, Nkem Osian, Aaron Pang, Dylan Park, Carl Pillitteri, Wang Ping, Jodi Powell, Sherman "O.T." Powell, Kemp Powers, Peter Pringle, Alan Rabinowitz, Anoid Latipovna Rakhmatyllaeva, Ashok Ramasubramanian, Isabelle Raphael, Kim Reed, Tomi Reichental, Cynthia Riggs, Boots Riley, Noreen Riols, Bill Robinson, Trina Michelle Robinson, John Elder Robison, Aisha Rodriguez, Suzi Ronson, Larry Rosen, Flash Rosenberg, Noriko Rosted, Martha Ruiz-Perilla, Suzanne Rust, Faith Salie, Chloe Salmon, Eva Santiago, Carol Seppilu, Vin Shambry, Saya Shamdasani, Gabrielle Shea, Nikesh Shukla, Lindiwe Majele Sibanda, Harjas Singh, Danyel Smith, Catherine Smyka, Andrew Solomon, Betty Reid Soskin, Judith Stone, Stephanie Summerville, Dr. Wendy Suzuki, Teller, R. Eric Thomas, Boris Timanovsky, Danusia Trevino, Jason Trieu, Kathleen Turner, Daniel Turpin, John Turturro, Sala Udin, Pegi Vail, Adam Wade, Diavian Walters, Sherry Weaver, Dame Wilburn, Jessica Lee Williamson, Carmen Rita Wong, Fatou Wurie, Joey Xanders, Musih Tedji Xaviere, Pamela Yates, Damon Young, Gloria Zhang

CONTENTS

FOREWORD

It was one of those unseasonably warm New York evenings. We were at Cooper Union, and it was my first Moth event. I had rehearsed several times with the other storytellers, including a comedian, a *New Yorker* magazine staff writer, and a firefighter. We were all there from our different walks of life to tell our stories. We were all in the same vulnerable boat. No notes, no memorization, nothing to paint with, except our memory, imagination, and courage.

I was terrified. I was in the middle of a story about the scar on my arm. It was so quiet. I could hear people in the first row of the auditorium breathing. Why the total silence? Why had I said yes to getting up in front of eight hundred human beings, who had paid good money, to lay myself bare and embarrass myself in this way?

I was there because I believe in the supreme power of storytelling. It's been the one through line in all my work. It's really the only superpower we humans have. *Think about it.* The cheetah is faster, the elephant stronger, the eagle can soar much higher than any Olympic pole vaulter. Storytelling is the best thing about being human. And I believe it can change the world. That's right. Stories can and do change the world.

I hope this book you are holding in your hands will help you believe it too.

The patient and professional story coaxers at The Moth know the power of storytelling. They assured me when I first met with them more than a decade ago that everyone has at least one story to tell. It's all in the way you tell it. You are encouraged to remember texture, detail, sense memory, and what you felt like when the story first took place. These exercises make you listen to yourself, and in doing so, they unlock the true power of storytelling.

And to understand each other better, we need a true diversity of stories, from a diversity of people. We need to hear, feel, and understand what it's like to walk in each other's shoes. This is what drove me to make my documentary series *Taste the Nation,* which is about immigrant and indigenous food and life in the United States. It was important to hear these stories from the people who actually lived them. Sharing their experiences on a mainstream platform helped viewers better understand their fellow Americans. The process of unearthing the stories left me with the belief that it's always possible to learn something new about the human condition.

Every time I hear a Moth story, I am reminded of this fact. For twenty-five years, The Moth has been uncovering the most compelling stories around us. It has brought so much listening pleasure as well as pathos to our ears. It has shown us, through real-life storytellers from all walks of life, what it means to be fully human.

Our stories tell us who we are, who we were, and who we hope to be. They're how we form our very identity. The stories we carry with us contain our lineage, hopes, dreams, and pain. They tell, too, of our anxieties about ourselves, the world, and our place in it. Stories are how we keep our collective history alive.

That night at Cooper Union, somewhere in the middle of struggling to find my way through the deafening silence, I knew that my story was about more than just the scar on my arm. The wonderful folks at The Moth had helped me trust myself, to believe in the value of my story in all its gory and glorious details. I needed to be brave. To be courageous enough to look at the truth of our lives through our remembered experience is to be changed by it.

My tale began with a car crash that led to the scar on my arm, but through my retelling that night, I realized it was about something much deeper than flesh. My story was about the often cruel and erratic nature of existence, losing faith in God, and the long path to finding my spirituality again through motherhood. That journey and the reliving of it on that stage also gave me newfound empathy for my own mother.

And the silence that terrified me? It was the sound of others listening. It was the sound of human connection. The audience was right there with me, suspended and bound in the shared experience of storytelling.

You don't need to be a writer to be a storyteller.

Your story is enough.

—*Padma Lakshmi*

INTRODUCTION

In June 2015, I was given the life-changing opportunity to pitch a story to Catherine Burns, artistic director of The Moth. As a longtime fan and audience member, I was thrilled—and terrified. I often listened to Moth stories to be transported out of my own life, and to be transformed by the entertaining, deeply moving, and amazing lives of others. Now The Moth was calling me! Did I even have a story to tell?

Adrenaline (born of excitement and fear) surged through my veins. This was a chance to hone my own storytelling craft with experts, and maybe even to be heard by Moth audiences all around the world.

Storytelling lies at the heart of my professional life. As a professor of critical media studies, much of my teaching involves finding stories that can transform abstract concepts and history into relatable and compelling experiences. As an organizer striving to make institutions more equitable, effective storytelling can not only dismantle false narratives but also cut through intractable political divides to reveal how power is currently working, how we got here, and what needs to be done. As a journalist, great stories are the beating heart of impactful reporting, essays, and narrative-nonfiction audio productions.

For all of these reasons, I enthusiastically accepted the invitation. But as soon as I hung up, I felt a fluttering of fear in my chest. My own stories had made friends and family laugh, but they were really just short anecdotes told to people who were being generous. To make matters worse, my experience as a hip-hop artist had taught me that there's a big difference between telling a funny story to a couple of friends and telling it to hundreds or thousands of strangers. On stage, everything but the power of your story is stripped away, and it is very easy to fall flat. The few times this happened to me, it felt like nothing could remove the stench of doom from the air.

After an hour, the fluttering in my chest turned into panic. Every time I tried to summon a potential story from my past, a crowd of critical voices in my head would quickly impale it with a flurry of criticism: *No one cares about this. Get over yourself. You've never saved a life. Why do you get to stand in front of people and talk about your weird silly stuff?* Jay Allison, the longtime producer of *The Moth Radio Hour,* had introduced me to the Moth team, and I reached out to him to explain my predicament. Jay told me, "Well, Chenjerai, Moth stories can be deeply inspirational, but they're very different from the exclusively heroic or positive tales that some other places invite you to tell. I don't know where you'll end, but as a place to start, remember that everyone is entertained by, and relates to, a train wreck. Stories about failure and learning can be powerful."

Failure! That was something I had a lot of. I could definitely remember and tell a story about that.

Up until this point in my life, I had presented myself, and been taken seriously, as a scholar, organizer, journalist, and hip-hop artist. Stories about the confusing, awkward, and downright embarrassing parts of my life, and the lessons that might be learned from them, had been pushed to the margins of my mind. They would spill out, poorly developed, at family dinners or on dates, or in the classroom. My friends and family and students welcomed the best parts of these stories and tolerated the rest.

The pounding in my chest calmed enough for me to start reflecting and jotting down some notes. My best bet was a story about some funny and painful moments in my career as a hip-hop artist.

By the time my group, the Spooks, finished our last tour in 2005, we had earned gold singles in three countries and a gold album in the UK, and had performed in front of more than a million people. After my music career slowed down, I was forced to learn new skills, figure out new ways to sustain myself, and forge a new identity—but I never really processed or properly mourned this tumultuous shift in my circumstances.

When I was ready, I called Catherine, and she listened closely and supportively as I ran through several story possibilities. Breathlessly, I shared the story of meeting Laurence Fishburne *on my own music video set* as the Spooks were taking off. But I took forever to get to the main point, losing the thread several times along the way. Another anecdote involved me botching an Excel sheet at a temp job. It was meant to illustrate the tragicomedy of my post-fame life, but I stretched it out far too long and included a wealth of irrelevant details. I also told Catherine about meeting Laurence Fishburne for the second time, while working as a security guard at a film festival. But this time I had hidden from him, ashamed of my humbled station in life (and my JCPenney suit). It was a meandering, sloppy affair with a sad, deflating ending.

After listening closely, Catherine recognized the seeds of a story—something that had elements of humor, tragedy, and drama, and would likely resonate with a lot of people. I use the term *seeds* because clearly my story wasn't developed yet. When I first shared my story, I thought that having been famous—and then not—was the point of the story, and that meeting Fishburne twice was the punchline. I thought the ending of the story was me in my humiliated state. None of those initial instincts was correct.

The lack of an ending was crucial. Laughing with me, Catherine pointed this out by saying, "Wow, that second time you saw Laurence feels so awkward and terrible. But I feel like that's not the ending. I mean, you seem to be doing much better now. What happened?" When she asked this, something emotional and planetary moved inside of me. I didn't know what happened. I didn't have an ending because, even though my life had moved forward, some part of Chenjerai was still standing there in that JCPenney suit, feeling defeated and small.

A day or so before the live show, the storytellers meet and share their stories for final notes and tweaks. This is a scary but ultimately beautiful part of The Moth's process.

I will never forget my first rehearsal. The day before, I was attending a protest in South Carolina. The rehearsal was going to be in person at The Moth's offices. This meant that I had to drive from Clemson to New York. The good news was that the twelve-hour drive gave me plenty of time to rehearse my story. But it also allowed time for doubt to creep in. Was I really driving to another state to tell a story in front of one thousand people? With no music? Because one person in New York told me that this story is interesting? Maybe I needed to tell a more political story. After all, I was not here to simply entertain people. I became so filled with doubt and confusion that I called Catherine and proposed telling a different story. Catherine listened and was fully open to this. But her questions helped me realize that if I was going to tell a political story, I should put the same time and effort into it that I had put into this one. I think she also understood that my sudden passion for this new idea was a by-product of second-guessing the story I was currently planning to tell.

By the time I arrived in New York, I was back to telling story number one. But my doubt returned when other storytellers started confidently weaving their own tales at rehearsal. This anxiety didn't last long, however. Moth listeners have a special way of holding storytellers up by laughing at what's funny, "wow"-ing at what is genuinely shocking, nodding in validating affirmation, and even shedding tears when moved. As soon as I shared my first punchline, the room laughed, and I felt better. Relief flooded my body and I felt that I was hanging out with friends—that we were all going to make each other stronger and support each other through the process. My point here is that the horrifying feeling of pressure was necessary, because by the time I got to the big stage, I had already faced my fears.

As I got closer to the show, I remembered a turning point in my story. I was applying for a new temp job, feeling defeated, wearing the same JCPenney suit, when I heard a Spooks song playing and I saw people in the temp office enjoying it. This reminded me that the power of my music wasn't contingent on my own fame or hanging with celebrities. It was about the joy of dreaming up and shaping my art. The office workers were enjoying what I had made, and they reminded me of the power and joy I had felt creating it.

In the final scene of my story, I talked about sharing a lesson with my students: Follow your passions, but be prepared to brace for impact. And after going to sleep thinking hard about the core message of my story, I woke up with the line "Sometimes you have to figure out who you're not before you can become who you are."

When I tried this line at the rehearsal, I felt the swell of recognition and affirmation wash over the room. Catherine nodded confidently in a way she hadn't before and said, "Yes! That's it. That's the ending."

The Moth team lovingly pushed me toward a stronger ending—the real ending—and helped me recognize when I had found it.

The Moth helped me understand that this was not simply a story about Laurence Fishburne, or even about fame. It was about being on the wrong path in life, having the courage to try things, and figuring out where our strengths really lie. It was about not letting the roller coaster of success and failure that all of us experience lock us into the wrong identity or kill the lifelong magic, wonder, and power that should continue to live inside of us.

This process helped me to understand this period of my life better, not simply by imposing a narrative on it, but by allowing me to see this broken part of myself as part of the journey to how I got to where I am now. I think that's true of so many Moth stories. People love The Moth because there really is medicine for others in each of our stories, and since I've shared mine, I've hugged, shaken hands with, and listened to so many people who related to my journey of discovery. Even friends and family members who knew some pieces of the story have told me that they understand me better after listening.

The Moth prompted me to take myself seriously as a storyteller. They asked me to reflect on my life experiences and consider how they might resonate with other people. This lesson matters tremendously in a culture where so many of us grow up learning that only certain people are storytellers and only their stories about their extraordinary lives are worth listening to and investing in. My first Moth invitation was the opposite of that. I was being told something that everyone should be told, something that this book is telling you right now: You have important stories to tell. They are stories that no one else can tell. But you have to be willing to do the work of developing them—and then work through your fears to share them.

What's crucial to recognize is that taking me seriously as a storyteller didn't mean that the Moth staff validated everything I said or propped up all my bad ideas and rambling, pointless anecdotes. In some ways, their commitment to me—and to all of us as storytellers—meant the opposite. I had an open invitation to tell stories, and they had my permission to listen closely and respond honestly, laughing at what was funny, wrinkling their faces at things that seemed problematic, asking questions about things that were unclear, and nodding calmly at things that were interesting but not essential. By the end of my first experience working with The Moth's directors, I would learn that, like all of us, I desperately needed to work through these uncertain moments, which were like raging wild rivers inside my body.

This book is an invitation for you to take yourself seriously as a storyteller—to discover your stories, center what's most important about them, initiate yourself in the fire of live performance, and use *your* truths to break down false narratives, whether that's on stage or over dinner with a friend. So, welcome! But brace yourself: This process will take you to new places, connect you to new people, and unlock new layers of who you are.

—*Chenjerai Kumanyika*

PART 1

EVERYONE HAS A STORY

CHAPTER 1

WELCOME TO THE MOTH

You are a multitude of stories. Every joy and heartbreak, every disappointment and dizzying high—each has contributed to the complex, one-of-a-kind person that you are today.

While your experiences are ephemeral, your stories can be eternal.

As we know from ancient scrolls, cave paintings, and the histories passed down by word of mouth from generation to generation, people have been telling stories since the beginning of time. The first utterance from one person to another is the earliest ancestor of The Moth.

What do you think the first story ever told might have been about? Maybe it was just a series of screeches and howls. Screeches, howls, and pantomime probably did an okay job in a pinch. Language developed out of necessity. "There is water over there. Look out for the bear. I found some berries. Damn, fire is hot." And eventually, "I went to go look for some berries, but I saw a bear, so I came back to sit by the fire, where I feel safe." Perhaps all the first stories were cautionary tales that helped save lives, and that's why we're so hardwired to want, crave, and treasure them.

Beyond the essentials ("Water here. Berries here. Bear there!"), we long for more to make sense of the world around us. Over time, storytelling has evolved to serve many purposes, some practical or frivolous, others righteous or evil, still others romantic, entertaining, cautionary, or incendiary. Sharing stories aloud is one of humankind's best attributes—our magical ability to shape-shift into each other's imaginations with the spoken word. Because we have the capacity for imagination, stories bring other people's experiences to life, so we can see, and very often *feel,* events that didn't happen to us.

When you choose to share a story, you share a piece of yourself. Stories explain your heart, decode your history, decipher who you are, and translate it all to whoever takes the time to listen carefully. They're what make families, friendship, and love possible. They're both ordinary and exquisite. Stories are the currency of community. They tear down walls, unite cultures, and help people realize they are more alike than different, all while celebrating what is unique to *you.*

Beyond survival, stories enhance our lives, deepen our bonds, and, if we tell them right, get us invited back to dinner parties. A well-crafted story helps you create a magical sort of clarity. It can illuminate an experience your audience could not have fathomed a few minutes before, or draw them so close that they imagine they can feel your heart beating. You could make them laugh out loud or bring tears to their eyes or stir them to action. You might make them feel seen.

Time and again, your stories will reveal larger truths about yourself, and sometimes they'll point you in the direction of where you'll want to go next. When you craft a story, you hold each piece of your life up to the light and say, "Yes, that mattered" or "No, that wasn't what I thought it was at all" and often "WOW, I did not realize this affected me so deeply."

Storytelling is vital to being alive. So know that you're not getting out of this! *You will be telling stories.* In fact, you *have* been telling stories. Every day. Since you started talking.

This book will help you tell *better* stories.

WHY "THE MOTH"?

A wise mattress salesperson once quipped, "You spend a third of your life in bed. Sleep in the best bed you can find!" Nobody can say for sure what fraction of your life you spend telling stories, but most would agree it's a significant and important portion of your self-expression, so it's worth investing your time and energy in the skills you need to be a great storyteller. The Moth is here to help.

Most of us have a few fun anecdotes that we end up telling again and again, the greatest hits that we pull out on dates or when meeting people for the first time. We tell them at parties and work functions and across kitchen tables. We might work them into the conversation at an otherwise boring cocktail party ("In case of social emergency, break glass!"). In the pages that follow, we will teach you how to turn those anecdotes into stories that mean something to you and give you the tools to deliver them with confidence and grace.

This book is not Aristotle's *Poetics,* Joseph Campbell's *The Hero's Journey,* or Scheherazade's thousand and one tales. There are plenty of books on storytelling through the ages (read them all!). In *this* book, Moth directors help you shape and tell your own personal story, using decades of on-the-ground experience as the guides and midwives of the stories that grew The Moth from an exclusively New York series to a renowned global arts institution dedicated to building connection and community through true personal stories.

When Moth founder George Dawes Green held the first official Moth event in the living room of his New York City apartment in 1997, it was with these expressed goals: Some people will tell stories. One at a time. No one will interrupt them. No one will interject that their uncle did the same thing. No one will one-up that person by saying they had *two* aunts and a brother-in-law who did that thing too. No one will ask to pass the gravy. The storyteller will have the floor for a time, and people will listen.

MOTH FOUNDER GEORGE DAWES GREEN, ON THE INSPIRATION BEHIND THE MOTH: It's hard to imagine now but back in 1997, when some dear friends and I launched The Moth, the idea that nights of personal stories might be worthy of assembling an audience seemed a reach. Personal stories were seen as just that: *personal,* not public, not to be shared with an audience. But all my life I'd noticed the mysterious power of the personal narrative.

A porchful of siblings and cousins at a beach house near Savannah, Georgia. My aunt Alice giving us her memories of our great-grandmother Big Inez, imperious matriarch of Waynesboro, Georgia. I remember noticing that the story seemed to be *happening* to Aunt Alice as she spoke the words. And happening to all of us with her, drawing us together as we listened.

A night when my shy father, after one and a half glasses of rye whiskey, conjured forth, for my neighborhood pals, a boyhood rafting trip on the Ohio River. Again: As lovely as the story was, I was even more taken by the silent hum of the *listening—* the strangely deep empathy of these ten-year-old kids for a man they hardly knew. Because his story transported them to that river.

And then once, in the early '90s, I was at a poetry slam at the Nuyorican Poets Café and a poet was reciting something long and surrealistic, in that dead-poetry singsong that was all the rage then, and I was drifting off—as the whole audience was.

Then a small thing happened.

The poet finished her poem, then paused and said, "So this next poem is about . . . when my grandfather used to take me fishing. He'd wake me at four A.M. and we'd get in his station wagon, and this was back when station wagons had real *wooden* sides, and we'd drive upstate to this stream, and we'd fish all day for brown trout . . ."

I looked around. Everyone was giving their full attention. For a moment, there was no trace of the sacred veil that separated artist from audience. We were all right there with her *as though her memories were our own*—and then she cleared her throat and went back to the singsong, and whoosh: Down came the veil again.

I thought, *Let's have a night of the stories that poets use to introduce their poems, without the poems.* I loved poetry, but how splendid to not have that veil!

The notion of nights of stories took root in my head and started to grow.

It was an idea I'd take down from its shelf in my skull now and then, to play with, to add to. When I was walking to a café in the East Village, or riding the subway, I'd be concocting these evenings. Each night could be anchored by a central theme: "Fish Tails" (stories of catching fish or cooking fish). "Cuba Libre!" "Civil Rights." "Sheer Survival." Each evening, I thought, should feature a guest curator, an artist or writer or dancer or fisherman; we'd help them find a slate of raconteurs and assist in giving the stories direction and shape. For almost all the nights, we'd have smallish audiences—intimacy was key. We'd find compelling music pegged to the theme. We'd look for outlandish venues: a barge for "Fish Tails," a Cuban bar for "Cuba Libre!," a graveyard for "Sheer Survival."

I started seeking advice. Many of my friends were baffled, resistant. They said, "Nights of *music,* sure, with maybe just *one* story—so people don't get bored?" Or, "Why not find 'traditional' storytellers, and gear it toward *kids*!"

But there was also steady, loving support, and gentle pressure. And finally, one night, at her apartment on West Fourth Street, Gaby Tana talked me into just going for it.

"Well, okay," I said. "One. We'll try one Moth. Just to see."

PEGI VAIL, FOUNDING BOARD MEMBER: We were all nervous as to how this first event would unfold, how the stories would be received, and if the format would work. It was appropriately titled "Finding a Place." The stakes felt high that evening. We were reintroducing the idea of storytelling, stripped back to its bare bones. Would they like it? We were telling people to just sit back and listen. When it began, George spoke passionately about his friend Wanda's porch in Georgia, where he spent many a night listening to people tell tales while watching the moths circling the light above. He wanted to re-create that feeling here in New York City. Suddenly it was so exciting.

MELVIN ESTRELLA, FOUNDING BOARD MEMBER: That first Moth was a gorgeous mess. The stories were so long, we ran out of wine! It was clear we would have to limit the amount of time for each storyteller for future events. But regardless! We knew we were witnessing something great, even though it wasn't fully shaped yet. The audience that night came back for years and years and years. They cheered the storytellers on, and they still do. The Moth audience wants you to take it high, and they'll help you get there. They are rooting for you. I've never seen another audience like that, ever.

PEGI VAIL: The format took shape over the next couple of years. On a night in 1998, I had the fortune of curating an evening of teachers' stories at Lansky Lounge. I remember my former high school teacher Luigi Jannuzzi told a story, along with Frank McCourt, who had just won a Pulitzer Prize for his haunting memoir *Angela's Ashes*. I called McCourt to invite him after finding his number in the telephone book, and was thrilled he said yes! The host was our friend and an early Moth collaborator, Roland Legiardi-Laura (Nuyorican Poets Café). It was exhilarating to hear such natural storytellers, who'd initially inspired people in classrooms, now telling stories to strangers, creatively directed by founding artistic director Joey Xanders.

What started in George's living room was moving further into the world with each event, growing the audiences with every story.

That first night was a bit bumpy, but by the end, everyone in the room felt they had been transported to new places. It felt like art, simply because stories, honored with space and time, are transformative. One night led to many nights and a movement took hold. And though those first few years were a little rocky (and nearly depleted George's bank account), the spirit of that first night can be felt on Moth stages to this day.

WHY TRUE STORIES?

There is a powerful connection that comes from hearing someone share their memories and lived experiences. Some Moth stories feature first-person accounts from people who've lived through events we've only read about in history books. Sala Udin took us deep into 1965 and the civil rights movement with stories of his life as a Freedom Rider. Dr. Mary-Claire King shared how she won the grant that led to her discovery of the BRCA gene. Dr. Kodi Azari took us through the harrowing surgery of the first transplant of a human hand. Flora Hogman told us about being a hidden child during the Holocaust. Hearing an eyewitness account from Rick Hauck, an astronaut who piloted the first shuttle mission after the loss of the *Challenger,* allowed us to be there with him when he landed in triumph.

You don't need to have made headlines to tell a fantastically gripping personal story. Eva Santiago told us of falling in love with her soulmate, Christopher, while he was incarcerated. Kim Reed shared what it was like to go home to Montana after her gender transition, where she was celebrated as the star high school quarterback. Jenny Allen described an embarrassing mishap with a wig while undergoing cancer treatment. Marvin Gelfand remembered the freedom and independence he felt after getting his first library card. Gabrielle Shea told us about the perils of messing up the Thanksgiving mac and cheese for her potential in-laws. We rode shotgun with Adam Wade on his teenage Friday evening drives with his aunt and his yia yia.

Some stories take a sweeping episode of history and break moments or interactions down into smaller, more intimate scenes. Others take what might seem like an ordinary event (getting your driver's license, a first kiss, the first time you voted) and imbue it with all the magic you may have felt in that moment. In both cases, the authenticity of the teller is vital. We listen with different ears when we can feel and believe that a story is true.

And so, *true* became the guiding principle for Moth stories.

NEIL GAIMAN, MOTH STORYTELLER AND BOARD MEMBER: How important is truth in these first-person stories? Lying is like playing solitaire and cheating: It takes the fun out.

WHAT HAPPENS WHEN WE LISTEN

As The Moth grew out of that cozy living room and onto stages around the world, the creative minds at The Moth listened to the stories. Tens of thousands of them and counting. And through it all, the people who created the space for these stories and directed the tellers and told that guy in the back on his cellphone to knock it off and take it outside—those people took note of what makes the strongest stories. What pulls at your heart, makes your blood boil, your belly laugh, your eyes widen, or your brain tick. The Moth learned secrets about stories that really make you *feel* something both familiar and foreign.

Some of the best nights at The Moth can seem as though the storyteller and everyone in the audience are breathing the same breath. With each story, every brain in the room fires together. The hearts share beats per minute.

Imagine how excited we were when we learned that this feeling is backed up by science! A study led by neuroscientist Uri Hasson found that when a person is listening and comprehending a story, their brain activity begins to couple, or align, with the brain of the teller. The scientific term is "speaker-listener neural coupling." MRI scans of two brains, one talking, one listening, showed that the brains began to sync. Where the teller's brain showed activity, or "lit up," soon after, the listener's brain lit up too. One catch is that this only happens when the listener is engaged and comprehending the story being told. In short, if you want to spark another person's brain, your story needs to be *good*. This book will help you light up some brains.

FATOU WURIE, MOTH STORYTELLER: We left Sierra Leone and were displaced for over eleven years because of the civil war. My mother, deeply connected to her family, was left figuring the world out without her safe place—her mother, aunts, father, brothers, and extended family—to guide her journey as a young mother and wife. She would spend the whole day singing songs or speaking out loud to herself in her native language, Mende. She would pull my sisters and me close and tell us about her childhood. We didn't always understand all the details, but seeing our mother light up while telling us stories made us light up too. Her excitement became our excitement, her sorrow our sorrow, and so on. Telling those stories is what kept my mother alive, kept her heart beating through loss after loss after loss—that is how I came to understand the power of storytelling.

Imagine a room full of people listening—their brains aligning. There is power in millions of strangers experiencing one person's story. These darkened theaters and airwaves where people of different faiths and backgrounds listen together push us all to question our long-held beliefs—and what we thought was true *before we listened* is cracked, crushed, or finally cemented.

At The Moth you can hear stories from people you know, people you *thought* you knew, and people you might never meet otherwise. We may start as strangers, but by the end of the story, we are closer—and that is the ultimate point. The act of sharing personal stories builds empathy, and out of many stories, we become one community.

It *starts* with a single story.

CHAPTER 2

NO NOTES, NO NET

Storytelling is sacred; it is how we keep the dead living, and the living thriving. It's how we show up as our most authentic self. It can permeate artificial boundaries of race, borders, gender, language, and unequal power. It is the language of the heart, reflecting the breadth of our humanity as individuals and as a collective.

—FATOU WURIE, MOTH STORYTELLER

There are many forms of storytelling across time and cultures; this book will cover what we call "Moth-style" storytelling: sharing a true personal story, out loud and without any notes.

It's not always easy to sell a potential storyteller on the idea that they should get up on a stage to talk about themselves. "Like, *why* would I want to do that?"

We tell them, it's different for everyone. For some it's the thrill of the ride and the opportunity to finally own the spotlight. For others, the more reluctant, we say, it'll help you look under your psychological bed and scare away what haunts you. It'll help you Humpty Dumpty yourself back together again. It'll help someone who's going through the same thing and could use a road map. It's your chance to change the tune, or set the record straight. It'll make you friends or help you identify your enemies. Instead of rushing through life, it's an opportunity to stop, sit back, and reflect.

Believe it or not, people you've never met will line up to hear from *you*. The *real* you. Over the many years of The Moth, we've seen audiences of millions from around the globe gather to hear individual stories that reflect the world we are living in.

What an extraordinary passport to experience the world from *your* point of view, to walk for ten minutes next to you and hear one of your stories.

Early on, we established and refined a few parameters for Moth-style storytelling. While rules may feel restrictive, we believe these limitations fuel creativity:

> Moth stories are true and told out loud, in the first person.
>
> Moth stories are not read or recited.
>
> Moth stories always involve stakes and some sort of transformation.
>
> Moth stories are told within a specific time frame.

We will explore the why and how of each of these rules in more depth, but in our experience—without a doubt—they are the foundation of what makes a story successful.

YOUR VERY OWN MOTH DIRECTOR

If you've heard a story that you loved on *The Moth Radio Hour, The Moth* podcast, or at a live Moth Mainstage show, you should know that most tellers weren't up there alone. What you heard was a collaboration. Each Mainstage teller—whether discovered at an open mic StorySLAM or on the Moth Pitchline, or overheard recounting a wild story while waiting for an oil change—is paired with a Moth director who helps uncover and shape the story, and shepherd it to the stage. (You should consider this book your own personal director!)

The process always starts with a conversation where we mine for ideas. Perhaps you've already scrounged around in the memory pantry and have an inkling of a story. Or perhaps you're completely stumped for ideas, so we ask questions like:

- What are moments from your life, big or small, that stick with you?
- What are the stories you can't wait to tell a new friend, or the stories your oldest friend or partner always asks you to repeat?
- What are *The Greatest Hits of You*?

We listen to your answers, and then we ask more questions, many of which you will find in this book. We ask about everything that was happening in your life when the story took place. Why was this significant for you? We ask about your backstory and the things that led to this particular moment. What was different? Why does it stand out for you? We'll listen for hesitations and stumbles— anything that indicates perhaps there is more under the surface. (There's gold in those pauses!)

Sometimes the answer will include "It was the *first* time," "It was the *last* time," "It was the *worst* time," or "It was the *best* time"—and we work from there. How was this time different from all the other times?

Once we start to focus on a story, we ask the teller to consider a few bigger, often harder-to-answer questions.

- What is this story ultimately about for you?
- Why is this story important for you to tell?
- How would you describe yourself at the beginning of the story, and who had you become by the end?

These questions aren't always easy to answer right away. The process helps you find the answers. By asking these questions, we are able to help you find the direction and heart of the story and get a general sense of how you changed, which helps to define the overall arc.

Once we get a good focus on *the story,* we start to look for the best way to tell it. We identify scenes and details that can bring the story to life. We ask you, "If this were a movie, what scenes would keep us glued to our seats?" Retrace every step, describe it in Technicolor. We often ask that you "blow it up big" and look at every detail you could play with, and then pick the very best and shiniest.

Then we work on structure. Is there a smaller story within the larger experience that might make the story more interesting or relatable? For instance, in Amy Biancolli's story about the death of her husband, we encouraged her to push into the detail of her wedding ring and use it to tell the story of their life together, bringing us to the moment she finally decided it was time to take the ring off.

After that first phone call or meeting, we create an outline with bullets of how the story might be structured, with questions to consider at various points. The bones of the story are identified, constructed, and reconstructed, because the outline might change as we uncover something new. Like shoes, you gotta try things on! Sometimes they look great on the mannequin but the heels are too high for you, or they make a clacking noise when you walk that would surely drive you crazy. Like the shoe, the story has to fit. What you learn through the challenge and process of "trying it on" is powerful.

Once the structure of the story is mapped out, we have you tell it out loud.

The director is the storyteller's first audience. We listen and reflect, with honesty, what we are hearing. As directors, we listen each time like it's the first time to see if anything is confusing to the ear or if there are any details that are unnecessary. Does the story feel slow in some parts? Does that moment about the neighbor's rooster really belong? We note what makes us laugh, makes our hair stand on end and our eyes fill with tears, what makes us cringe with dread or gasp in surprise.

We ask you to punctuate with emotion. And yes, just like a therapist, we'll ask: *How did it make you feel?* You want your listener to feel it too!

We help tellers focus their stories to make the overall arc as clear as possible, which helps determine what details need to stay, or go, or be saved for another story.

Integral to the Moth process is a time limit. All storytellers, no matter the venue, should be mindful of time. On the Moth Main-stage we aim to feature stories that are between ten and twelve minutes long. (At our open mic StorySLAMs, tellers only get five!) We take timekeeping so seriously that a musician timekeeper is actually on stage with the teller. If the storyteller goes long, the musician will play a little note to signal that it's time to wrap up. The playful threat is that if the storyteller continues on for more than a minute, the musician will play again, and louder. The time-keeper strikes fear into every teller! That is by design. Completing a story within a given time frame takes a lot of consideration and planning. Mark Twain is said to have quipped, "I didn't have time to write a short letter, so I wrote a long one instead." The same is true with stories. It takes practice to tell a ten-minute story and not include every ingredient. We can't send a violinist to your house, but we'll give you the tools to help you be mindful of the ticking clock.

The last step in The Moth process is our in-person group re-hearsal. All of the tellers in a show gather together, and we ask them to stand up, one by one, and share their stories. A mini-audience of fellow storytellers and Moth staff listens intently. This run-through gives storytellers a chance to experience a live audience. People often tell us that the rehearsal is the hardest and most intimidating part, but we can't stress enough that it's essential. That's why, even-tually, you'll need to find a trusted person to act as a sounding board for *your* rehearsal run. It will show you where the nerves or emotion might hit, what scenes you might forget, or which details were confusing for the audience. More than anything, getting through the rehearsal will build your confidence.

You may be thinking, *I don't have a director to help me.* Well, now you do! The people writing this book *are those very people.* We (Meg, Catherine, Jenifer, Sarah, and Kate), along with The Moth's artistic and workshop teams, are here to give you the tools you need to guide *yourself.* We have broken down our process in this book and have posed all the same questions we would ask if you were on the other end of the phone with us. We'll walk you step-by-step through the process in detail and throw in a few tricks for good measure!

THE RULES WE PLAY BY

In 2001, once again inspired by elements from the popular poetry slam model, we decided to provide a stage, a theme, and a host, and open up the evening to *any* ten people who had a story. We called these StorySLAMs. We made a few simple rules, set up parameters for crowd-sourced judges, and asked aspiring tellers to put their names in a hat for a chance to share a five-minute story. As we listened to thousands of stories in rapid succession, we noticed patterns and pitfalls. Killer beginnings, glorious landings, and common stumbling blocks. Each StorySLAM was a crash course, and we made note of what worked and what didn't.

In the early days of the SLAMs, we heard about Boris Timanovsky hunting down his grandfather's headstone in Russia; Andy Christie staving off a midlife crisis with a jump from a plane; Faye Lane being cast as a string bean in a school play in Texas; Jen Lee selling Mary Kay products in the Midwest; Dion Flynn bonding with his stepfather while his mother was dying in the hospital; Jerald Hayes nearly missing his brother's wedding; and Sherry Weaver, single mother of four, hopping on the back of a motorcycle and falling in love.

JENIFER ON STORYSLAMS: These weren't people we'd worked with prior to the show. It was an uncontrolled environment. What happened was a roller coaster: some thrilling parts, some super-harrowing turns, bumps, a few sleepy sections, and of course, some stunning highs and some spectacular fails. But each story, limited to just five minutes, was over soon, and we were on to the next. It had a sort of jukebox feeling: What story will be next?

The audience kept coming back, and a culture grew around what happened in the room. We started off simply wanting to hear the stories, but we also got hooked on the electricity between tellers and listeners. A community was born.

JON GOODE, MOTH HOST AND STORYTELLER: Stories are what turn friends into family.

Decades later, these open mic nights are in cities all around the world. The unpredictability can make the evenings magical. But, as you can imagine, there are many factors that can break the spell.

We truly have no idea what stories people will bring to the SLAM stage. We've been knocked out by the tenderness and vulnerability of absolute strangers, and wondered how it is possible that an accounting admin from Detroit doesn't have her own comedy special on HBO. But we've also had some record-scratch moments.

From the start, the content at the StorySLAMs was unpredictable and unruly. Not every story heard was one we'd want to hear, given a choice. A *not-so-fun* fact: Across this great land, there are thousands of people willing to take the stage to confess a story of a time they weren't able to make it to the bathroom. Incontinence stories from Miami to Melbourne. (Technically, this does fall under the category of "vulnerable," so hats off—pants off?—but we so dearly wish people would keep it above the belly button and bring the vulnerability of their hearts or minds and not their behinds.)

We made a poster of how-tos that outlined the parameters for

Moth-style storytelling and placed it in a prominent space on the stage so tellers could look it over when they signed up to tell.

THE MOTH StorySLAM

Telling a story tonight?

It must be TRUE.
The Moth is strictly nonfiction.

It must be ON THEME.
The story you've prepared should be intrinsically related to the theme for tonight's show.

It must have STAKES.
A story needs action and the action must have consequences. What is gained or lost? What is the urgency? What is the conflict? What is the goal and who or what is blocking it? How did the trip from Point A to Point B change or shape you?

It must be YOUR STORY TO TELL
Were you there? Are you one of the "main characters"? Your involvement in the events as they unfold is essential. No journalism.

Finally, it must be **ON TIME**. SLAM stories should be 5 minutes long, plus a one minute grace period.

GOOD LUCK!

What we don't want: Stand-up routines. Repeat stories. Stereotypes. Rants. Essays. How-tos. Confessions. Lectures. Fictions. Gratuitous anything. (SEE MOTH DON'T LIST.)

What we do want: Hook us in. Make us care about you. Paint the scene. Clearly state your fears, desires, the dilemma. Make us invested in the outcome. Introduce the conflict. Make us worried for you. Impress us with observations that are uniquely yours. Rope us into the moment when it all goes down. Conclude as a different person: Triumphant? Defeated? Befuddled? Enlightened?...**CHANGED**.

Wish we could say that the bathroom stories were the worst things we have heard on a Moth StorySLAM stage. Not so. It is an open mic. While the majority of people bring warmth, humanity, madcap adventures, and heartfelt content, there have been some pretty painful, insensitive stories told.

One ugly storytelling premise we've seen a lot is using another person as a prop in your story. *I was feeling low and empty and hopeless. Like a real loser. And then I saw Julie bravely fighting through her very obvious obstacles, and I thought, Julie's life is an absolute wreck. Poor thing. And yet she has the courage to face each day. I can't imagine how HOR-RIBLE it must be for her to get up and face herself in the mirror every morning. I feel so much better about myself when I see her courage. Julie, you are my hero.*

Consider how this "story" sounds if you are Julie. Julie does not want to be your hero or the worst-case scenario you compare yourself to. Nobody wants that. (Also, hello! Julie may be blissfully content!)

More disturbingly, we noted something deeper. To name the sins openly, we've been disheartened and aghast to hear occasional open mic SLAM stories that include blatant racism, sexism, ableism, and homophobia. All the negative -isms and -phobias. We needed to ask potential storytellers to truly examine what they were saying before they took the stage. To practice empathy.

The things *we didn't want* couldn't squeeze on the poster of the things we *did* want. So eventually we made another poster for tellers to peruse as they signed up to tell. It was a step in the right direction.

We advise everyone (including you!) to consider these rules as you craft your story.

As the poster states, we celebrate the diversity and the commonality of human experience. (It's in our mission statement!) Night after night, we watch as shared experiences between strangers are recognized and celebrated—but we cannot ignore the fact that we all hear and tell stories through the lens of our own experiences and our own internal and external biases. We exist as the culmination of all our experiences, so we'll receive stories slightly differently—in some cases, profoundly differently.

THE MOTH
StorySLAM Don'ts

The Moth's mission is to promote the art and craft of storytelling and to honor and celebrate the diversity and commonality of human experience.

Below are a few things that we believe are counterproductive to this effort.

If your story suffers from any of these problems, please go back to the drawing board. **We promise your story will be better for it!**

Please don't caricature or "explain" a culture that is not your own (e.g., putting on fake accents of telling us about the "customs" of a community you don't belong to).

Please don't make another person's identity (class, gender, race, orientation, body type, etc.) the punchline ... or the story line. **Your story, your struggles.**

Please don't use another's identity as a prop or plot point. (If you choose to include another person's race, orientation, physical appearance or able-bodiedness, be sure that it is intrinsic to the story.)

Please don't celebrate unwanted sexual advances in your story.

And of course, **NEVER** use racial slurs or hate speech.

As Always...

Please don't repeat a story you've previously told at The Moth.

Please don't use notes or props.

For us to honor and celebrate your experience, we, your listeners, need to trust that you honor and celebrate ours. That's your responsibility as a storyteller.

EVERYONE HAS A STORY—YES, EVEN YOU

In 1999, we started Moth storytelling workshops, where we reached out to people who we weren't hearing on our stages. We gathered with local communities—nursing associations, veterans' halls, local libraries, and so on—to craft stories in small groups. Time and again, people would tell us that they didn't believe they had a story, but after a few sessions, one story sparked another and another, until everyone was sharing. At The Moth, we believe that everyone has a story, and we love helping people find theirs.

JUDITH STONE, FOUNDING MOTH BOARD MEMBER AND STORY-TELLER: Instructors in The Moth's Community Program like to start each storytelling workshop by saying, "Sharing a story is an act of courage and an act of generosity." Both are spectacular components, but it's the second that moves me most—the gifts storytellers bestow on an audience. Thanks to the generosity of storytellers, we listeners are almost always granted the pleasure of simultaneously losing ourselves and *finding* ourselves in the story. We're restored to compassion and possibility and reconnected to our messy, marvelous, exasperating, exalted human community. For a while, at least, our hearts and minds are open. That's good practice for after the stories are over.

Most stories aren't told on stage. Maybe you are hoping to tell a fun story at your next high school reunion or on a date or to get people excited about a new idea at work. Maybe you want to share a story more formally in a keynote, toast, or eulogy—or find the words to motivate others to advocate for a cause.

Using real examples from beloved Moth stories to illuminate the path, we'll teach you our methods and techniques for unearthing, building, and sharpening your stories. We'll offer you practical applications for everyday storytelling moments. You'll be able to use these tools on all your stories going forward. "*All* of them?" Yes, you have more than one! No doubt.

You don't have to have a story ready to go as you're reading this now! You're just getting started. For some folks, finding a story is easy. You may already have one in mind and come to this process full of enthusiasm. Perhaps you lived through an extraordinary or historic event. Fantastic. This will be fun. But for the rest of you, *most of you,* don't feel intimidated! It's perfectly fine to feel stumped. *We have ways of making you talk.*

Identifying the story you want to tell can be challenging. Expect some trial and error. Many are convinced they simply don't have a story, some might not think their story is important enough to be told—but storytelling is for everyone. Your memory is a pantry full of ingredients. You might not have a recipe in mind yet, but dinner *will* be served. The first step is to take yourself seriously as a storyteller. No matter which direction your life and your choices have taken you: If you have lived and breathed, you have a story.

But remember, this is not always a linear process; discoveries happen along the way. We've ordered this book logically, but know that you may jump backward before you turn the page—it's all part of the (beautiful) process.

Now, let's open the pantry of your memories. That proverbial eleven-year-old can of sardines way up on the top shelf behind the cranberry sauce? That just might be the genesis of your greatest story.

PART 2

DEVELOPING
YOUR STORY

CHAPTER 3

MINING FOR MEMORIES

A well-crafted story requires thought and care, but take a deep breath and revel in some good news! Your stories are like finger-prints; they are unique to you. Only you can tell them.

—SARAH AUSTIN JENNESS

Finding your story requires the hard work of sifting through all your life experiences, all the phone calls, alarm clocks, and deadlines; the sunsets and taxes; the breakups and stumbles and epic fails; the home runs and stupid luck. You look through all that and try to identify the significant moments when you felt most like yourself, or the self you could finally see you wanted to become.

Think about sitting down with an old photo album or scrap-book. (If you don't have one, you can create one in your mind. What pictures do you dearly *wish* you had?) The photos and arti-facts in your album, real or imagined, will conjure memories of people and places and situations. A postcard from a family vacation, a ticket stub from your first concert, photos from the summer of your first kiss, the tent falling down at your cousin's wedding, the day you met your brother for the first time. Notice the wallpaper in your grandmother's house. Smell what's on the stove. Remember how much you hated her meatballs? Each of these memories can help you find, and refine, your story. (Sorry, Grandma.)

You are looking for the moments where perhaps something happened that showed you glimpses of who you truly are. Moments that altered your life's course or led you to discover something new. Turning points have occurred multiple times during your life, from big obstacles to seemingly mundane choices; these turning points have affected and ultimately changed you.

> **NESHAMA FRANKLIN, MOTH STORYTELLER:** I believe we're like Russian nesting dolls and everything we've done is still inside us. Just twist off the top, and there it is.

Consider just one vivid memory. What about that time you had a run-in with a mime on your lunch hour? Or that Mother's Day weekend you were asked to sing a solo hymn at church and forgot all the words? Or that time you found a plastic bag full of little toy cars you loved as a child in your grandmother's closet, years after she died?

If you have an inkling of an idea, explore it. Don't be shy. The process of excavation will help you decide whether to pursue it. There is value in rejecting a story idea, but only if you take the time to really mull it over. In your head, a story idea is just a theory. Test it by saying it out loud. Often when you say something out loud, it changes shape. When spoken, a story can feel less silly or scary. Remember, there is a good chance that someone hearing your experience will say, "Hey, me too."

Look for a place, an object, a friendship, that meant a lot to you. Or the opposite: a place, an object, a friendship that almost destroyed you. Try to focus on just one moment!

Think about a time when you . . .

- Felt an emotion: doubled over with laughter, burst into tears, or lost your cool.
- Did something you never thought you'd do.

- Tried to be something or someone you aren't.
- Discovered something about yourself, your environment, your family, or the world.
- Changed your relationship with someone—for better or worse, a little or a lot.
- Had a secret revealed—by you or someone else.
- Stood to gain or lose something that mattered to you.
- Made a tough choice for the right (or wrong) reason.
- Found yourself saying, *I do! I won't! Hell no! I dare you. You couldn't pay me to. It would be my greatest honor.*

The truth is, our lives are made up of a million stories. Trying to stuff your whole life into *one* story won't work. To cover many years in only a few minutes, you would need to reduce the story to a list of events that lack detail and are all given the same emphasis, with no emotion or meaning. At The Moth, we refer to this phenomenon as feeling too "and then, and then, and then." Long lists without much detail are boring.

Focus on a time frame—whether it's an afternoon from your adolescence or the week leading up to your fortieth birthday—and tell us about it in detail. In Moth storytelling workshops, we begin by identifying a scene. "In the movie of your life, what's one scene you'll never forget?" One brave participant might say, "The time in sixth grade, when we moved."

Great! Now tell us for one minute: What was the moving day like? How did you feel as the car drove away? Put us into that place. What do you remember seeing, smelling, touching? What did you hear? What do you remember saying? What kind of thoughts were running through your mind? Now, tell us again, but for *three* minutes. Really zoom in and stay in that day.

The more you do this exercise, the more your memory will actually start to come back, and seeds for stories will start to emerge.

MEG ON MINING FOR STORIES IN A SOCIAL SETTING: A few years back, a friend of mine invited me to her apartment in Manhattan for an informal cocktail party. She said that everyone she invited had some connection to our home state of Arkansas. When I arrived, I recognized one or two friendly faces, but everyone else was a stranger. I typically find these kinds of events difficult, with small talk and trying to find a way to connect, but the genius idea of our hostess, creating a theme for the evening, gave the guests a perfect entry into conversation. "So what's your connection to the Natural State?" Everyone's introduction turned into a little story about them. They went to college there, they worked on the Clinton campaign, they'd dated the hostess and had flown there to meet prospective in-laws. Each story gave context and a perfect place for the conversation to start. The real beauty was we already had something in common. It turned out to be one of the best cocktail parties ever! You may not always be given a perfectly themed evening, but when faced with the daunting task of making conversation with someone new, try to think of a question that might bring about a story from them. The tried-and-true "How do you know our host?" is an easy place to start. Compliments are always nice and can often break the ice. "Where did you grow up?" or "What's something you're looking forward to?" But try to steer clear of the "What do you do for a living?" question. (New Yorkers love to ask this one, but in other parts of the world—not so much!)

YOU ARE THE MAIN CHARACTER

Moth stories are personal; in other words, they are *your* stories. Resist the urge to tell a story where you have no personal connection. You don't want to tell the story about the time your aunt Alma went to Jamaica unless you went with her, or unless that story directly affected you. Were you a witness? Did you have the ackee and saltfish too? Does this story relate to how you were raised or how your aunt loved you? Consider how the story is personal to you. It's okay to tell us about something that happened to someone else, as long as there is a correlation to how it impacted you.

People are often drawn to the idea of telling a story that includes a loved one who passed away, and the same rule applies. If you can put the story of this person in the context of your life, in a tangible and emotional way, that's a good place to start! But don't forget that stories need a plot. Your uncle fueling your passion for biking is great, but that's an observation, not a story. Better to focus on a specific bike trip.

When mining for potential material, out-of-the-ordinary events stand out in our memories and leave footprints. People naturally draw on injuries, calamities, disasters, and heartbreak for ideas. While personal struggles can be part of a story, they do not make a good story on their own. A rule of thumb is to not let the trauma or the struggle be *the* story, but rather to make it the context of the story. Stories always need to go beyond "a bad thing happened." (And now, a rhyming Moth proverb: *All ouch and no yay? Hard to make the listener stay.*) Which is not to say that all stories need a happy outcome! But be careful not to make a laundry list of your woes. The point is that a lengthy account of all the ways your day/year/marriage is terrible isn't a story, it's a catalog of grievances—and the audience isn't your therapist.

THE KICKOFF

Not all stories are epic. They can be born from the simplest of origins: getting summoned for jury duty, accidentally dropping your keys down an elevator shaft, dialing a wrong number.

Stories happen when expectations meet reality. Sometimes stories take place during an exception, an outlier event.

Think back to those moments when you encountered something a little out of the ordinary:

- Getting off at the wrong stop or exit.
- A phone number found in a pocket.
- The eyes meeting across the room.
- The last—*I swear, the last*—shot of tequila.
- A kiss.
- A lie.
- A promise.
- A betrayal.
- A windfall.
- A comeback.
- Your ex at the door.
- The final straw.

Or think of it this way: Remember a time you broke a pattern
or a habit. What was different from the everyday? A moment that
interrupts the normal routine may be your *inciting incident*—"the
thing" that kicks off a story, the first moment that shifted everything
or set things in motion.

Consider moments in your life when your patterns were broken:

- "I'm never without my phone, *but one day* I left it in my
  car . . ."
- "I always walk this way home, *except the time* I decided to
  take a detour . . ."
- "I told everyone that I would never sign up for speed
  dating—*but then* . . ."

An unexpected event usually kicks off the journey of a story—
and the choices you make along the way lead to a bigger, lasting,
overall change in you. Without this "out-of-the-ordinary happen-

ing," the story could not have taken place. Here are some examples of inciting incidents from Moth storytellers:

> *I'm commuting home from work. And when I walk into BART, San Francisco's subway system, I am instantly annoyed, because I walk with a cane and I wear leg braces, and I noticed that the elevators and escalators are out of service. Which means that after sitting on my butt in my office for eight hours, I have to start off my commute by walking down three flights of stairs, down to the platform. And there's nothing I can do. That's the only option. So I walk up to the mouth of the stairwell and I take a deep breath, 'cause I ain't afraid of no stairs. And I put my hands on the inevitably sticky hand rail. And I begin my descent.*
>
> —Aaron Pang, "Balancing Act"

> *They had a display up for Black History Month that said, "From Bondage to Books: Black History Month." And it had a picture of Harriet Tubman and a picture of Colin Powell. And I looked at the sign, and I looked around the store like* Is *anybody else seeing this?* I *started to get heated. Like, the sign hurt my feelings, because it said to me in those few words that the history of Black people, of my people in this country, could be boiled down to the middle passage, slavery, and whatever it is that Colin Powell means to you. From bondage to books. "You were enslaved and now you can read. Congratulations." I felt like I was in an argument with this sign, and I was losing, but I realized the sign didn't have to have the last word. So I walked to the campus newspaper office, and I said, "I'm writing an editorial!" and they're like, "Aren't you the movie review guy?" And I was like, "I've changed."*
>
> —R. Eric Thomas, "A Sign, a Satire, and a Scandal"

> *The week of April Fools' Day of 1981 began badly. That Sunday night, my husband told me he was leaving me. He had fallen*

in love with one of his graduate students, and they were headed back to the tropics the next day.

—Dr. Mary-Claire King, "Who Can You Trust?"

When I was fourteen years old, I had a deeply meaningful experience, something so real, so raw, almost divine, that I knew it was going to shape who I was to become for the rest of my life. I saw the Spice Girls on MTV.

—David Montgomery, "Spicy"

I walk to the elevator, and I press the button, and as we're waiting for the elevator to descend to the lobby, the lights go out. We're all looking around. We don't know what happened. It's two years after 9/11. Everyone's a little jittery. We're thinking, Hey, maybe this could be another attack or something. *It's 2003, most people don't have cellphones. I don't have a cellphone. About ten minutes later, they say, "It's a blackout."*

—John Turturro, "Stumbling in the Dark"

One Sunday, I went to a picnic organized by Arab and South Asian students. As soon as I arrive, I meet the cutest guy. And this guy, his eyes were this beautiful green color. They were like the color of expensive olive oil. Now, this guy is talking to me, words are coming out of his mouth, but all I'm thinking is, Please be Christian, please be Christian, please be Christian. *Somewhere in the words were "Pashtun" and "Pakistan." My heart sank. Olive Oil is Muslim. You have to understand, we were absolutely forbidden from falling in love with Muslims. I mean, by the time I was ten, I knew that when a Christian Arab girl falls in love with a Muslim, one or all of the following would happen: She is disowned, her mother gets a heart attack, or she dies in an honor killing. And I had always obeyed my parents, never considered dating a Muslim. But when he asked me to dinner, everything went out the window, and I said yes.*

—Suzie Afridi, "Olive Oil Eyes"

When you start mining for story seeds, memories might suddenly pop to mind. Don't dismiss them as insignificant before you think about *why* they come to mind. What is it about these moments that sticks with you?

All you're looking for are ideas at this point! Maybe you've already decided on one, and you're raring to go. We knew you had it in you! No idea yet? We've just begun!

> **TOASTS:** Toasts are more observational than traditional first-person stories. You are *in* the story, but your subject is the main character and hero. Whether the toast is for your best friend's wedding, your nona's ninetieth, or your beloved colleague's retirement, think of how this person has directly affected you (and others too)! You may have knowledge of the hearts they've touched, their madcap adventures, the punchlines and the punches, the way this person has shown up for you and for their community. Choose scenes and examples that tether us to who you're toasting. A beautiful toast gives the subject the gift of being seen.

CH-CH-CH-CH-CHANGES

Do you remember a moment that rocked you to the core? Curled your toes? Made you vow to *never* take a road trip with Ricardo again? That *EUREKA!* moment? Or softer epiphanies: a time you were humbled, a heartbreak it took years to fully understand, or an act of kindness that still resonates in your life to this day.

All Moth stories involve some shift in the storyteller's perspective as a result of something that happened. When mining for stories, consider moments of change in your own life. How have you grown over time? Think back. What was the catalyst?

Was there a time that you . . .

- Changed a belief you held?
- Had a moment when everything came into focus?
- Discovered you were stronger than you thought?
- Realized you were just plain wrong?
- Tried a new haircut that gave you wings?

At the end of your story, you are a different *you* than you were at the beginning. *I used to be like this, but now I know different!*

> *Nobody told kids anything in those days, so you just tried to figure it out. We found out what polio meant was hospitals, and hot packs, and painful therapies, and iron lungs. I stood in the doorway, and I was watching my mom, and she picked up my little sister's shoes—her little summer sandals—and she held them in her hands for a moment. She held them like they were birds with broken wings, and she put them in a drawer. And she shut the drawer, and I saw tears in her eyes, and I knew.*
>
> —Sister Mary Navarre, "Catholic School Dropout"

Think back to moments that built you up or tore you down.

> *I was fourteen years old when, suddenly and disastrously, I fell in love with a girl in my class. She and I had been in school together since we were little kids, but we never really interacted there. And I don't know why I felt so strongly so quickly, but I did, and I knew that she sometimes went to church down the street. So every Sunday I started walking over, and if she was there, I'd sit for the whole sermon and take notes. And if she wasn't, I played pool in the basement with my best friend, Paul.*
>
> —Max García Conover, "Kid Religion"

Was there something you were adamant about only to one day discover you were so very wrong? Did someone tell you something that suddenly made everything shift into perspective?

I got to know some of our clients. One of them was this therapist who came in for a few years in a Land Rover. And one day, he comes into work and he says, "John, I've thought for a long time whether I should tell you about this, but you've told me so many times how isolated and alone you feel. And there's a reason for that. There's this thing they're talking about in the mental health world called Asperger's syndrome. It's a kind of autism, and you could be the poster boy for it." And he says to me, "Normally, therapists learn not to diagnose their friends, or pretty soon they won't have any friends." But, he said, "I think this could mean a lot to you." And he handed me this book and I looked in it, and I saw how people with Asperger's can't look other people in the eye. We're uncomfortable. We can't read body language. We say inappropriate things because we don't understand social cues. And everything I read about this? It was me. And that truly transformed my life at age forty.

—John Elder Robison, "A Complete Correct Human"

Perhaps you spent your life following someone else's rules and then decided you'd had enough. What happened then? How are you different now?

In her story "The Curse," Dame Wilburn and a friend decide to visit a psychic. As Dame walks into the storefront, the fortune-teller welcomes her.

She locks me in a gaze and says, "You're cursed. You're cursed! You'll never find love. This is the worst curse I have ever seen. Your whole family—this is generational. I am floored by the level of curse that's hanging on you." And I'm standing there. And I gotta tell you, I'm pretty excited about this. Because all these years, I thought it was me! I thought I was too loud, too fat, too Black, too whatever. But if I'm just cursed? Hallelujah! Yes, that means we can fix it. All right, here we go.

Sometimes a change is sudden, and sometimes gradual. *One day I woke up and realized I hadn't thought of my ex for quite some time, and it didn't hurt anymore.* Explore this! Hypothesize why. You might find a great story there.

CATHERINE ON STORIES DURING JOB INTERVIEWS: In a job interview, your prospective employer might say, "Tell me a little more about yourself!" or "Tell me about a work moment you wish you could do differently now." This is an invitation to tell a very short personal story that illustrates your character, work ethic, or ability to problem-solve. Think through the stories in your arsenal before the interview and have one or two prepped. In an interview for a TV producing job, I once managed to work in a story about me surviving a runaway camel in Morocco without dropping the expensive camera I was holding. (I got the job!) But one of my favorite on-the-job stories is told by my friend Tim Bartlett. He once spent a year traveling solo through rural England, shooting a documentary. He took buses from town to town, and stayed overnight in the small villages where he was filming. One cold winter night, he missed the last bus that would take him to the next town. There were no taxis or hotels in the tiny village where he was shooting. In the end, he ordered a pizza, asked if it could be delivered to the place in the next town where he was staying, and then said, "Uh . . . can I go with it?" The delivery guy took Tim *and* his pizza to the hotel in the next town. The story demonstrates that Tim is a creative problem solver, with an adventurous spirit and great sense of humor. I'd certainly hire him! There's no one right story. All job interviews are about determining two things: Does this person have the skills needed to do the job, and do we want to spend every single workday with this person? Choose a story that will make your prospective new employer think: I want this person on my team.

DECISIONS, DECISIONS

In your quest to find your story, think back to those turning-point moments in your life. Often they start with a decision. After you decided to do X, your day (week, year, life?) was different. Was there a time when you said YES! or vehemently NO!? Moth stories are all about agency—where something happens as a direct result of something you did or did *not* do. Think of those specific moments in your life when you made a choice that altered your course.

DECISIONS AT WORK:

To quit your job.

To fire someone.

To switch career paths.

To go back to school.

To speak up or step back.

DECISIONS WITH YOUR FRIENDS:

Falling in friendship-love.

Letting people in.

Shutting people out.

Acknowledging jealousy or competitiveness.

Discovering the dynamic that needs to change.

DECISIONS WITH YOUR ROMANTIC PARTNER:

Beginning to date.

Taking things to the next level.

A breakup and a make-up.

Redefining boundaries.

Or ultimately calling it quits.

DECISIONS ABOUT HOME:

A big move to a new place.

Finding a community or choosing to leave one.

Saying goodbye to your childhood home.

Inviting someone in or throwing them out.

Rolling up your sleeves for a transformative deep clean.

DECISIONS ABOUT FAMILY:

Starting one, or adding to one.

Breaking with one.

Reconnecting with one.

To loan money or not to loan money.

Leaving or recommitting to the religion you were raised with.

GEORGE DAWES GREEN, MOTH FOUNDER: Every good story, I feel certain, hinges on a decision. Sometimes there'll be lots of decisions in the course of a narrative: backtracks, double-downs, veerings off, choices made by other characters, your replies to those choices. But always, at the story's core, will be *one key decision*. In the most powerful stories, your decision will be a tough one. (Some of your audience will concur with your choice, some will be appalled!) Good storytellers soon learn that what *happened* is of less importance: Your audience really wants to know what you *decided to do* about what happened. I've often been told stories of harrowing auto accidents. I usually find these tales kind of dull. But once, a man told me of a long icy skid that took him over a bridge and into a small river. The car was completely submerged, but the windows were shut and he had plenty of air—and so he had to make a choice. Should he lower the window, let the river come rushing into the car so he could try to escape, or just wait in that air-bubble for help? The story instantly took power. *The decision.*

When you consider potential stories, it's important that you think back to your frame of mind at the time. Decisions that seem minor now, like deciding what to wear to the school dance or asking for time off work to see a Spice Girls concert, might have felt monumental in the moment. As an adult, we know that it is a very bad idea for a nine-year-old to attempt to drive a two-hundred-pound motorcycle. But if you are a daredevil nine-year-old, *of course* you know you can handle it! It's fun to hear from both perspectives. Your nine-year-old self is still inside you. Let her speak!

You are always making decisions that change the course of events. The decisions can be as enormous as a move to another continent or as small as a shift in perspective, as illustrated in Peter Pringle's story.

We first met Peter through the Innocence Project, and his Moth story "As If I Was Not There" was about being in solitary confinement for a crime he did not commit. He is in a small cell, with no physical freedoms, and yet the story explores agency.

> *When I heard these jailers discussing their role in my execution and the fact that the authorities had told them there would be a role for them in my execution, there was no doubt in my mind that I was facing death. And I tried as best as I could to distance myself from that, and as best as I could to curb my anger. . . . And while I knew with certainty that the worst thing that they could do to me would be to kill me, until they did that, I was my own person. While they could imprison me physically, they could not imprison my mind or my heart or my spirit. And so it was within those realms of myself that I determined that I would live. And within that death cell, in that small space around myself, I had my own sanctuary. And I learned to almost totally ignore what was around me.*

In "Being a Foot Soldier," Dr. Sybil Jordan Hampton describes being a fifteen-year-old in 1959, on the front lines of school desegregation at Little Rock Central High. She was the only Black student in a class of 544 people. At graduation she was sure she would never return:

> *I thought to myself, "I'm not going to miss anybody. This is over for me. I am going to go on with the rest of my life. I am not coming back in this building, and I am certain I will see none of these people again in life." And then, there is this invitation to return to the twentieth anniversary in 1982. And I decided that, yes, I wanted to return because I needed to know what, if anything, had changed.*

Remember: *Choosing inaction* is still a choice. There are plenty of Moth stories that have been built entirely around the decision not to act. How about the critical moment in time when you froze and did nothing at all, or the knowledge you kept to yourself, or the big leap you decided you were better off skipping?

SARAH: Taking ownership over the choice *not* to act is rare, and can make an impactful story. I'll never forget hearing Megan McNally at a Moth GrandSLAM in Seattle. She told a story about how her close bond to her grandma was strained when Megan decided to give her baby up for adoption. She and her grandmother never talked about the decision in the aftermath. In "Things Left Unsaid," she said:

> *When my daughter turned eighteen and found me on Facebook, I told a staff meeting, but I didn't tell Nanny. And a few years after that, when I learned that she'd graduated college, had moved to New York, and fallen in love, I didn't tell Nanny. There were so many times I visited Nanny, when I tried to will myself to tell her about her first great-granddaughter. How scared I had been, wondering if I had made a mistake, how grief made me into something I wasn't proud of, how my daughter turned out just fine without me, and mostly, how sorry I was that I had left her out of all of*

this. But the longer you wait to do something, the harder it is to do. In the last years of her life, Nanny and I talked all the time. We talked about everything except this one thing. When she had a stroke, I sat with her, and I knew it was my last chance, and I said, "Nanny, do you remember that I had a little girl and I gave her up for adoption?" And I never imagined that she would say, "No." And when she died the next day, I became someone who had waited too long.

Megan's decision not to discuss her daughter with her grandmother until it was too late results in her change. Megan's inaction revealed a larger and irreversible truth to her. This was one of the deepest stories of her life, and we, in that Seattle audience, were witnessing it. I contacted her before we aired her story on *The Moth Radio Hour* and asked her a few questions. Megan told us that she's lived with years of regret. She said, "I regret that I didn't understand grief. That I never asked for help. That I let fear win out over love. I was so afraid for people to know how broken I was, and I was terrified to learn how much I had hurt the people I love. With Nanny, I regret that I never mustered the courage to bring it up, to just talk about it. And now there will never be that opportunity. It is, literally, too late."

Think back to that proverbial fork in the road, the path least traveled. You made a decision to act or not—where did that decision take you?

LOOK FOR THE OUCH

Our biggest mistakes often lead to great stories, the kind that you are always asked to repeat, or that arrive at the party before you make your entrance: "OMG! *You're* the one who fell through a skylight at a rooftop party! I've heard about that wild night!" Sometimes that fame can feel more like infamy, but the beauty of a well-told story is that it can turn your most embarrassing moment into something you're proud of. "Whoops, I accidentally sexted our rabbi" could end up as your most requested party story!

Mistakes are universal. Sharing our missteps and epic fails reminds people that it's okay; we are all fallible. These blunders are our chance to learn or grow, to be better and sometimes not take ourselves so seriously because, if we're honest, mistakes can be downright hilarious.

Does thinking about a particular incident make you a little embarrassed? A bit worried? Ashamed? ("I couldn't possibly. What would people think?") *Go there!* At least explore it! What you are reluctant to share might be *exactly* where you need to look. What do you have to lose by being honest with yourself?

> **MIKE BIRBIGLIA, MOTH HOST AND STORYTELLER:** What I've found over the years is, you know you're on the right track with finding a story if it makes you very uncomfortable to tell it. If you want to bail out at many stages of it, you know you're going in the right direction.

People often want to tell a story that makes them look good, but to the listener it can feel self-indulgent and braggy. "I benched my bodyweight/won a Peabody/sailed a sea/successfully completed a sixteen-hour surgery/memorized a concerto." Extraordinary accomplishments are a potential *setting* for your story, but not *the* story. Telling people about all the big wins in your life is a very easy way to lose your listener. You're talking *at* them, you're not inviting them in.

We've all been at dinner with the person who found themselves intoxicatingly *fascinating* and know the feeling of relief when it's over. It's okay to celebrate success, but that success will be more interesting if you tell us about your stumbles along the way. What was in it for you? What would happen if it didn't get done? If there is a story in there, it exists in your relationship to what it took to get there, how you felt about it, and why.

When working with Chenjerai Kumanyika on his story "The Two Times I Met Laurence Fishburne," we wanted him to talk about being a hip-hop star in the '90s, and what happens when you get your dream job at a young age, only to see it all disappear.

Chenjerai was reluctant to appear too braggy or full of himself, which is tricky when you are talking about actually becoming a music star! So we decided to start the story with an embarrassing scene about him screwing up at a job he was forced to take after his group broke up.

> *Now, when I say "my job," what y'all should know is this was a temporary job. And when I say it was a temporary job, what you should know is that my performance today determined whether I would be asked back tomorrow. So when I went in the boss's office, here's what she said: "Hi, Chenjerai. Yesterday I asked you to make two hundred* Gilmore Girls *Thanksgiving Day Special DVDs. But the Excel spreadsheet that you made ordered more than that." "Okay. How many more?" "One million* Gilmore Girls *Thanksgiving Day Special DVDs. Can you explain that, please?" I could: I have no idea how to use Microsoft Excel. And I lied about my skills to get this job.*

Because we meet him when he's down on his luck and failing at work, we're already on his side when we get to the later scenes with him riding on private jets and performing in sold-out arena shows.

Another musical example is Rosanne Cash, who, in "Until the Real You Shows Up," could have spoken about her multiple number one hit songs. Instead she talks about an album that did not produce hits:

> *I was in the studio, waiting to play it for the head of the record company for the very first time. I was so proud. He came in, and he sat down at the recording console and we played the album start to*

finish. He didn't say a word in between songs. And I thought, "He's speechless with the sheer beauty of this record. He's stunned into silence." As the last note faded away, he turned to me and he said, "We can't do anything with this. What were you thinking?"

KATE ON MOM FRIENDS: A few weeks after I had my son, I went to a meetup I found online, because I desperately wanted to meet other new parents. We met in a sunny corner of a biergarten where everyone drank water and made small talk as they showed their babies to each other. I was on the cusp of a massive life change, sleep deprived and full of big feelings, but everyone kept talking about "favorite products," and I had little interest in chatting about Boppy pillows. It was not for me. Shortly afterward, a mom emailed me a picture of her baby in mid-acid-reflux-vomit. It turned out that our boys were born a day apart and we started to get together to mostly stare wide-eyed as we confessed our darkest feelings about new motherhood—our fears, our failures, everything we were doing wrong, and how full of anger we were about it. After one playdate she texted, "I've never related to you more than when you rage-kicked the air at the end of your story today." A few days later, we brought our kids to the playground just before sunset. She handed me a tiny baby food jar she'd filled with some red wine. "Cheers," she said. "This is hard." It was. It is. But it was the brutal honesty of the stories that we shared that made me feel like I wasn't alone. I've sought out these conversations in the years since then, and built a community that feels like family and makes me a better parent.

Even when real-life heroes tell Moth stories, they connect with the audience best when they reveal their less heroic sides, rather than talking about how they saved the day.

When astronaut Michael Massimino started working on his Moth story "A View of the Earth," he said, "I could tell you about the time I broke the Hubble Telescope." *What?? Yes, please!* Mike was assigned to a shuttle mission to fix a problem with the Hubble Space Telescope. He and his fellow astronauts had spent years preparing for the mission—training for each step of the repair and planning for every possible problem. Without exaggeration, millions of taxpayer dollars had been spent. After years of training, Mike finally found himself tethered to the shuttle, floating in space, a foot from the famous telescope—armed with his trusty tools. He started to remove the panel that protected the telescope and that's when it happened—he stripped the screw. He couldn't get it out. Removing the panel was supposed to be the easy part, so much so that they never even considered it might be a problem. Years of training to fix a telescope that they now couldn't get to because he'd stripped a screw. It was a simple thing, but in this instance, it threatened the whole mission. As he floated in space, he pondered the possible consequences of his mistake.

> *I can't get to the power supply that failed, which means we're not gonna be able to fix this instrument today, which means all these smart scientists can't find life on other planets, and I'm to blame for this. And I could see what they would be saying in the science books of the future. This was gonna be my legacy. I realized that my children and my grandchildren would read in their classrooms, "We would know if there was life on other planets . . . but Gabby and Daniel's dad"—my children would suffer from this—"Gabby and Daniel's dad broke the Hubble Space Telescope, and we'll never know."*

Most of us will probably never be sent to outer space by NASA. But who can't relate to spending many hours of your life preparing for something important, only to be undermined by something as tiny and common as a stripped screw?

Spoiler alert: Mike ultimately figured out a way to fix the problem and the Hubble repair was completed—the day was saved! But the fact remains—the story's hook lies in one small mistake.

What it really comes down to is vulnerability. There is something comforting when people are willing to share the not-so-pretty sides of themselves. It's as if they give the listener permission to relax. This is not a competition or an exercise to impress—*I'm not perfect, so it's okay if you're not perfect too.* When someone makes themselves vulnerable, the listener leans in, and a quiet bond is formed. It's trust. *This person trusts me enough to admit they screwed up or got it wrong.* And that trust is the gateway to great empathy and memorable storytelling. It's almost a cliché to say it now (thanks, Brené Brown) (seriously, thanks, you are very smart) but vulnerability is power, especially when it comes to story. When we share our stories, we open ourselves to the opportunity to connect with each other.

DIRECTOR'S NOTES

- You are bursting with stories! Where will you start? Think back through the moments in your life you'll never forget—big events or smaller ones that changed you. If you have an inkling of a story idea, don't shoot it down too quickly. Ponder it. Why does this moment stick with you?

- Think of moments where you made a conscious decision, big or small. What happened as a deliberate result of something you did or did not choose to do?

- Consider how the story is personal to you. If you're including something that happened to someone else, remember it must have a direct impact on you, or the other person should be telling the story.

- Can you remember a moment where it all went horribly wrong? How did you recover? What did you learn? Don't be afraid to explore those uncomfortable moments and share the not-so-glamorous sides of yourself. Our biggest mistakes often lead to great stories! Those missteps make us human, and that vulnerability creates connection with your listener.

- Remember not to let a trauma or a struggle be *the* story, but rather the context of the story. Stories always need to go beyond "a bad thing happened."

- What was the inciting incident that set everything in motion? Perhaps you broke a pattern or interrupted your usual routine. What happened that shook things up?

- Think about moments that might have pushed you or pulled you in a different direction than you had planned. How might that moment have changed you?

CHAPTER 4

THE FOUNDATION

Honesty and empathy do not flourish in the expectation of perfection.

—MEG BOWLES

Once you have the germ of an idea for your story, it's time to start construction. You need no permits or hardhats, but you do need the general blueprints. It's vital that your story has a strong foundation. A big part of the foundation is what the story means to you.

Moth directors begin working with storytellers by listening . . . and then asking open questions. Big questions. Little questions. Many questions. As we listen, we dig deeper, drawing connections and identifying patterns and themes. Why does this story, of all the stories in your life, resonate with you? Why do you care? What about it stuck with you? What effect did it have on you—big or small? By answering these questions, you are beginning to identify the stakes in your story.

SARAH ON THE FIRST CONVERSATION: As a director, my heart flutters before the first phone call with a potential storyteller, even though I've coached many hundreds of stories. The very beginning of story crafting can be daunting, but we have to start somewhere.

STAKES

Stakes come from moments where you *feel* you have everything to gain or everything to lose. You might be fighting for your life, or you might be startled to realize that—*oh no*—you've slept through your alarm clock and you might not make your flight to your sister's wedding.

Stakes are defined by you, the teller—not your mother, brother, sister, or friend—and are born out of what you want/need/must have/can't live without OR desperately want to avoid. Some stakes seem universal: "I do NOT want to fall off the edge of this terrifying cliff." But *all* stakes are personal. For someone else, the stakes might be "I *need* to visit the edge of this terrifying cliff and take a selfie to prove to Carlos that I am adventurous and I'm doing *just fine without him.*" Your stakes resonate deeply within you, and part of your job as a storyteller is to make us understand your why. Sometimes stakes exist in smaller, narrowly defined situations, such as "I *will* get the bag of pretzels I paid for out of this *%#$# vending machine, even if I have to knock it over or break the glass. Go ahead, call security! JUST TRY TO STOP ME!" In more rational moments, you might just opt for some chips instead, but in the parameters of your story, it is the pretzels or Armageddon. On principle!

Stakes are what give a story urgency and energy. They create tension. They fill the listener with excitement or dread, and they give them a reason to go on this ride with you. Clear stakes establish why *you* care, which tells us why *we* should care.

In "The Duel," Jonathan Ames, longtime Moth storyteller and host, sets up the stakes clearly when he tells us of his epic fencing match.

> *I had a secret goal that sophomore year at Princeton while train-*
> *ing, and that was to beat the number one sabre fencer at Colum-*
> *bia, Robert Whitson. My lifetime record against Robert Whitson*
> *was 0 and 13. I had been fencing him all through high school. I*
> *had been fencing him at Junior Olympics. He was always beating*
> *me. Once at a party, he snubbed me socially, which only added to*
> *my growing wound. He trained in New York City with expatri-*
> *ate Russian coaches. He had incredible skill. He was snobby, and*
> *he had these sophisticated moves—so his whole worldview was*
> *opposed to mine, and I was always losing to him. So my secret goal*
> *sophomore year was to beat Robert Whitson.*

And then Jonathan, who wants to support his beloved coach, raises the stakes even higher.

> *And my coach also wanted me to win terribly, because his wife had*
> *left him and was shacking up with Columbia's coach—she had a*
> *thing for swordsmen, I guess—so he really wanted me to win. We*
> *both had a vendetta.*

In "Unhooked," Nathan Englander is a young tourist who finds himself being kicked off a train in Eastern Europe right after the fall of the Soviet Union.

> *I'm terrified because this is a part of the world that swallows Jews.*
> *That wall came down in a day, it could go back up in a day. Half*
> *the world was trapped behind it for all those years. And I think,*
> *"What have we done?"*

Clear stakes compel the audience to champion you, root for you, and cheer you on. When working on a story, it is essential to keep asking yourself: *What are the stakes?* Identify the moments where you felt you had something to gain or lose.

MEG ON CONVERSATION AROUND A TABLE: Making conversation at a dinner party can often be daunting. When you're the host, it can fall to you to keep the conversation going. This does not mean you have to take the stage and regale your table with tales of your most recent vacation. Sometimes the trick is knowing how to engage people and get them talking. While attending the Toronto Film Festival, I was invited to a dinner with Quentin Tarantino. Most of us around the table were complete strangers, so, as a way to break the ice, Quentin asked everyone to tell their favorite joke—and we went around the table one by one. I must admit it was intimidating being put on the spot in front of a legendary director like that, but in a way it bonded us, because we were all a little unsure. Some of the jokes were comically terrible, while others were hilarious! But it didn't matter because it changed the dynamic, and suddenly we were all friends. Posing a question to the table can be fun: What's your hidden talent? What's the story of your name? Tell us about a time you pushed your limits. Many of the same prompts we use to find a story can be used to get the conversation flowing.

THE WHAT AND THE WHY

Often, there is a struggle between what you want and what's working against you. Ask yourself: What did I *most* want? Who or what was challenging me? A story is more compelling when it is clear what a storyteller wants and why.

> *I was an expert on long-term memory. I knew everything about the anatomy and physiology. But I couldn't do one thing to cure my father's memory problems.*
> —Dr. Wendy Suzuki, "Saying I Love You"

Stakes require tension. Where can you find it in the story?

- A problem that needs to be solved.
- A struggle over a tough choice.
- A question that needs to be answered.
- A mystery you're trying to get to the bottom of.
- An unexpected event.

Tension keeps the audience on the edge of their seats. Your listeners wonder: *What happens next? Will they or won't they? How will this end?*

> *I was twelve years old and I was in my third foster home, and my very first foster father had just called. He called to say that he was very sorry to hear about my mother. But what he didn't know was that nobody had told me that she was dead.*
>
> —Samuel James, "Jenny"

Explore how the moment challenged or jeopardized your chance of success, your safety, your innocence, your faith—and what you risked physically and/or emotionally gaining or losing as a result. Is it your happy life, your carefree view of the world, your stability? Help your audience know what's important to you.

> *I was the first trans person through the Washington, D.C., police academy, and the path for me was going to be a little different. I would have to be excellent. I would have to be perfection, because they were going to judge every trans person who came after me by the standard I set.*
>
> —Morgan Givens, "Police Academy"

Stakes help the story become more than just a list of things that happened or a series of musings. They show the listener why the story is important for you to tell, and will ultimately support the overall arc of your story.

Many stories are some version of SNAFU: Situation Normal, All Fudged Up. The trip to grandmother's house through the forest isn't a story. It's an essay about gathering flowers and a grandchild's sense of obligation. But introduce the Big Bad Wolf into the mix, and suddenly we have stakes! Danger, an obstacle, a foe, something to overcome.

> *All of a sudden, a rush of fire comes into the room, lights up over our head and banks down the walls. I mean, everything is on fire. It got so hot so fast that it forced me down to my knees. I turned around thinking I could go back out the same way we came in, but that exit was blocked by fire as well. I didn't even see where the other firefighter who came in behind me was. I knew I was in a bad situation and I probably had to go through the rest of this house to get out.*
>
> —Sivad Johnson, "To Bravely Do or Bravely Die"

Say you have a story about a hellish airport experience where you end up losing your luggage. Okay, but people lose their luggage every day—so what? If you tell us that the luggage contained the only photograph you owned of your grandmother, suddenly you have given the story much higher stakes. We understand why this is more than a mere inconvenience. Your story of a hellish experience becomes more than just "this bad thing that happened."

Perhaps you begin by describing the scene of you packing, and you mention sliding the picture of your late grandmother, who raised you and loved you, into the pocket in the lining in the luggage. (You never travel without it.) Then tell the story of the hellish adventure, and when you get to the scene where the agent tells you your bags have been lost, you immediately bring us back to the image in our head of that photo tucked safely inside—the only photo you have—and suddenly you have given the listener a reason to care about you losing your bags (outside of just "well, that's awful/horrible/annoying").

By weaving in the detail of the photo, you've brought meaning to the story. Your listeners instinctively put themselves in your position. They remember similar instances from their own lives. They connect with you.

In his story "Have You Met Him Yet?," former White House staffer David Litt has the simple task of handing over headphones . . . to President Barack Obama.

> *I reached into my pocket and pulled out what looks like a hairball made out of wires. I don't know what's happened. I guess somewhere in that waiting room, I have just worried this thing into a hopeless tangle. And now I don't know what to do, so I just hand the entire thing to the president of the United States. Now, if you work in the White House, you will hear the phrase "There is no commodity on earth more valuable than a president's time," which I always thought was a cliché. Until . . . I watched Barack Obama . . . untangle headphones . . . for thirty seconds . . . while looking directly at me.*

Stakes can be magnified by smaller moments, simple twists of fate: missing the train stop, taking a wrong turn, being seated next to someone from your past at dinner—something that came out of the blue and tested you.

> *I'd just moved to New York. I didn't have a job. I didn't have any friends. I didn't know what I was doing, but I had a lot of laundry. So I spent the days going up and down the elevator to the laundry department downstairs. And one of these days, I was going back up in the elevator, swinging my keys around my fingers, and the keys, as if by magic, dropped down the shaft between the doors and elevators. So I heard them clank clank clank clank. Down the shaft. To the bottom. And I just stood there and was like, "Oh my God, I have no wallet, no phone, no keys. I don't know anyone." I had met a very nice girl on the plane, but I didn't know her number by heart. I did not know my neighbors,*

I had no bra on, and I had no shoes. And I was so hungry. I had
no idea what to do.

—Isabelle Raphael, "Shoeless and the City"

INTERNAL STAKES VS. EXTERNAL STAKES

Some stories explore internal stakes, in other words, what's going on inside your head: *Will I feel alone forever? Do I have what it takes to pass the test? Am I strong enough to forgive my mother?* Others deal with factors outside yourself: a bear, an audit, an irate neighbor. But many of the best stories are a mix of both.

Stakes are defined by context. Where were you in your life at the time? About to graduate from high school? Hitting a rocky patch in your marriage? What things were happening in your life that were (or could have been) altered by this moment? What had you taken for granted? What had you spent too much energy on? Show your listener what was going through your mind—what you felt you had to lose or possibly gain. What put everything in jeopardy?

In Karen Duffin's Moth story "The Speechwriter's Lament," Karen skillfully builds the stakes with every detail she chooses. She starts by telling us about her job, giving us the context of her story and what she stood to lose if something went wrong.

> *I was the speechwriter for the CEO of a very large company for*
> *several years. The thing about being a speechwriter is that it isn't*
> *just about being able to write well, it's kind of like being a profes-*
> *sional best friend. You kind of have to be able to finish their sen-*
> *tences, be able to channel their voices. So you spend a lot of time*
> *together, you travel a lot together, you learn how to speak in their*
> *voice. Also, if you happen to be able to afford a speechwriter,*
> *you're probably pretty busy. We might go to four or five countries*
> *in one week. We'd get on the airplane, I'd be like, "Where are we*
> *going? We're going to Saudi Arabia?" So I pull out all the mate-*

rials and teach him how to say hello in Arabic. So he's placing an enormous amount of trust in me to be able to pronounce things correctly and tell him GDPs and things like this. You spend several years building up this kind of trust. I've seen people fail not for lack of talent, but for lack of ability to build a relationship.

Karen has laid the groundwork for what is important to her. The trust she describes is what she risks losing. She goes on to tell us about working on a speech with her boss the night before the annual shareholder's meeting. (More stakes!)

I drop him off. I say, "I'm going to pick you up at six o'clock tomorrow morning, we're going to rehearse, and you're going to be great."

I go home, finish the script, send it off to the producers. I go to sleep, set six alarms, just in case, for five o'clock in the morning, and I wake up the next morning without the alarm, which is strange, because I never wake up without the alarm. There's sunlight streaming through the windows. I'm thinking, "That is so weird. I'm in California, I'm not in Alaska. Why is there sunlight?" And then, it's that movie moment where the audience would be screaming, "No!" And in my head, I'm screaming, "No!" I'm in slow motion leaping out of my bed, probably tucking and rolling and grabbing my cellphone, and it's 7:30. And he goes on stage at eight o'clock in the morning.

Thanks to the earlier context, we feel the consequences (stakes) *with her* in this moment. She's on the verge of losing not only her job but also her boss's trust.

There's also probably twenty-two text messages, four voicemails, some of which are from him, and he's seriously the nicest man on earth, which is what makes this story so much worse. Because he's like a father who's not angry, he's disappointed in you. He's like, "Hi, Karen. It's 6:04 or 6:12. I assume maybe your car broke? I

don't know. I'm just going to drive myself." So I have six of these
voicemails. So I call [the director of communications] and she says,
"It's okay. I'm just so glad you're alive, because John had to stop
rehearsal this morning and tell everyone, 'I'm very, very sorry
that I'm so off today and so flustered, because I think that one of
my communications people died. I don't know where she is.'"

He trusts her so much that the only explanation he can find for
why she hasn't shown up is that *she must be dead*.

When she finally gets to the event, hours late, she describes it
like this:

This was an audience of everyone who mattered to my career, all
the executives in the company, all of the communications depart-
ment, everybody's there. So picture your worst personal walk of
shame. This is like a professional walk of shame. Everybody
knows, because first of all, they thought I was dead. And now
they know I'm alive and that I just slept in like I'm seventeen.

The beauty of this story is the way Karen builds the stakes. With
each added detail, the stakes change and turn and elevate. Like a
roller coaster, the action rises; you climb up the track *click by click*.
She is creating and playing with the tension the listener feels, and
she uses the tension to pull us through, until the moment we find
out what ultimately happens.

If she hadn't successfully built up the stakes, it would have just
been a story about sleeping through an alarm clock—which, ultimately, it is—but the stakes invest us in the outcome.

When you build out the stakes of your story, how can you set
them up so the audience knows what's important to you? Can you
reveal something deeper about yourself through your motivation?

A story that lacks stakes has no tension, and will fall flat. Find
the moment—the unique and personal detail—that helps them feel
what is at stake in the same way it felt for you. You want them to be
on your side, cheering you on!

PITCHING A NEW IDEA: For a while, nobody believed that we would all be carrying computers in our pockets, yet here we are putting on a rainbow filter and FaceTiming our friend Claude. What if *you're* the one with the next great idea? How will you get your stakeholders to believe in you? Tell the story about the moment you realized the idea was brilliant, even though no one believed in it. Use your story to set up the world before your idea, guide them through your aha moment, how it will change everything, and land on where you are today. Your story can be the tool that gets everyone excited about your idea.

ANECDOTE VS. STORY

People tend to use the words *anecdote* and *story* interchangeably, but actually they are quite different. An *anecdote* is a short, amusing account of a real incident or person. A *story* is beyond a string of occurrences; it deals with evolution. If you don't want or need anything, it's not a story. A good story builds. By the end, things have intrinsically changed. Something about it has a lasting effect. You can't go back. You can't unsee it. You can't un-be it. You are a different person because of the events that unfolded.

Our anecdotes might have some dramatic or entertaining details, but they usually lack true depth. These anecdotes are worth mining, because often there is more to these frequently repeated moments if we dig into them. Quite a few beloved Moth stories started out this way!

When Ellie Lee was in college, her father's grocery store—the largest Asian market in New England—burned to the ground. There were a lot of details that made the terrible event memorable: Among them, the city of Boston had done work in the area a week before and had forgotten to turn the hydrants back on, so there was no water to stop the fire. Here's what she originally told us that made it into her story "A Kind of Wisdom":

> *It was just a disaster. They were trying to rig something from a nearby hydrant ten blocks away, and if things couldn't get worse, the fire jumped an alley and the building next door caught on fire. On the top floor were ten thousand square feet of illegally stashed fireworks . . . and it's a surreal moment, because things are exploding, like in celebration.*

When Ellie dug in, she saw how this event changed her view of her father. Up to that point, she had seen him as a little ridiculous (the way many teenagers view their parents). Over the course of the fire, she came to see him in a new light.

> *I remember seeing three elderly women, and they were crying. And so I went up to them and I said, "Is everything okay? Why are you crying?" And the lady looked at me, and then she looked at my dad's burned-down store, and pointed, teary-eyed, and said, "Where are we gonna go now that we don't have a home?" And that was a turning point for me. I hadn't really thought about my dad's store in that way. I just thought it was something he was doing to provide for the family, but in fact he was providing for a greater community.*

Ellie's Moth story includes the anecdote about the exploding fireworks, but with a richer, deeper context about family, respect, and community. The best stories are not just about the facts of *what happened*. We want to walk next to you through the story and *understand*.

Say you get the wrong bag at the airport and finding the owner to return it to is an ordeal. Or you sit next to someone on a bus who, it turns out, was your deceased father's best childhood friend. There is a beginning, middle, and end, but what's the larger point? Action, characters, setting—all of the boxes are checked *except for* what it all means. The *why* of why you are telling it.

Often the stories that we repeat again and again to our friends and family seem just fun and amusing ("Tell the one about how everything went wrong at your rehearsal dinner!"), but when we step back and reflect, bigger themes emerge ("The bride and groom were nervous about two very different families joining"). Why does the teller want to share the story again and again? Is there something deeper that's drawing them to it? If you dig a little, there's often meaning to mine from them, which is why they are important to you and get repeated ("The disastrous rehearsal dinner bonded the two different families").

We're not just exploring "this thing" that "happened" to you. Dig deep to find the roots of how and why it mattered to you.

DON'T THROW AWAY YOUR ANECDOTE: Sometimes your amusing or illustrative anecdotes are the seeds for something bigger, but sometimes they're perfect just as they are. In casual settings, like in the waiting room at the doctor's office or at your company picnic or at a PTA meeting, you may not have the time for a fully rounded story with big stakes and a tender, reflective ending. If Taye Diggs took mercy on you and your crying baby on a flight to LA, and said, "Hand him over," then rocked him to sleep in two minutes—there's your story! You can leave it there; no need to go into the insecurities you were having at the moment about your parenting. These social interactions and conversations are typically brief, and nobody gets the floor for five uninterrupted minutes. And yet these brief moments have impact, build connections, and invite others to share their experiences. One anecdote begets another, which inspires a volley of sharing and perhaps the beginning of new friendships, business relationships, and romances.

A BIG LITTLE STORY

Sometimes a small story will tie into a bigger event that inspires a change in the teller. That seemingly minor story will then be elevated into something with more meaning. We have a shorthand for this—we call it a Big Little Story.

In "Head of Clay," Jay Martel has to figure out what to do with a very heavy and ugly statue he inherits from his mother. The bigger story, the emotional story, is that the statue is a clay portrait of Jay's own head when he was a teenager. Although he doesn't want custody of the statue, he ends up feeling kind of hurt that neither of his parents have room for it in their downsized apartments. If he doesn't take it, will they just put it out on the curb?

Ishmael Beah's story "Unusual Normality" is about trying to fit in at a new school by playing paintball, a game his classmates enjoy. The bigger story is that, unbeknownst to his fellow students, Ishmael is a refugee from a war where he was a boy soldier. "Playing" war is in sharp contrast to his lived experience and gives him a window into the innocence of childhood.

SUZANNE RUST, SENIOR CURATORIAL PRODUCER, ON THE ORIGIN OF THE BIG LITTLE STORY: In a showcase featuring stories from women and girls, Mmaki Jantjies told the story "Meeting Nelson Mandela," about being a fourteen-year-old student in South Africa.

Going into high school, I really battled with my self-confidence. I didn't believe in myself, and I didn't feel that I had much to offer the world. This despite my mom's continuous words that "Mmaki, I believe in you." "Mmaki, education is so important." "Mmaki, hang in there. One day, all of this will make sense." I remember the first day of school, getting there with my skinny self, with a school uniform so big and so baggy that the little dress went over my knees. And I remember looking at all the other girls—their moms had agreed to alter their school uniforms to fit their little bodies. And on top of that, they had the trendiest hairstyles.

Mmaki's mother had read about an essay contest in the local paper and encouraged her daughter to enter. The theme was *If I were king or queen for the day*. With no mention of a prize of any kind, Mmaki reluctantly wrote the essay, sent it off, and forgot about it. But a few weeks later, she was called to the principal's office.

> *I head off to the school principal's office, and to my amusement, he was so excited to see me. He wanted to tell me that I had won an essay-writing competition, and that as part of the prize, I would be whisked off to the capital city of South Africa, Pretoria, to go to an award-giving ceremony. That essay-writing competition had a prize after all! Anyway, I rushed home, told my parents, told my family. So much joy, so much excitement. My mom and I were then taken to Pretoria to a plush five-star hotel. Upon arrival, we were briefed on the award-giving ceremony and how it would go. We were then informed that as part of the prize, we would meet Queen Elizabeth and President Nelson Mandela!*

Mmaki's story is special not just because she got to meet these icons but because of how the event transformed the way she thought about herself.

> *I looked up. There were all the other finalists dressed in their baggy school uniforms with their traditional hair plaits. So I took my place in the line in my baggy uniform with my traditional hair plaits. I stood there and waited patiently. Queen Elizabeth came down the line, greeting every single finalist, until she got to me. I reached out, I curtsied, and we had a conversation about leadership, and what I thought about leadership at that time. She went off, and my heart started to pound. I was overflowing with emotion. As I heard Nelson Mandela's voice come closer and*

closer to me, this voice that represented freedom for so many years was about to stand in front of me. And as I picked up my head, there stood this towering figure, Nelson Mandela. At that moment, it came to me, my mother's words: "I believe in you. One day, all of this will make sense. Focus on your education." I stood there and I realized that I had so much to offer the world. Because despite the baggy uniform, despite the traditional hair plaits, I was standing in front of Nelson Mandela because of what I had to say.

It struck me on first listen that Mmaki's is a "big little story." In theory, a story about a schoolgirl winning an essay contest might seem pretty small, but because it connects to something bigger in the world that inspires a change in the teller, it's elevated. And so the Big Little Story became part of our vernacular at The Moth.

(But a word to the wise: Just running into a celebrity does not qualify as a Big Little Story. It's very cool that you met Beyoncé, but beyond the giddy rush of excitement, did it really change you or the trajectory of your life?)

FINDING YOUR ARC

Moth stories involve change and evolution. The change is the structural frame that helps you build out your overall arc in the story. An arc, put simply, is: Who were you at the beginning of the story, and who were you at the end? How do you live your life differently as a result of the events in the story, and why is that consequence meaningful to you?

If you're telling the story about the time you dropped your keys down the elevator shaft, did you always keep your keys in your pocket after that day? If it's about families bonding after a disastrous wedding rehearsal dinner, did you feel less fretful about attending family gatherings after that?

All Moth stories document a storyteller's transformation. The change can be:

Physical (out of shape → now running marathons)

Situational (terrible marriage → divorced and fancy free)

Emotional (dreading each day → now happy to wake up)

Behavioral (lover of bacon → vegan)

Attitudinal (hated dogs → now you have three)

The change feeds the stakes of the story. It can be the discovery you made or the habit you broke, but ask yourself: Why should we care about this shift in you? Why do *you* care? (Maybe those dogs filled an empty void?)

> **SARAH:** If nothing changes, you're sharing a recap, or an eloquent summation. Stories hinge on change.

One of the most rewarding things about crafting a story is recognizing the significance of an experience that has marked you. There's a difference between the events of the story (the plot) and what the story is really *about*. As storytellers, we see how those pivotal moments continue to influence and alter us.

> Faith Salie's Moth story is about choosing a dress to wear to her divorce proceedings, but the emotional core is about wanting to be fully seen by her former husband, one last time.

> Nikesh Shukla shared a story about learning to cook his mother's recipes for chana masala and dal bhat after she died, but on a deeper level, re-creating those dishes was a way to conjure his mother's memory and make him feel closer to her.

Noriko Rosted told a story about choosing a pet sitter for her beloved cat, Spencer—but the story is really about finding an unlikely connection with her young neighbor.

When you allow yourself the space to revisit these experiences from your past, you'll begin to see patterns and themes emerge. Often a storyteller will say, "I never realized this about myself." By truly looking at your life, you start to connect the dots and find meaning in the story.

MICHELLE JALOWSKI, MOTH DIRECTOR: I love when a storyteller calls me and says, "I remembered something!" As they thought about whatever experiences are part of their story, something occurred to them that shifted their perspective and brought them some new level of understanding.

KATE ON TOASTS: Moth stories hinge on change. A toast may not. I approached my father in the line for one of our StorySLAMs. He was smiling, proud to tell me that he was going to throw his name into the hat and tell the toast that he'd given at my wedding a few months before. He knew it was great; he'd had the room captivated and in tears. One friend was so moved that she had to excuse herself for a walk around the block to gather herself afterward. In the toast, his love for me was clear from the beginning—but there was no change. He never once doubted it! I looked him in the eye and said, "Dad, your toast was perfect, but if you're going to tell it at a SLAM . . . I have notes." Your toast can earn a standing ovation without an arc. Keep your toast celebratory, brief, and full of vibrant scenes. (Worry about the arc the next time you're at a SLAM!)

YOUR ONE SENTENCE

At this point you're on your way to developing a story. You've identified a moment or two, you have an idea of the stakes, and you feel deep down that *something* changed for you as a result of the events in the story. The next thing to try, before you build the story, is to distill it down to *one* sentence.

What's the trailer of your story?

The sentence you choose will act as your road map. You don't need to include it in the actual story—there's no need to start with a stated premise. (Please don't!) Just think of it as a path to help guide and focus your story. You can revisit the *one sentence* as you go along, using it to edit out details that might be distracting or take the story off course.

Let's look at a *one sentence* for "A Kind of Wisdom," Ellie Lee's story that we talked about earlier in this chapter.

> *It took a disaster for me to appreciate the important role my father played in our community.*

Inherent in this sentence are the plot *and* her arc.

- There was a disaster in the community. (In this case, it was the devastating five-alarm fire in Boston's Chinatown.)
- Ellie's father is somehow important in the community.
- Her father's importance was not evident to her until the extreme circumstances of the fire made it clear.
- Ellie gains a whole new level of respect and admiration for her father when she sees him through the eyes of the community.

The story would be *so* different if just one word of the sentence changed. The one sentence acts as your *lens*. You can tell several different stories about the same life event, but knowing what *this* version of the story is about will give your story focus. For instance, if it involves going to a fancy New Year's Eve party, the details you choose to highlight will be different if the main through line is about confronting your fear of crowds versus realizing your date is the love of your life.

> **CATHERINE:** Occasionally, after one of the storytellers I'm direct-ing tells their story, Meg will ask (either in the moment or later), "Well, what do you think the story is about in one sentence?" My heart always sinks, because I know it means what the storyteller is trying to convey is getting lost. I always dread that question, even though finding the answer will always (always!) make the story much better.

Remember, Moth stories are about *you,* so you'll only be using *your* point of view. To choose the angle of *this* version of the story, ask yourself:

- Is this story about you versus yourself—an internal struggle (e.g., realizing and admitting your addiction to Twitter)?
- Is it about you and your evolving relationship with another person (e.g., learning your son neglected to mention you were going to be a grandmother)?
- Is it about you versus the world around you (e.g., navigating a busy rush hour commute as a person who uses crutches and leg braces)?

Defining what the story is really about early on helps you choose the details and moments to best support the story as you build it. We'll revisit your *one sentence* later during the editing process, when it will help you choose between details that support your story and those that distract from it. For now, consider it your blueprint and refer back to it frequently.

DIRECTOR'S NOTES

- Ask yourself: What are the stakes of your story? What did *you* feel you stood to lose or gain as a result? What did you most want/need/must have/couldn't live without? Remember, stakes show us why *you* care, which tells us why *we* should care.

- Does your story go beyond anecdote? You might have dramatic details or a string of amusing events, but it must go deeper! Ask yourself why this moment left a lasting effect on you so you can transform your anecdote into a story.

- What is the arc of your story? Who were you at the beginning and who were you at the end? How were you changed? How do you live your life differently as a result of the events in the story?

- What is the story ultimately about for you? How would you distill it down into one sentence? Remember, you can tell various stories using similar events—boiling it down to one sentence will give you the focus and clarity to guide and shape the story you want to tell.

CHAPTER 5

THE MATERIALS

When I first speak to a new storyteller, I ask them dozens of questions. We talk through what stories they might want to tell, and I want to hear every detail. I sometimes refer to this as "dumping their bag out on the bed." We sift through everything, then decide what to keep and what to toss.

—CATHERINE BURNS

As you continue to build your story, you'll need supplies. Good news: You have everything you need, but you're going to have to scrounge around in the beautiful junkyard of your memory to find the pieces. Get out your metal detector. We're digging for treasure, but we'll hit a lot of pennies and bottle caps along the way.

NARRATIVE STEPPING STONES

You may know where the story starts and where it ends, but between those two points are a thousand choices. What critical pieces of the narrative puzzle do we need in order to follow along? Try making a list of bullet points that includes not only specific moments but also the backstory and important thoughts or realizations that lead you to the climax and resolution at the end.

But remember: Moth stories are *not* all plot (this happened, and then, can you believe *this* happened?); they always alternate between action and reflection. The action may take the form of a specific moment (or scene) or perhaps a series of moments. Reflection may include reactions to what is taking place (i.e., thoughts and feelings), or it may be background information that helps us to better understand the action and the stakes involved.

Each of these beats is a potential stepping stone in your story. It's a little like an outline; every step is important to the narrative flow. If you leave any one of them out, the story will be tough to follow.

Have you ever heard a story and thought, *Wait, how did they get there?* Were you confused by some detail that suddenly seemed important to the story? Chances are the teller missed a narrative step. If the story starts with you flat broke in Detroit but in the next scene you are suddenly shopping for fancy perfumes in Paris, the audience will be confused. You have to include the scene where you get that big unexpected tax refund right after your girlfriend tells you it's her dream to see the Eiffel Tower.

As you share the story, it's as if you, the storyteller, are driving a car, and we, the audience, are in the passenger seat. You know exactly where you're going, and which turns to take. Some houses you just drive by en route to the next turn. But sometimes you slow down and stop to tell us about what we're seeing and maybe how the person who lived in that house was the only person who really *saw* you for who you are.

You do not need to literally include every step of the journey or every turn you took along the way. Jump cuts are allowed! You can tell us about the car ride without including that you got in the car, put the keys in the ignition, started the car, put it into reverse, and backed out of the driveway. You just need to think about the important steps that will take us through your story. What info do we *need* to know to understand the bigger picture?

For example, take Jackie Andrews's story "Feedlot Calves," about getting pregnant at sixteen and struggling to make ends meet, but succeeding with the help of the community. The stepping stones might go something like this:

- Jackie opens in her family's dining room, telling her parents she's pregnant and wants to keep the baby.
- Next, we are in the hospital, where Jackie is holding her newborn daughter for the first time, realizing how much she loves her, and how determined she is that they will make their way in the world together.
- She gives us the context of her daily life, successfully juggling high school, chores, and a job at Wendy's, all while caring for her daughter.
- She explains how her ability to care for her daughter was challenged when a wave of hospital bills started to arrive, and she couldn't pay them on her salary at Wendy's; she had to find another source of support.
- She provides context and backstory that show how she was raised by a fiercely independent father who would not allow her to seek public assistance.
- Then she introduces her father's detailed plan to rescue newborn calves from feedlots, raise them, and sell them at auction (including important background info on how feedlots work).
- She tells us the farm crisis hits, and the price of cattle plummets (important context that raises the stakes).
- In the end, she takes us to the auction, where the mood is ominous. But when Jackie's father tells other farmers about her efforts to pay her bills, they are deeply impressed. Despite their hardships, they bid high, and Jackie earns the money she needs.
- The resolution comes when Jackie is able to pay all of her bills and expresses her deep and lasting gratitude for the community who rallied to help her.

Once you have all your stepping stones in order, you may find that you can completely skip some. Sometimes you need to see everything to realize the fastest path to where you're going. You can often jump-cut from one plot point to another without hurting the story. We don't need to see you measuring flour and mixing the batter, just take the cake out of the oven.

We'll talk about various structures you can use in a later chapter, but for now, as you're beginning to build your story, you just need to identify the important pieces of information. Which parts of your story absolutely must have close-up detail, and which parts can you condense?

In a Moth story, the teller uses three elements to get us from beginning to end:

1. **SCENES** illustrate parts of the story that are both compelling *and* critical to the arc. The climax of the story is almost always a scene.

2. **SUMMARIES** move us through the time line and connect us to the next step ("three weeks later," "after a lot of trial and error," "I completed my master's degree and was finally ready," "two kids and a mortgage later . . .").

3. **REFLECTIONS** share your feelings and insights about what you learned, concluded, deduced, decided to change, or accepted.

In Jackie's story, outlined earlier, she opens with a short scene of the inciting incident that sets the stage for the rest of the story.

> *In 1979, I was standing in the dining room of our western Nebraska farmhouse, and I was crying. I was telling my mom and dad that I was pregnant.*

Her opening scene places us firmly in the moment and introduces the stakes of the story right out of the gate. She goes on to summarize her father's reaction and then takes us quickly to the next scene.

> *It was my father who brought my daughter to my bedside, and he placed her in my arms, and he said, "Jackie, here's your daughter, and you do the very best you can with her. But no matter how hard you try, you're going to mess her up." He said, "We all do. But if you love her and you let her know how much you love her, she'll forgive you."*

She reflects on her feelings.

> *The easy part was loving this baby. From the minute I held her, I loved her more than I loved life itself. And I knew that she and I were going to fight our way through this world.*

She then summarizes the context of the life that she settled into.

> *I'd get up in the morning and I would do chores, and then I would go off to band practice and to school. And I would race home after school to see her before I went off to work at Wendy's. At night, I would come home and I would do the chores for the night and start my homework. And I would learn to sleep with that little baby right here in the crook of my arm. It wasn't easy, but I felt like I was keeping my head above water until that wave of hospital bills hit, and they were enormous.*

She provides context and important backstory about how she was raised.

> *My dad was the kind of man who loved democracy, and he loved children, and he respected people who made an honest living with their hands. But he hated capitalism, and he distrusted institutions, and he was scornful of a wasteful society. So he had said that*

we would live on this farm and everything we needed would come from the farm. And if we couldn't get it from that farm, then we would barter for it.

And she throws in a little scene to illustrate.

I can still see my father standing there with a piece of rotten fruit that we had gotten from a dumpster behind the Jack & Jill grocery store. And he'd say, "Jackie, look at this. Seventy-five percent of this pear is good, and someone's thrown it away." Then he'd cut off the bad part and we'd eat it. He just had this way of looking at the world.

She continues, summarizing the plan to rescue newborn calves, raise them, and sell them at auction, explaining how feedlots work. She weaves in scenes to illustrate how they put the plan into action and the obstacles they encountered, including the 1980 farm crisis.

Then Jackie brings the story to a close with one final big scene at the cattle auction after her father shares her story with his fellow farmers, many of whom are struggling financially themselves.

And that sale starts, and herd after herd is just coming through this sale ring, and the price is so low that they're practically giving these cattle away. And I get that feeling in my stomach that's just tightening because my fate is kind of marching toward me. And my herd comes into that ring. Those farmers started bidding, and then they kept on bidding. And they started bidding on those cattle like they were some kind of prize breeding stock. And that price, it went so far beyond what those cattle were worth, because those farmers were voicing their approval of my ability to try and pull myself up and pay off these bills. And they voiced that approval with wallets that had been emptied in this farm crisis. They didn't give to me from their surplus, they gave to me from their hearts. And I walked away with enough money, and paid that hospital bill off in full.

She lands her story with a final summary, including her reflections looking back on the experience.

> *A couple weeks later, I graduated high school, and my daughter and I took off out of western Nebraska, and I went on to earn a college degree. I joined the army, and I was awarded a bronze star for my actions in Desert Storm. I have been able to travel the world, and I have seen magnificent things, but a part of my heart has never left western Nebraska. It will always remain with the farmers who gave me a chance in life.*

As the storyteller, you are in charge of how you use scenes, summaries, and reflections. You are driving this tour bus through your story, and you choose which scenes your "passengers" see—what we cruise past or where we pull over for a closer look. If your story is about applying for your dream job as a law clerk, it's probably okay to skip the fact that your parents ran a clown school. Or maybe, for the purposes of the story you are trying to tell, that is *exactly* where you metaphorically stop the bus and have everyone get out and take a closer look. "I had learned to walk on my hands but couldn't figure out how to put on a tie that didn't squirt water."

SARAH ON STORIES DURING JOB INTERVIEWS: My father spent his career in executive leadership, and he believes in connecting the dots on your résumé through story. He says, "When you look at your résumé, what did you learn in each position that led you to the next? What is the story arc of your career, and why is this new position the right next step?" For example: Maybe you were a bassoonist who then became a conductor and then ultimately interviewed to become a music educator because you wanted to inspire more young people to choose a career path of music. You might not know where the story of your career is going, but when you look back at all the different jobs, there has to be some connection. What did you learn in one experience that narrowed down what you wanted to do next?

When Travis Coxson, The Moth's executive assistant and office coordinator, applied for his job, he had just spent years traveling as a stage manager for Broadway tours. We worried that he'd miss being on the road. But in his interview he told us that when the pandemic shut down theaters, he was suddenly at home for long stretches of time. He found he loved quiet mornings with his longtime partner. What used to be a crash pad became a home. He settled into a routine and realized how much more grounded he felt. He wanted to pivot, and find a way to use his organizational skills for live theatrical events without living out of a suitcase. His story resonated with us, and we offered him the job. A person who can turn job changes into narrative stepping stones that relate to one another will distinguish themselves. Telling the larger story of your work thus far is an impressive way to show the prospective employer who you are and why you are the perfect person for this role.

FINDING THE SCENES

Finding the scenes in your story brings it to life. What do these moments look like cinematically, as little movies? Reconstruct them in your mind and recount them vividly, so we can see and experience them with you.

In "My Dangerous Beauty Mission," Esther Ngumbi describes a familiar rite of passage: ear piercing.

> *I was growing up in a Kenyan village where there's no Walmart or Claire's to go get my ears pierced, so I had to do it the old school way. I locked the door, and I took that needle and thread, and I*

*placed the wall mirror so that I could see what I was doing. I start
pushing the needle and I'm feeling pain, but my pain is overshad-
owed by the beautiful Esther I'm imagining I will look like. Oh,
my first kiss, my first boyfriend! After a minute the needle pierces
through my earlobe. I tie the thread and I repeat the process. I start
pushing again. And after what seems like eternity, my second ear
is done. I take a big sigh and take a minute to appreciate my beautiful me.*

By bringing us into this detailed scene, she makes the audience
feel both the pain and the joy she experiences from taking matters
into her own hands.

In "This Is Going to Suck," Matthew Dicks tells us about being
sent to the emergency room after a near-fatal car accident.

*A nurse comes over and asks me for my phone number, and I give
her my parents' number. Then I give her the number for McDonald's, because I'm supposed to be working that night. She scoffs at
it, but I say, "No, that drive-through does not run well without
me, and they're gonna have to get someone in," and, bless her
heart, she calls McDonald's. My parents, they don't show up. I
find out later that when they heard I was stable, they went to
check the car out first. I'm waiting for a surgeon, because it's December 23 and they're hard to find, and I'm feeling alone. But
I'm not alone, because when she called McDonald's to tell them I
was out, those people started calling other people, and the waiting
room is now filling up with sixteen- and seventeen- and eighteen-
year-old kids. They roll my gurney to the other side of the emergency room and they open a door, and one by one each of my
friends stands in the door, and they wave and they give me the
thumbs-up, and they say stupid things to make me laugh.*

Matthew could have just said, "My parents were absent and so
my coworkers and classmates became my chosen family." Instead he
lets us experience the beauty of that realization with him.

In her story "Before Fergus," Lynn Ferguson tells us about a takeout dinner that she and her husband will never forget.

> *We arrived back home, my husband decides he wants some take-out food. I have this bizarre thing where I want to do a pregnancy test. It's positive. So my husband arrives back with his little brown paper bag to be greeted with the immortal phrase, "Put your curry down, sweetheart, there's something really big I have to tell you!"*

Lynn uses the simplicity of this scene to underscore a moment that changes the trajectory of her whole family.

In her story "Cast in Bronze," Trina Michelle Robinson talks about researching her ancestors and describes a scene from her journey to Kentucky to retrace their steps.

> *We finally get to the homestead where my family was enslaved. We get out of the car, and everything is largely overgrown with wild flowers and tall grass. Scott [our guide], he starts pointing everything out to me, like where the main house used to be, the native grass and plants and trees, just so I can get an idea of what my family would have seen. There were these beautiful ancient oak trees and cherry trees and goldenrod. It was fall, so things were starting to fade, but when they were hit by the sun they were just so beautiful. I hated it, because how could beauty live here?*

Scenes like Trina's keep us present. They drop us into the story and let us experience it. Because we can envision the sun on the goldenrod, we can better understand her struggle to reconcile the physical beauty with the historical ugliness. Which of your stepping stones could be told in a scene? Perhaps you start with a particularly exciting moment in your life or getting some surprising news—for example, the day you discovered you had a winning lottery scratch ticket. Push in and describe the actual moment:

- Where were you?
- Do you always buy a scratch ticket on the same day at the same location?
- Were you alone or with friends?
- Did you believe it, or did you have to ask someone to look at it and tell you it was true?
- Were you stunned into silence, or did you do a rowdy victory dance?
- Then what happened?

. . . And so on and so on.

GIVING SPACE TO A MOMENT

Scenes can be drawn from the active moments, places where something happens in your story and you want to slow down and explore. For instance, if your story begins with you quitting your job, don't just tell us you quit. Show us where you were—sitting anxiously in your boss's office or losing your cool next to a frozen yogurt machine that just erupted with raspberry swirl. Was there a phone ringing or a kid standing nearby laughing uncontrollably? What happened next? Did you stumble over your words, or did you take off that purple apron covered in yogurt and throw it on the floor before you stormed out?

In "Rich City Skater," Jacoby Cochran drops us right into the moment he's called to perform in the high-stakes world of competitive roller-skating circa 1990.

> Now, if you've never been roller-skating in your life, a National Party is like the Grammys of roller-skating. I'm talking about some of the greatest roller skaters in America, all in one place, showing off their moves, their music, their style. At that moment, we were going through a roll call, which means every city comes on the floor and represents. So, you got people from Texas doing the

"Slow Walk." People from Detroit doing "The Ballroom." Folks from Kentucky doing crazy between-the-leg throws. They were here from California to New York City to Florida, each with their unique flair, and the place was packed. The classic music was thumping. The synchronized lights were blaring. The fog machines were humming. At that moment, a song by the Godfather of Soul, James Brown, came on. And once you hear that "woooooo" in the intro of "The Payback" you knew it was time for Chicago to get on the floor.

In "A Soldier's Story," army veteran Ray Christian talks about confronting his post-traumatic stress disorder (PTSD) with a few disturbing scenes where we see him quick to anger, confused, and even delusional. Then he shares this:

I find myself at the mall, and I'm sitting on the bench, just trying to gather my thoughts, and a middle-aged lady, she shows up, and she's got her very elderly and frail mother with her. And she says to her, "Mama, I have to go to the bathroom. I want you to sit right here and don't go anywhere until I come back. Okay?" And she leaves. And this old lady is staring at me and staring at me. I try to look away. She keeps staring at me, and then she slowly moves her trembling, frail old hand next to mine, and she holds it. And I start to cry.

Her daughter comes back and she sees this and says:

"Mama, what are you doing? You can't be just touching people like that. Sir, are you okay?" I said, "I'm fine." And her mother looks up and says, "It's what he needed."
It is what I needed.

Earlier in the story, Ray had shown us his erratic behavior. When we see him take comfort in a stranger's gesture, we know he can no longer ignore the signs of his PTSD. It is the moment he sees it too.

Scenes *show* us important moments, instead of simply conveying facts. Ruby Cooper does this in her story "Kirk's Christmas Gift," which explores her relationship with her son.

She could have told us: My son had charisma.

> **But instead, she shows us:** *He was seven years old when I took him to school for the first time. And I pushed him down the hallway in his wheelchair, and he was going, "Hi! I Kirk. Hi! I Kirk." And waving like he was running for office.*

She could have told us: I had a hard time saying no to my son.

> **But instead, she shows us:** *When he lost his tooth that year, I said, "Here's what's going to happen. We're going to put your tooth under your pillow, and then the tooth fairy is going to come and exchange it for money." And he said, "No. Mine bring pie." I said, "No, no. The tooth fairy doesn't deliver pie. The tooth fairy's a little thing with a sack of coins." And he said, "No. Mine bring pie." I said, "Okay. . . . What kind of pie?" "Chocolate." So the next morning, the tooth was gone, and there was a box with a chocolate pie in it, delivered by a fairy at the local bakery.*

This little scene of Kirk calling the shots and Ruby's inability to resist paints a picture of the dynamic that plays out later on in the story.

In "Shawnees Never Quit," Alistair Bane recounts a time he was asked to sing a hymn in church.

> *I turned to the organist, who was waiting patiently. I was like, "'Michael, Row Your Boat Ashore,' please, ma'am." She smiled, nodded. "Good selection." The music started, and about the place I felt like there should be some words, I started to sing. "Michael, row your boat ashore, hallelujah. Michael, row your*

boat ashore. . . ." It was about the time that I reached the second hallelujah that I realized that was, in fact, the only line I remembered. But Shawnees have never been quitters. So I decided there can be different versions of the same song. There can be, like, extended dance remixes, where vocals are looped repetitively. I closed my eyes, 'cause sometimes it's better not to see your audience. And while I stood there singing, I had plenty of time for existential questions, like Who is Michael? Why does God want him to row his boat ashore? *And then finally I hit that line for the sixteenth time, and I stopped. The organist, who was not quite sure what was happening, continued to play for a minute, but when she realized it was finally over, she stopped in kind of an abrupt way. And then there was silence, and in that silence, I walked back down the center aisle. I started to climb back over my friend's knees. As I did, our eyes met, and he just said, "Dude."*

In Alistair's story, the scenes build toward him giving in to the pressure of performing in church, in an attempt to make his host happy. In sharing his inner thoughts, Alistair strategically slows his story down—thus building the tension, anxiety, and dread that he felt in that moment on the pulpit. Using this technique, Alistair not only reveals his vulnerability—he helps the audience *physically feel* that same dread.

Some stories might be chock full of small scenes, while others may have only two or three more detailed, impactful scenes. Usually there is one *big* scene (or the "main event") that the entire story is building to, which includes the climax. This is the scene without which there *is* no story.

In James Braly's "One Last Family Photo," his family has gathered at the deathbed of his sister Kathy. The story comes to a head as they witness Kathy's wedding held in the hospice room.

My dad stands up. The nurse walks in to make sure Kathy's not being coerced. Steve walks over to the corner and takes Kathy's hand, and the preacher opens the bible and begins speaking very

quickly, "Dearlybeloved, wearegatheredheretojointhismanandthis
womaninholymatrimony"—like an auctioneer. Because he needs
to finish before Kathy falls back asleep.

Kathy says, "I do." My dad looks at Steve, and they shake
hands.

My mom says, "Congratulations," and gives him one of her
bony osteoporosis hugs. I pop open the champagne and pour it in
the paper cups from the water cooler.

And everybody is drinking a toast to the bride and groom
when someone says, "How about a picture of the kids?"

I walk over to the corner and stand on one side of Kathy's bed,
and my brother and sister stand on the other, and we pose for a
photograph. We're looking out at a giant poster of the same pose,
taken twenty years ago at my sister Corinne's wedding, the only
photograph of the four of us together ever taken. Corinne had it
enlarged and put on Kathy's wall to remind her of home.

So, I stand there staring at how we used to look, posing for the
last photograph we'll ever take. My mom and dad looking on, all
of us together in a room for the first time I can ever remember, and
probably the last—because of Kathy who, in the end, is showing
us all how hard it is, but how beautiful it can be, to let go.

BIRTHDAY CELEBRATIONS: On her fiftieth birthday, Mary Domo, an early volunteer at The Moth, threw a party, and asked everyone invited to come prepared with a two-minute Moth-style Mary story. Mary has many friends from vastly different parts of her life: her Hoboken crew, East Village neighbors, career friends, people from The Moth, people from Burning Man. The idea was for each guest to share stories. "That's very Mary" could have been the theme. Each person only had a minute to paint a scene that showed her quirky genius. The little stories acted as introductions between people who had never met before. Mary felt loved, celebrated, and *seen*. All her guests felt more connected.

On the other side of the world, in the Embakasi neighborhood of Nairobi, an eighteen-year-old birthday girl asked each adult guest to tell a memorable story of their eighteen-year-old self. Stories were shared by the girl's grandmother and grandfather and everyone who was there to celebrate. The best story was the one her grandmother shared about how her husband (the girl's grandfather) taught her how to drive a car. Moth instructor Maureen Amakabane, who was there, said, "It was so beautiful. The grandfather said that he'd tell his version of the story at next year's birthday celebration! We all laughed. I was there with my young daughter, and not only did we get to know the family and neighbors better, but my daughter asked if we could do the same for her next birthday."

BEFORE WE EXIT SCENE

As you craft your scenes, make sure to stay in the action and describe them from the inside. Be an active participant rather than a passive observer, and avoid telling from hindsight. Allow the moment to unfold the way it happened for you.

Consider the difference between

> *I was scared when I walked in the room because I heard a noise.*

and

> *As I opened the door, I heard a growling noise in the corner—and my heart started racing!*

Tell it as if you were standing in it and feeling it now.

If a detail or scene is surprising, don't ruin the surprise by telling us it's coming! Give us the gift of feeling surprised along with you. Lose the preamble "and then the most amazing thing happened."

Setting the expectation might actually dilute it. Resist the urge to tell a listener what to think or feel, and let them come to their own conclusion.

If your story is feeling flat or you notice your listener is tuning out (or maybe *you* are!), try finding a scene to make it more engaging.

DETAILS

The brand of margarine, the song on the radio, the texture of the blanket, the fragment of crime scene tape still on the doorframe, the feel of moss beneath your bare feet—details turn your scenes from black-and-white into Technicolor. They make the story vivid, real, and tangible. They are often the juiciest part. Believe it or not, even the most obscure details can make your story feel *more* relatable. They highlight moments, create emotion, add tension, and ultimately support the stakes and the arc of a story. Details make your story unforgettable to the listener.

> **MEG:** I often tell people to blow it up big—look at all the details and moments you have to play with. The first step is to assess everything you have and then decide which of the details really support the story you are trying to tell.

In Leland Melvin's story "A Moment of Silence," he tells us about arriving at the International Space Station and being invited for a meal in the Russian segment by the commander. She told him to bring the rehydrated vegetables and they would provide the meat. He described the evening like this:

> *The smell of meat getting heated up. Their beef and barley, and our green beans with almonds, all being shared with people that we used to fight against, the Russians and the Germans. As we*

*broke bread at 17,500 miles per hour, going around the planet
every ninety minutes, seeing a sunrise and a sunset every forty-
five, I thought about the people that I'm now working with and
trusting with my life. African American, Asian American,
French, German, Russian, the first female commander of the International Space Station. Breaking bread, floating food to each
other's mouths. All while listening to Sade's "Smooth Operator."*

The specificity of details brings the scene to life. Instead of *it was
raining*, tell us about the noise of the rain on the roof or the puddles
that blocked the path.

In Trisha Mitchell Coburn's story "Miss Macy," she describes
the journey from her small Southern hometown to the big city like
this:

*Miss Macy and I boarded the train for New York City with a
bottle of Drambuie and a brown paper bag filled with Southern
fried chicken. Thirty hours later, we walked into the Waldorf As-
toria hotel. We had never seen anything like it. It was out of a
movie or something. And people sounded different, and they
looked different. And our room was a far cry from the cinder block
walls of my bedroom back in Alabama.*

You draw these details out from any (or all) of your senses. How
did something feel, both emotionally and physically? Was there a
sweet smell or an eerie whistling sound? Did someone use a turn of
phrase that sticks with you? Was there a thought that ran through
your head in the moment?

In Shaun Leonardo's story "El Conquistador," he paints the picture of what it felt like the first night he got in the ring as a luchador.

*The night comes, and it's a rickety ring in some makeshift arena
with folding chairs, and the mariachi music is blaring, and it feels
glorious. And they call out my name, and all the blood rushes*

*right out of my body. But I pull myself together, I get pumped, and
I step out in all white and gold. The knight in shining armor with
a fourteen-foot velvet cape. I hit that ring and I'm looking good,
and then I get my ass kicked.*

JODI POWELL, MOTH DIRECTOR: We often forget the inner dialogue. It is equally if not more important to let us know what you
are saying to yourself in the moment as it is to hear what you are
saying out loud to everyone else.

In discussing his story on *The Moth Radio Hour,* François Clemmons, a Black man, takes us to *Mister Rogers' Neighborhood,* where in
a now iconic scene, filmed at the height of the civil rights movement, he and Fred Rogers, a white man, soaked their feet in a kid-
die pool.

*So I took my boots off, put my socks over there, and we indeed put
our feet in that same tub. I get chills thinking about what a statement it was. And he cared enough to say something. So we put
our feet in the water together, and he had a little hose, and he ran
some water there. Once again, you think about what the police-
men did with the hose when they were so powerful, knocking
people down. And here were two people in friendship using the
hose to wet our feet.*

There are events or situations that a vast number of people have
experienced: falling in love, losing a loved one, being diagnosed
with cancer, coming out, the birth of a child. Many of the "stepping stones" in these stories will be the same for everyone. The
challenge is to find the details that make your familiar life experience *remarkable and uniquely yours.*

Consider the difference between "We kissed" and how Moth
storyteller Jeni De La O described her first kiss with her husband.

> *It was a kiss I could feel in my toes. A kiss I can* still *feel in my toes.*

Many people have been through some harrowing moments while driving, but in "That Thing on My Arm," Padma Lakshmi takes us from being a passenger eating lunch in her mother's car to the moment the car was hit.

> *I was eating this rice. Suddenly I heard a loud* bang*! And I looked up, and I can remember the plate flying . . . and yellow rice everywhere, like confetti. And as the rice came down, all I could see was this beautiful, crystal-clear blue sky. No clouds, no cars, no road in front of us, no trees, nothing. Just endless, miraculous blue sky with these kind of yellow grains flying all around. Then, all of a sudden, I heard another* thud*. And then it was just stillness.*

When you dig into the scenes you've identified, details begin to emerge that might be interesting and bring more meaning to your story. Those tennis shoes that you wore every day for all of 1986 might tell us a little bit about who you were in your youth; the random man at the grocery store who was laughing uncontrollably in the produce section might illustrate how you thought everyone around you was acting unusual.

Consider how Danusia Trevino shows us she didn't want to be picked for jury duty in her story "Guilty":

> *I got dressed for jury-picking day. I spiked my hair. I made sure my bat tattoo was in full view. I put on motorcycle boots, jeans with holes, and a T-shirt that said* I Wanna Be Your Dog.

Each of these storytellers used specific details to bring their scenes to life. Try it in your story. Instead of "I was nervous about a meeting," share the playlist you blasted in your headphones to get you *pumped* as you walked into your boss's office to ask for a raise. Make us root for you to get the R-E-S-P-E-C-T you deserve!

MOTH FOUNDER GEORGE DAWES GREEN ON "BURIED TREA-SURE": There's a bit of magic that raconteurs use, which I call "buried treasure." Early in your story, in the first minute or two, you bring up some small detail—usually something physical, talismanic: "So that was the day Uncle Wilkins took us to Coney Island. We all rode the Cyclone and the big Ferris wheel, and then crammed into a photo booth to take a strip of photos. Four shots, and before each one Uncle Wilkins called out a pose for us to assume. 'Surprise!' he said. We all tried to show surprise. 'Fury! Sorrow! Exultation!'"

Then, as your story goes on, you palm that detail. Forget it, leave it alone. Till you come to the end of your narrative, when you produce it again:

". . . And the cop handed me Uncle Wilkins's threadbare wallet, and I looked through it. There was a twelve-year-old gym membership, his expired driver's license, and nothing else—except a long, folded cardlike thing. Which I unfolded. It was a strip of four photo-booth snapshots. The four of us assuming those poses. 'Surprise. Fury. Sorrow. Exultation.'"

Your listeners will have completely forgotten that photo strip—until you bring it up in this entirely new context. And now that that they know the characters involved, the photo strip—the "buried treasure"—will be laden with new meaning. If you pull off this sleight-of-hand nimbly, it can be a powerful and moving device.

DETAILS BUILD CHARACTERS

When describing other people in your story, try looking for details and choices that will help us understand the character of that person the best. In "GFD," one small detail says a lot about Micaela Blei's classmate.

> *She is a lipstick girl and I am a ChapStick girl. So she knows more than me, right? And she's not nervous about ninth grade at all.*

In "The Gig," Christian McBride remembers meeting legendary musician Freddie Hubbard for the first time.

> *Freddie Hubbard was a man with a huge spirit, very macho kind of guy, almost had, like, a mob boss mentality. To be a good musician wasn't enough. He was very dramatic; he didn't make the rehearsal, didn't make the sound check, just showed up for the gig. I'm in the dressing room, shaking in my shoes, and Carl says, "Hey, Freddie, this is Christian McBride." I was seventeen at the time, and Freddie just kind of looks at me and says, "Yeah, nice to meet you." We go on stage and we play and to hear his horn up close like that, I almost had a heart attack. I thought, "Oh my God, I'm playing with Freddie Hubbard. I can't believe this."*

Many stories include a colorful family member. Instead of saying "My uncle was eccentric," in her story "Ashes and Salmon," Joan Juliet Buck quotes her uncle Don.

> *"When I was bringing your grandmother's ashes down to Cannes to bury them, somebody gave me a smoked salmon to cheer me up. I was not going to pack it in the suitcase, so I left the smoked salmon in the carrier bag, and your grandmother was in one of those pale-blue Pan Am overnight bags. I put them both above my seat in the plane, and when we landed at Nice, I collected the smoked salmon and I forgot your grandmother."*

In his story "The Met, Mrs. Vreeland, and Me," about working for the legendary *Vogue* editor Diana Vreeland, Andrew Solomon could have stated that she was opinionated about fashion. Instead, he gives us this:

> *We were walking through the Great Hall of the Metropolitan Museum. And she put one of her small, clawlike hands on my arm. And she said to me, "Young man, stop for a minute. I want you to look around this room, and contemplate the fact that every one of these people went into a store* in which other things were available *and selected what they're wearing right now."*

We asked storyteller Carl Banks to render the twin sister he lost to suicide more clearly in his story "Over the Bridge." With limited time, he only had a few sentences to do it, and yet, a lifetime of memories to choose from.

He went with this:

> *She was an amazing visual artist. She was an unrepentant radical with a touch of anarchist, but she had an extremely tender heart and was incredibly sensitive.*

He could have left it there but chose to add this rich detail:

> *She used to draw caricatures of tourists at Six Flags, and she was so sensitive that she couldn't make any money doing it. She would always give the drawings away, either thinking it wasn't good enough or thinking it was so good that they should just have it for free.*

The summary of his sister was good, but the Six Flags detail really paints a picture.

It's another way of connecting and engaging with your audience. We feel closer to his sister, and to Carl, because of this story detail.

JENIFER ON RIBBON-CUTTING TOASTS: On occasion, you might have to toast not a person but a place or thing, such as a hospital wing or a new branch or brand. In this case, you are likely toasting and celebrating the team responsible. What is the "personality" of the team? (Scrappy, diligent, magically creative, fierce, intimidating!) How is that "personality" reflected? Shed some light on how the team found each other and found unity in its purpose. Remember to focus on the *why* of their venture: "Now we can heal more people/serve more clients/sell more." Sometimes there is a very clear story arc. You can nod to the process of development: from seed to plant, from blueprint to brick and mortar. Make sure to include the challenges, because the valleys make the mountains seem higher, and a toast is a mountaintop-worthy celebration.

THE PERILS OF DETAIL OVERLOAD

Details can offer useful color, but don't go overboard! Too many details can be distracting and fatigue a listener. If you go into great detail about something that doesn't really connect to the rest of the story (e.g., if you digress and tell us about your uncle Al, when he isn't particularly relevant), it can be confusing. Anytime a detail raises a question or causes a listener's mind to wander, they're off trying to figure out the answer to the question in their head while you've moved on. You lose your connection.

It's like having too many vases on the mantel—you can't fully appreciate the beauty of one when there are others competing for your attention. When directing a story, we'll sometimes say, "The audience won't know where to look." Choose a few details that really shine and capture our attention, and save the others for a different story where they can get their due. You are a multitude of stories; they won't be in storage forever.

When debating whether a detail is relevant, go back to the *one sentence* of your story. If the one-sentence summary of your story is: *This is a story about a dog who finds a home,* you won't want to include the details about the cat unless they directly support the story of the dog.

More *details* on the detail pitfalls to avoid:

- **TOO MANY SPECIFIC DATES.** Mentioning multiple dates can make a story feel long and tedious. The listener might think the dates are important and get frustrated thinking they have to keep track. *On March 9, 2009, I did this, then on September 21, 2010, I did this, then on November 24, 2021 . . .* Are the dates really important? Is one crucial? Don't tell us over and over what time it was or a specific date, unless that's a driving force of the story.

- **TOO MANY NAMES AND CHARACTERS.** It's enough to know you have twenty-three cousins, we don't need all their names and ages. Say the name of a person in the story only if they are a *key character.* Once you name someone, the audience will think they need to remember that person because they're integral to the story. Even if a person *is* a central character, it can sometimes be easier to refer to them by who they are (e.g., "my dentist" rather than "Nancy") for the sake of simplicity. Any added characters must have a functional purpose in the story.

- **TOO MANY GRAPHIC DETAILS.** Don't go into the gory details of an injury (or the intimate details of a romantic encounter) if they aren't what the story is ultimately about. Sometimes people will add in details they think are cool or shocking, but they end up distracting the listener. The teller has moved on with the story, but the listener is still back there thinking about the gratuitous image you've conjured. Make sure the details you choose support rather than compete with the story.

- **DETAILS THAT MIGHT BE AT ODDS IN YOUR STORY.** Situations are often complex, but make sure your story makes sense. If your story is about the time your father drove four hours in a snowstorm to pick you up after a bad date, it might not be relevant to share that he plagiarized his paper on *Romeo and Juliet* in high school. We only need to understand his character as it relates to your story.

- **MISLEADING DETAILS.** Don't mention that your uncle just finished plumbing school unless a pipe is going to burst. If you put too much emphasis on a detail, the listener will hold on to it throughout the story and be disappointed when you never come back to it. *Whatever happened to the plumber?*

- **QUESTIONING DETAILS IN YOUR OWN STORY.** Saying something like "I can't remember the details of the argument" or "I was *probably* driving to school" might cause the listener to question whether you are remembering everything else correctly. Better to say, "Before class, we fought like cats and dogs!" Include the details you *do* remember instead of pointing out the ones you don't. In most cases, the ones you remember will be enough to move the story forward.

- **USING DETAILS TO SETTLE A SCORE.** This is not the time to grind your axe. We have found that when a storyteller shares a story and bad-mouths someone—an ex, a friend, a parent—they run the risk of putting the listener on the defensive. Human nature wants to protect people who aren't there to defend themselves. Your neighbor might very well be a jerk, but unless we know and care about *you,* we will most likely question your motives for telling this story. It's important that you show the listener who *you* are first, and gain their trust, so that when you introduce this bad element, they will already be firmly on your side.

THE TRUTH ABOUT DETAILS

At the end of every episode of *The Moth Radio Hour,* we hear producer Jay Allison say, "Moth stories are true, as remembered and affirmed by the storytellers." Memory is imperfect, and sometimes the way we remember our experiences is different from how the events actually unfolded. Think of Moth stories as an artistic time capsule of one person's emotional experience of events.

FRIMET GOLDBERGER, MOTH STORYTELLER: Stories are not static; they grow, they shrivel, they stretch on one side and shrink on the other. Like people, stories evolve—even, and especially, our own stories. Memory is unreliable; we tend to remember things based on present perceptions. And in that sense, no person's story stays the same.

It's impossible to remember our experiences with scientific accuracy. Stories rely on memories, not court reporters, and rarely can we roll back the tape. Memories are porous and imperfect, and can be deeply influenced by internal bias. The truth we see, and therefore the truth we tell, is colored by every single experience we've lived through.

DR. WENDY SUZUKI, MOTH STORYTELLER AND NEUROSCIEN-TIST: Our memory is precious because it provides the scaffolding for who we are as a person, including defining our own personal histories. However, at the same time, our memories don't act like a YouTube video, recording every move in precise detail. Instead, our memories are fallible, inaccurate, and can be modified literally every time we recall them.

To complicate matters further, the details and pictures that you've had etched in your mind for all these years could be protecting the innocent, fanning the flames of a grudge, or clouded by nostalgia.

As you're considering and constructing your story, acknowledge that what you remember about these events is not *all there was to remember*. This experience left a lasting mark, but every time you recall it, you're recalling a memory of that memory. Details are bound to shift. Some may get lost, but some long-dormant details may also be brought back to light.

We often have complex and conflicting opinions about events as they unfold. It is rare that we feel just one emotion. Multiple truths can exist in tandem, and you can acknowledge two or three (or more!) in a story.

It is possible to be incredibly grateful for a lifeboat but also deeply resentful. Say you thought you weren't actually drowning and you didn't need it and wished you could have proven how strong you were, but you're also relieved that you didn't have to exhaust yourself. It all depends on the thrust of the story. Is this relevant to your arc? Sometimes that complexity *is* the story. The contradiction can be the focus of the story, but if it isn't, it's best to leave it out.

TMI: Divulging too much information in social settings can be uncomfortable. Think twice before adding a TMI laundry list of pet peeves, the saga of your bum toe, or a trilogy of pet tragedies. (God, I miss Fluffy.) Be conscious of what you're sharing and the themes within these stories. With too many distracting details and digressions, your neighbor, fellow PTA parent, or potential new partner will wonder: What is this person trying to say? What is the point?

CATHERINE: I was on a blind date, and in the first minute, he told me the story of being fired just hours earlier. That was bad enough, but then he told me he was fired because, in his words, he was "grumpy, lazy, and likes to complain." It didn't make me eager to sign up for a second date.

SARAH: Years ago, a first date told me a very serious story of his favorite vacation. He'd unexpectedly found himself at a nudist resort where he spent his days playing volleyball (!) and his nights at a club on-site, where the dress code was "sport coat only." He said this resort at first seemed strange but quickly became his favorite place. At the end of the story, he looked deeply into my eyes and asked, "Does this sound like something you would be interested in?" He purposefully used a story to illustrate something that brought him joy. It was a test to see if I might share that same interest. But—much respect to nudists— I politely said no. I loved the story, we just weren't a fit—but I won't soon forget him.

TRUTHS TO CONSIDER

- **OUR MEMORIES ARE A LITTLE FAULTY (AT BEST).** What if you don't exactly remember a few of the details? *Was it Wednesday or Friday? Was I eight or nine years old? Was his name Joe or John? Did I receive the care package from Mom before or after I filed for divorce?* This is a time to make a choice about what is *most likely* true. If this detail is not factually correct, will it make a difference to the essential truth of your story?

- **REAL LIFE IS MESSY.** On Tuesday, you were sure you were in love. On Wednesday, you knew it would never work, but by Friday, you were engaged. Depending on the story you're telling, do you need to include Wednesday? Is the story still true without the day of doubt? If the Wednesday blip is of no consequence, leave it out, or it'll just confuse the listener.

- **UNCOMPLICATE THE TRUTH.** It is okay to simplify if the simplification feels honest. If your story has multiple details that happened at different locations or times, you can condense them into one scene or location. Say there's a part of your story where something is mentioned at a church service, and then a few days later, something else was said at Bible study, and then at the next church service, another thing was said. It's perfectly fine to take a little artistic license and just condense all the things that were said into *one time at church.* Otherwise it will be confusing.

- **EDIT TO MAKE THE TRUTH CLEARER.** You might find omitting a character or streamlining events might make it easier to follow along. Do we really need to know that the cab driver heard the whole exchange? Does he recur as a character, or is this his only appearance? Grouping people together rather than listing them off individually might be less confusing: *my theater tech crew, everyone in Accounting.* Or perhaps you reorder a chain of events or even leave a whole chunk of action on the cutting-room floor. (It might be interesting that you stole the getaway car from your ex-father-in-law, but if we don't have a ton of time, it is enough that you just have a getaway car.)

- **OWN IT.** Part of the honesty in a story is also taking stock of *your* part in it. What have you done or not done to land you in this predicament? Aunt Ethel was cranky at the family reunion? Well, did you leave out the part about when you were twenty and ran over her foot with your car? Showing your honest, banged-up self will generally make us trust you and want to root for you.

- **IS THE POINT OF VIEW EVEN POSSIBLE?** It's hard to believe that you could remember a ton of detail from a story that happened when you were four, or in a coma, or asleep. Don't strain your credibility by telling a story that starts with your alleged thoughts in your mother's womb.

- **STAY IN YOUR OWN EXPERIENCE AND FEELINGS.** If you say that someone was thinking this, that, or the other thing about you, your listeners are taken out of the story. They stop and question whether your assumption is plausible or not. *How do you know what they were thinking?* To stay on track, tell us what you *knew* to be true: "John looked at me, and I instantly *worried* that he thought I was a fool" is probably more accurate.

    MEG: I once had a storyteller tell me something awful that another person thought about him, and I said, *They told* *you that??* and he said, *No.* So then I asked who told him and he said, *No one, I just have a feeling that they think that.* So I said, *Okay then, just say that. Let it be YOUR feeling, don't state an assumption as a fact!*

Moth stories are not fiction, and perhaps more important, human beings are smart. When we're truly listening—as Moth audiences do enthusiastically—we can sense when a teller is lying, and it pulls us out of the story. In film and literature, this is sometimes referred to as an "unreliable narrator," someone speaking in the first person whose version of events seems distorted, untrustworthy, or otherwise questionable.

Details, when used well, can make your story not just interesting but also harrowing, exciting, rich, fun, and colorful. They engage your listener on a sensory level and *show* us who you are and what you've experienced.

Stories are the original version of virtual reality—no goggles necessary.

SARAH ON FAMILY STORIES AND ARTISTIC LICENSE: My grandma Harriet told stories, many times with events just slightly out of order. I'd say, "Grandma, I was with you. That's not *exactly* how it happened," and she'd crinkle her nose, point her finger at me, and say, "I know. *I spiced it up.*" When you tell stories, some things may get switched around. If you get a big reaction for those Technicolor details, the narrative can grow and grow over the years—as you tell and retell—to become a "big fish" story or one that could *seem* like a tall tale even if it's true. You can spice your story up, like Grandma Harriet, but keep the plot grounded in your lived experience. The essence of the story can still be truthful, even if you skip forward, omit a beat, or reorder things slightly.

BACKSTORY

When something happens, and you just *have* to call your friend to share it, remember that your friend knows a lot about you—your background, opinions, and shared experiences—and it informs how they receive the story. Your listeners will only have the backstory you provide, unless you are famous—and even if you are, the audience probably knows nothing about you and your inner life. In iconic rapper Darryl "DMC" McDaniels's story "Angel," it's important for us to know that while on a world tour with Run-DMC, he'd been suffering from debilitating depression, and had recently found out he was adopted. This is information the audience needs to know in order to fully understand his story.

You have an endless backstory; the art is figuring out which parts are relevant. It's hard to imagine telling a story about being fired that would *not* nod to your extraordinary history of thirty-seven firings, but we can't possibly hear about everything from your childhood paper route to your corporate gig. Most people would instinctively gravitate to the biggest, boldest, or most outlandish firings, but sometimes it might be the smallest firing that has the most impact, such as being fired as the merchandise wrangler of your kid's Little League team. Perhaps being fired from that volunteer gig says more about your character and your emotional state than anything before.

Backstory can be dropped in or woven through—you don't need to start with it. Downloading *all* the backstory at the very top is exhausting and usually a bit boring. However, your audience also doesn't want to feel lost in a story out of the gate. They want *in*! Providing some backstory is an invitation. It lays the groundwork, giving listeners the context they need to interpret and understand the events with you.

Decide how best to parcel out what the listener needs to know and when. Sometimes you might share the backstory before a crucial moment to allow your audience to fully savor that moment when they get there. Other times, you might start with a scene, and then back up and reveal some important context from before this moment. It's like saying, "When someone cut off my great-grandmother in the church parking lot, I was worried. I should back up and tell you that in 1944, she was arrested for uttering profane language in a public place and was released under a thirty-five-dollar bond."

Early in Vin Shambry's story "Outdoor School," he lets us know that he, his mom, and his little sister were struggling and had to live under a giant tree, and that he considered himself the man of the family. Then he introduces the exciting week that all sixth graders in Portland look forward to throughout elementary school: a week in the woods, living in cabins, with teachers and instructors. Because we already know Vin's living situation, we really get to enjoy him describing his bunk, the meals, the joy of just being a kid. He doesn't need to give a ton of detail about the contrast . . . we get it.

> *I only had two pairs of pants and two pairs of underwear, and no quarters for the laundromat. Matter of fact, I don't even know if they had a laundromat. So I went to the counselor and I asked him. He told me that they would wash and dry my clothes for me, and I didn't have to worry about it, and it was okay to run and jump in the river. I felt taken care of. At Outdoor School, I didn't have a care in the world.*

We appreciate Vin's carefree camp experience so much more because we know his backstory. And because he shared the closeness of his family at the top, we also understand his ending, that though he loved Outdoor School, he was also haunted by worry about how his family was coping.

Each story will be different! Decide how best to arrange the details for your story—and if all else fails, always err on the side of keeping your listener *in the know*!

GETTING TO KNOW YOU: What if you had just one short "greatest hits" story in your back pocket on a date? Something to lighten the mood and show your sense of humor or your adventurous side? We're not suggesting you over-rehearse before meeting your could-be soulmate, but to calm your jitters, you could think of a story or two. Small decisions that at the time felt monumental may make good stories for a date. Think about the choices you made when you were growing into the person you are now. What about the time you switched your lunch table to sit with the chess club—or got busted copying CliffsNotes word for word? Did you tell a dad joke at your neighbor's funeral but found the family loved it because they just needed a laugh? How about that one time you tried hitchhiking? Or the story of your dog Foxy's adoption? Did you just drive from Taos back to Baltimore straight through the night and only make it through by blaring '90s pop hits on repeat? A very short story will give a new romantic prospect (or new friend!) a glimpse of who you are. Stories invite conversation. They encourage your "plus-one" to ask questions and share stories of their own.

UP AND OVER

At this point, like a roller coaster ride, you have your audience traveling up, up, up with all the tension you've built. You have the scenes and the backstory. The temperature is rising. The *action* is rising. But where is it all leading? The last and perhaps most important piece you'll need is the apex of your story: the "main event"! Your entire story is built for this moment. It's why we're all on the edge of our seats.

WE NEED A RESOLUTION

In the main event of your story, you come face-to-face with the dragon. This scene is the energy shift; it's where the story turns the final corner and your resolution is apparent. Something is achieved, insight is gained, and you metaphorically win or lose what you set out for at the start. We now understand how the you at the end of your story is quite different from the you we met at the beginning.

In David Montgomery's "Spicy," David's shattered confidence builds and builds, until he finally gets to meet Victoria "Posh Spice" Beckham, famously the most aloof Spice Girl.

> *Before I know it, I am thrust into brightness, now three feet away from my idol, and she squeals, "Oh my God, it's you!" She seemed genuinely excited to see me. At these events, she sits at a little table, and she does not stand up for anyone or anything. If you want to get a picture, you have to lean across the table, and they take a Polaroid from the side, real personal-like. She asked how many shows I was actually seeing and did not believe me until I pulled out the evidence of the twenty-two ticket stubs. She got up out of her seat, grabbed me by the hands, pulled me to the red carpet, and said, "You are fabulous. We've got to get some pictures." Mind: blown. And it started to click. You know what, David? You're not better off dead. You might even be special out-side of Spice World, too.*

Consider how you will illustrate what changed for you. How will you land your arc? Do you get what you want in the end? Or are you—our fearless hero—back to square one and ready to start again?

At the end of "Guilty," Danusia Trevino is lovingly confronted by her fellow jurors.

> *Each one of those eleven people talked to me. They didn't say that I was wrong. They said they understood where I was coming*

from, but they didn't think that the prosecution made their case beyond a reasonable doubt. And when I was still not convinced, they sent that older gentleman juror to talk to me. And he sat across from me and very gently said, "Maybe one day someone that you love very much will be in this situation where it will look like they committed a crime, but they are innocent, and this law that states that a person is innocent until proven guilty beyond reasonable doubt will save them. It's not a perfect law, but it's the law we were asked to follow in this court today. So please consider that." And I couldn't believe how much thought they all put into this. So I changed my vote.

Danusia goes into the story thinking jury duty is pointless and rigged. Her entire mindset is changed by the morality of her fellow jurors, the people she previously thought of as "square" and small-minded. She leaves with new respect for the system and especially her fellow jurors.

In Dr. George Lombardi's "Mission to India," the resolution happens in a strange and rather reverential moment while operating on Mother Teresa.

I said, "Let's get that pacemaker out." And they looked at me and said, "You want it out, you have to take it out." I said, "I've never done that before." I got a charge nurse and a basic tray, and I prepared the patient. The pacemaker box came out readily, but the wire, the wire that had been sitting in her right ventricle for several months, was tethered into place, and it would not budge. I twisted and turned and did all kinds of little body English. This thing was stuck. I started to sweat. My glasses fogged over. There had been stories that if you pull hard enough you can put a hole in the ventricle, and she could bleed into her chest and die within a matter of minutes. So in the most surreal moment, I said a prayer to Mother Teresa, for Mother Teresa, and the catheter came loose! I took it out. I cultured the tip, and I

proved that this pacemaker was the cause of her infection. She got
better. Her fever broke. She woke up. A couple of days later, she
was sitting in a chair, eating.

The tension that Dr. Lombardi creates as he describes performing the procedure on Mother Teresa's heart pulls us into the stakes
of this crucial moment. With the wire removed, he runs the final
test, which confirms his initial diagnosis. Our relief breaks along
with Mother Teresa's fever, bringing us to a natural resolution. And
note: This peak *usually* comes toward the end of your story, but it
doesn't have to. Where and how you order these narrative stepping
stones is entirely up to you.

~~AND THEN I REALIZED.~~ (YES. IT'S CROSSED OUT ON PURPOSE.)

By following the arc to the conclusion, we do not mean you should
say, "And then I realized . . ." Please avoid this phrase at all costs.
Often, people will cue the change in the story by saying "And then
I realized" or "In that moment." As clean and neat as it would be for
us as storytellers, very often the big moments of our lives don't immediately change us. Sometimes they're the catalyst for change, the
first domino in a beautiful cascade. We may realize the magnitude
of an experience only in hindsight.

The truth is, you most probably did *not* realize it then. It would
take years of meditation, the death of a toxic cousin, and a divorce
for you to *actually* realize what happened. Having your bike stolen
was a story-worthy start, but you cheapen your story by shoehorning enlightenment into a moment that's not there. Think about
language you can use that is efficient and true. "It would take me
years of therapy and two more broken hearts before . . ." "Sometimes I wonder if that was the beginning of the end . . ." It's more
truthful and possibly even more fun!

And a magic trick: You can just lift out "and then I realized" or
"in that moment," and the story will still work as is!

> *When the doctor said I needed a kidney transplant, my boyfriend*
> *immediately volunteered. ~~It was in this moment I realized~~ he*
> *loved me. He loved me so much he was willing to put himself in*
> *harm's way.*

> *As we summited the mountain, I could see for miles. I wasn't*
> *afraid. ~~And suddenly I realized~~ I had let go of my fears one by one*
> *as I made the climb.*

Or you can try giving the transformation more real estate in the story. Extra details act like a highlighter. Dress the moment up a little. Let it wear mascara or a bow tie.

> *I was nervous, but I let him know I was moving out.*

Versus:

> *I agonized about letting him know I was moving out. Each week-*
> *end I was sneaking a box of my most precious belongings into a*
> *storage space. I was only able to find the courage to tell him after I*
> *had put the down payment on the moving truck and the date was*
> *set. I felt like he might be able to talk me out of it if the plan wasn't*
> *solid and already in motion.*

It's the same moment, just fully dressed. It directs the listener: Look here!

Sometimes the change in the story may not feel true to you in the present day. "That was a long time ago. I've changed. So much has happened since! My waking hours are no longer consumed with a burning desire to finally beat smug Yolanda at tennis." You may have long ago moved on (we hope so) and not even know Yolanda anymore. But there could still be a great story there! Place yourself back in that time, and maybe perspective will reveal the real reasons why it was so important to you then. You may have processed and grown, but the passion you once felt for the game and for vanquishing Yolanda can live on. (Take that, Yolanda!)

It's fine to end the story anchored in how you felt at a particular moment in time. We go through many changes in life. Where one story ends, another begins.

You, right now, are all of the stories that came before you.

PERSONAL STORIES FOR COLLEGE AND GRANT APPLICATIONS: Kendi Ntwiga, a Moth Global Community Program graduate and instructor, told a Moth story of being picked on by the local schoolchildren, but working day and night to score the top marks that eventually make her the hero of her Kenyan village. She uses this story as the basis for every grant application she writes for her organization, which encourages young women entering STEM fields. The story helps potential new funders understand her drive and commitment to the next generation. She says, "Given the high number of applicants these days, going in with a personal story from the beginning helps you stand out and get shortlisted." Aisha Rodriguez, Diavian Walters, and countless other graduates of Moth high school workshops used their Moth stories for their college essays to showcase their character and how they see the world. The stakes are high in all applications, so show your potential new school what was once on the line for you in another area of your life, and how you came out on the other side!

DIRECTOR'S NOTES

- Identify the important information you need to build the arc of your story. Create a bulleted list of these narrative stepping stones. Which will become scenes, and which will be summaries or moments of reflection? What is your whole story building to? How will it resolve? Remember, you do not have to plot every literal step—jump cuts are allowed!

- Once you determine which of your narrative stepping stones could be potential scenes, decide how you will bring them to life cinematically. Recount them so we can see and experience them with you. Some stories might have many small scenes, others might have only two or three, but remember there is usually one pivotal scene that your story builds toward.

- Make sure to stay in the action and describe the scene from the inside. Allow the listener to experience your story by taking them through the events, the way they unfolded for you. Avoid telling from hindsight.

- What are the details that will make your scenes (and your overall story) memorable and uniquely yours? Draw from all your senses. Choose specific details to highlight important moments, create emotion, and build tension in your story, but don't go overboard with distracting or overly specific details that might risk confusing your listener. When in doubt, revisit your *one sentence* and determine if the detail supports the overall arc of your story.

- Is there important backstory you need to drop in or weave through in order for your listener to understand the context of the story?

- How will you land your arc? How will you illustrate what changed for you? Can you *show us* how you are different now than you were at the start of your story?

CHAPTER 6

MAGNIFYING THE EMOTION

If you don't feel it, the audience won't feel it.

—JENIFER HIXSON

We are emotional beings. We feel nostalgic about people and places, sentimental about childhood. We cry at weddings and revel in surprise. We love passionately and mourn deeply. Beyond eloquent and invisible construction of the story, *emotion* is the glue that connects storytellers and listeners.

Emotions are our common denominator. Listening to a story that is absent of emotion is like hearing an instruction manual read out loud.

Your story explores universal feelings, but it will be told in a way that is unique to you. The listener will recognize your willingness to be vulnerable.

MARINA KLUTSE, MOTH DIRECTOR OF FINANCE: No two journeys are alike. Our stories are unique, complex, and nuanced, but we can often find pieces of ourselves in the reflection of others.

Shades of emotion color everything. Consider a simple sentence: "I wanted him to come over." Now contemplate that sentence in the context of how you could have been feeling at the time: grumpy, pessimistic, skeptical, tormented, ashamed, elated, invigorated, focused, prepared, delighted, anxious, stunned, livid, burned out, bummed out, confident, crushed, motivated, cherished . . . on and on. All our favorite stories bring the listener along to experience a range of emotion.

ALFONSO LACAYO, MOTH STORYTELLER: I was part of one of the first-ever Moth high school StorySLAMs. Hearing some of the stuff my peers had been through gave me a different outlook on things. You never know what others might be going through, how they could be in pain and how they have grown from those times.

By deepening the emotion, you allow people to experience your story. They may quietly empathize, or they might have a physical reaction to what they are hearing—they might get a chill, tear up, or laugh out loud. By sharing what you felt in the past, you are creating a connection with the listener in the present.

Even a simple description of an emotion can bring a smile to your listener's face.

> *About two hours later, my roommate comes home. Joy is a concept that's very hard to pin down, but you know it when you see it, and I saw joy in the eyes of my roommate. The dude is clearly excited about something.*
>
> —Ashok Ramasubramanian, "Joy"

Stakes aren't possible without emotions. What's in jeopardy is tethered to your frame of mind: embarrassed, elated, fearful. Make us *feel* what you were feeling.

Frimet Goldberger, in her story "My Knight in Shining Sidecurls," gave this detail when talking about her first-ever trip to a water park in Florida, where she broke from the traditional rules of modesty that her Hasidic upbringing dictated:

> *It was a cloudy and muggy day, and I was wearing a bathing suit for the first time. On my head, I wore a chin-length wig with a Yankees sun visor securing it. So we make our way through the park, and I am wandering on my husband's tail, ogling this bevy of bikini-clad shiksas in all their tanned glory. I keep my arms on my chest, alternating between that and my thighs and knees and elbows, until I realize I am practically in the nude, and I just walk around in a self-conscious daze. My discomfort was so palpable. It was a constant reminder of the grave sin I was committing. I felt like everyone around me could see right through my shame.*

Frimet brings us into the tension by describing how vulnerable she felt in this moment. With each futile attempt to cover herself, we, too, can feel her shame and embarrassment.

In "Quiet Fire," Phyllis Bowdin is assaulted by a street performer and walks away in shock.

> *I had just been blindsided, bullied, and blatantly violated by a strange man in the street with the approval of hordes of other strangers. And the thought that I had no way to protect or defend myself made me feel so powerless that I wanted to cry.*

Phyllis lets us in on her emotional state. We are with her in her despair, which is what makes the plotting and execution of her eventual revenge so deeply satisfying. The delight of the audience is palpable, because the mime deserved it! The joy at the end of the story is earned.

While few listeners have ever been bullied by a mime, they know what it feels like to feel frozen in humiliation. They may have never delivered a big wallop of righteous revenge, but they know how good it feels to see a bully get their due.

Scenes can help you get in touch with your emotions. As you actively remember the moment you're describing, the listener can hear the emotion in your words and also your voice.

When storytellers allow themselves to be vulnerable, to admit their flaws and anxieties and showcase their not-so-pretty sides, they allow the listeners to see themselves in the story. Take, for instance, Martha Ruiz-Perilla's story "Opposing Forces." As a dental student, Martha is forced to perform a complicated procedure at gunpoint.

> *I was shaking. I had an idea what had to be done. I had seen it in books and in enormous slide projections in our oral pathology classes. But I had never done anything like this before. It would be really the first time. What I did know, though, was that if I made a mistake in my incision, and I touched the nerve that runs by that area of the face, I could cause the paralysis of half of this kid's face for life. I also knew that if I let that infection progress, this kid could go into sepsis and die. And I also knew in the back of my head that if the army had been informed that the rebels were in the hospital, they could burst in at any time. There would be a cross fire, and I would become collateral damage by the end of the morning.*

The emotions in this excerpt also elevate the stakes. You can feel the tension and grasp what's in jeopardy.

> *And the man, the commander who had been pointing a gun at me this whole time, broke his silence, and he said, "Almost there, mi hijo." And I was petrified. Because it was then that I realized whose child I was cradling in my arm. This was the commander's son. I couldn't screw this up. I had to do this right. I knew that if this kid got worse or if he died, this guy would come back for me. I was sure about that.*

It's one thing to describe how something looked or sounded, but when you punctuate with emotion, you bring us into how you were actually feeling in the moment. If you *don't,* the listener might misinterpret the truth of your experience. Consider the sentence "I signed the divorce papers." Perhaps you were delighted: free at last! But if you don't share your emotions, the listener may presume you were devastated.

A study by a team of scientists in Denmark looked at how listening to stories, especially emotional parts of a story, can trigger emotional and physical responses in the listener. Their results, published in the October 2011 issue of *Neuroimage,* found that listeners' heart rates might increase; they might have facial reactions, raised eyebrows, or increased blinking of their eyes; their palms might even get sweaty. All of these are signs that the listener engages with the emotion in a story.

SARAH ON DATING: On a first date, a man and I were talking about what we did for work, and he told me that as a boy, he dreamed of becoming a firefighter. As he grew older, everyone told him not to do it, so he went to college and became an engineer. His parents were so proud! But as the years went on, deep down, he knew he'd made the wrong choice. When he quit his engineering job at almost thirty and told his family he'd passed the civil service test and was accepted into the fire academy, they disapproved. They reminded him of the danger, but he knew that being a firefighter was his calling. He told me he put everything he had into the grueling training, then graduated and proudly joined the FDNY. He said he wouldn't trade it for the world. His parents are his biggest supporters now—and he's FDNY for life. Then he asked me on date number two. (And *of course* I said yes. Come on! I was so moved by this story!) When you're on a date, tell on yourself a little. Invite people in. A short personal story can calm your nerves and help your new potential partner to feel closer to you.

Many of us have been taught that hiding our emotions is a survival skill. We've been told, "Hold it in, don't show your cards. Don't signal weakness." However, in storytelling, bringing the full breadth of your feelings to the table is the power move!

> **ALISTAIR BANE, MOTH STORYTELLER:** If telling a story makes me feel vulnerable, it's because I'm being real about who I am and what I experienced at a certain point in my life. When I am real, that's when the audience will connect with me. If I hold anything back, there will be a distance between myself and the audience. If I'm developing a story, and it feels safe and easy to tell, I know I haven't looked deep enough yet.

It's all right to cry, tremble, woot-woot, steam in fury, or sing hallelujah while you tell a story. Actually, we typically discourage singing, but a modest and well-placed hallelujah never hurts if you're genuinely a hallelujah-hollering sort of person. (Not recommended for beginners. And only one hallelujah per story, please.)

HUMOR

Humor is a tempting and tricky force in storytelling. It can magnify your emotions or push them away.

So often people will use humor to protect themselves from feeling vulnerable. They will get to an intense moment and throw in a joke, and the audience suddenly doesn't know what to think or feel. It can end up creating distance from your listeners rather than drawing them in. It might make us laugh, but it might be an uncomfortable laugh of confusion. Ask yourself: Are my jokes integral to the story arc? Am I avoiding something here? Am I distracting the audience (and myself) from a larger truth?

Over the years, we've been pitched many stories of heartache and tragedy. Sometimes the teller will say, "But I wish my story could be funny. I'm afraid of bringing everyone down."

We get it! There's immediate validation in laughter. It's fun to bring joy and make people laugh.

But you can't force funny. Shoehorning a joke into a sad story doesn't work.

Humor shows up in varying degrees in many stories, even if they are harrowing or tragic, because life is strange and surprising. Humor can live in the details you remember, the observations you make, the absurdity of it all.

We laugh when something is funny, but also when we are nervous or stressed. Laughter can erupt out of disbelief, from fury, in camaraderie, even through grief. Laughter can release a pressure valve and make an intolerable situation suddenly bearable. Some things are so awful you just have to laugh—*did I seriously just get a parking ticket while picking out my mother's casket?*

(An informal and unscientific poll of the authors of this book determined that all of us can remember hilarious moments from the funerals or deathbeds of our most beloved family members. Five for five. The facts don't lie. Even the saddest days have moments of levity.)

In Andrea King Collier's "Meeting Miles," she tells us about her reaction to the shocking news that her son, unbeknownst to her, had just become a father.

> *So what do you do with this news? You go to Target . . . because you can work out a whole lot of sh*t in Target.*

You may find that an event that is serious and important, even stressful to you in the moment, might end up being a hilarious romp of a story once you've gotten a little distance.

Take Michelle Murphy's "Do You Know Who You're Buying This For?," a story about falling victim to a scam caller who claimed to be running a federal investigation.

The "federal agent" tells me that with my identity, a car has been stolen in Texas. A woman is missing, the car crashed—and the missing woman's blood and eight pounds of cocaine were found. I was like, "Holy f***!" I haven't been to Texas in ten years. My sister lives there, but I would never murder her and then get blown out on a baby's weight of cocaine. That's not my style. I was very upset by this news. I just started crying because I was like, "This is really intense. It wasn't me, man, I didn't do it."

They're like, "Okay, first thing, you have to do everything we say to a T, and you can't tell anyone, because we're handling this at the federal level, we don't want to involve the state." First of all, what? Second of all, I'd already Slacked eight of my co-workers being like, "I'm under federal investigation." They tell me this, and I'm like, "Okay, okay, from this moment forward, I will not break the law. I will keep this secret." My dad even comes downstairs. He's like, "Who are you talking to?" I'm like, "Get out of here, Dad! This is a federal investigation!" I'm taking this very seriously.

In "Good News Versus Bad," Erin Barker finds humor in a story about a disruption in her family when she was twelve years old.

Because my dad and I were so close, I knew what ice cream meant. Every time my dad has bad news, he takes us out for ice cream. It's kind of his MO. Don't ever go to the Cold Stone Creamery with my dad, just don't do it. Unless you want to find out that Grandpa has cancer, or your dog's been put to sleep, or your nanny's been fired for stealing your mother's jewelry. Just don't go.

Not everyone is naturally funny. Maybe you will surprise yourself when you accidentally stumble over "the funny" in your story. Humor shows up in the details or the emotion of a reaction. It's almost always authentically, organically baked in. Your stories should always follow your natural conversational style and rhythm.

We've seen attempts at comedy bring the house down—and we've seen them land with a thud. While we can't teach you to be funny, what we *can* do is help you figure out how (and if!) you should use humor, and when to avoid it at all costs.

TOAST DOS: If you've been chosen to give a toast at an event, everyone knows that you have a connection to the subject. Tell us something lovely we might not know about them. The details you include can bring the subject of the toast alive for your audience, whether you're reminding everyone of the time they sank the basket that clinched the playoffs, thanking them for insisting that you swipe right on the beekeeper, or lovingly revealing that, when your sister was three, she spent two months insisting she *was* a cat.

TOAST DON'TS: This is not the place to enumerate the subject's shortcomings. Some gentle ribbing may work, and an ancient vendetta featuring a botched cheerleading routine might be hilarious. But it *could* also potentially open up a wound that hasn't quite healed yet. (Don't mess with cheerleaders. They can bench press a human!) If you roast, make it a loving roast, not a biting takedown. Sure, one time your brother might have ratted you out to your mother for backing into the neighbor's car, and you were livid that you got grounded and had to drop out of your senior year production of *Sweeney Todd.* Maybe this makes it into your best man speech. But for the most part, if you've been chosen to give the speech, you probably have a whole lot of love for the groom (even if you still want to give him a shave). You may take a few jabs or share a moment where the two of you were at odds, but most of the speech will be a series of loving stories.

WHERE'S THE PUNCH?

As we've probably all experienced in real life, one of the easiest ways to get people on your side is to have a sense of humor about yourself. It shows the listener that you trust them. It creates intimacy.

> **TRISHA MITCHELL COBURN, MOTH STORYTELLER:** It was 2012. A sold-out show at the Paramount Theatre in Austin, Texas. It was my first big Mainstage show, and I was the last storyteller. I was really anxious. I even asked the director if I could go in the beginning of the lineup so I would not have to wait through the whole show. I had an out-of-body experience while I waited for my name to be called. When the host introduced me, I stood up and walked toward the stage. There were six steps I had to climb, and I tripped on the third one. I reached forward and caught myself before I did a faceplant. I heard a loud gasp throughout the audience. I stood up, turned around, and faced the audience, and a voice inside my head said, *Bow.* I took a huge bow and the auditorium broke out in applause. They began to hoot and holler. I stood on that stage and told my story as if every person in that room were my best friend.

In "The Bad Haircut," Alfonso Lacayo speaks to the audience like we're all friends. He gives us a glimpse inside his mind as the events in his story unfold.

> *My cousin starts cutting my hair. There was no mirror. You know how, like, when you go to a barbershop, there's those giant mirrors? So while you're getting your haircut, you can kind of look up and check. I like that. That's nice. There was none of it. So my cousin's cutting my hair for, like, twenty-five, thirty minutes, and all of a sudden he stops, and he's proud of his work. He's like, "Dang, there you go, I got you, little man." Gives me a high five. And I get up, I'm like, "Okay, now I'm ready for school."*
>
> *But I knew there was something wrong, 'cause as soon as I*

stepped foot into the house, my other cousin around my age looks at me and starts dying, crying, laughing all over the place, hysterically. I like jokes, you know. I want to know what's funny, too. So I go to the bathroom and I come face-to-face with the mirror. I couldn't believe what I saw. My new hairline was really far back, and my forehead was all shiny. I had, like, this windshield thing goin' on. If you look closely enough into my forehead, you can see your own reflection in it. It was crazy. It was just glistening.

Sometimes, your most vulnerable moments, in retrospect, have a lot of humor. In "Maybe," Jessica Lee Williamson helps us laugh at a previously humiliating experience, singing a song from the musical *Annie.*

When I was in the third grade, I decided to sing "Maybe" for the school talent show. And the moment I stepped up onto the stage, I found myself pondering some maybes of my own. Maybe I should have put some thought into it before I volunteered to sing alone in front of hundreds of people. And maybe I should have bothered to memorize the words to the song that I volunteered to sing alone in front of hundreds of people. I had seen the movie five or six times over the course of my entire life and somehow figured that would be enough. So I only focused on the feelings I would have while singing the song. And I only asked the important questions like, "Should I wear a curly wig, or will my short, newly permed hairdo suffice?" There was an instrumental version of the song playing over the PA system. And every time a new verse would kick in, I would take a deep breath and brace myself like I was getting ready to sing, sending out these tiny ripples of hope that I might just pull it together. But I never did, you guys. I just stood there and cried for two and a half minutes while the audience watched in a horrified silence.

This isn't to say that you should default to making yourself the punchline of your story. Owning your flaws or onetime mistakes can be a way to create a connection—to paint a funny, honest picture of who you are and own the whole you. Sometimes it can even feel powerful. In "Modern Family," Sara Barron wonders if she should be more generous with her husband's ex.

> *But the worst part of me . . . which is,* basically, *me . . . really wanted her to go away.*

But there is a fine line between playful self-deprecation and disparaging yourself with words or ideas that have been used against you. If a detail has caused you to be targeted or bullied, making light of it as a form of protection can be harmful to you and others who have similar experiences.

In her groundbreaking Netflix special *Nanette,* Hannah Gadsby says, "Do you understand what self-deprecation means when it comes from somebody who already exists in the margins? It's not humility, it's humiliation."

Your humor should come from honesty and create a bridge from your experience to your audience. If you find yourself sharing personal details to beat your audience to a joke, or if you're sharing details that you actually do not find funny yourself, choose a different tactic. Your story should create a connection with your audience, and that should never come at your own expense.

SUCH A CHARACTER

Humor, when used properly, can show your point of view and deepen the characters in your story. In his story "Broken Heart," Brian Finkelstein says:

> *I haven't had a physical since high school, for like twenty-five, thirty years, because my grandmother always said, "Don't go to a doctor, because they'll find it, and then you die," which is crazy, except for . . . Grandma was ninety-nine years old.*

To show someone's complexity, you may choose to mix a few serious details about the person with something lighter. Take Tig Notaro, in "R2 Where Are You?"

> So when I was little, I made a mess of my room, like any other child my age. . . . And when cleaning up my room, I was given an allotted time, and [my stepfather] Ric would come in, and whatever was out of place, he would put in a large trash bag. And then he'd lock it in the trunk of the car. Then I had to do chores to earn money to buy my toys back. I know, it sounds harsh, because it is. But to be fair, they were priced fairly. I could buy an entire Millennium Falcon, windup Evel Knievel, and stuffed monkey for, like, a nickel each. Totally reasonable.

Ric was not cruel, so Tig's levity puts the listener at ease and lets us laugh.

Or consider the ribbing Tara Clancy gives her family in "The Moon and Stars Talks."

> I am a fifth-generation native New Yorker. And while there is certainly something cool about that, there is also a downside. There was a moment when it occurred to me that while many other American families also first landed in New York, for the most part, at some point, they kept going and pioneering their way west with little more than the rags on their backs. And meanwhile, my own family got off a boat, took two steps, and were like, "Good enough for me," you know, forever. All of that is to say that I come from a place where discovering the great unknown means New Jersey.

The humor makes it clear that while Tara may have a complex relationship with her family, she also has a deep love for them.

In Phill Branch's story "If the Suit Fits," he overplans for his prom by designing a coordinating outfit for his date. While he sets the situation itself up as humorous, it is filled with myriad teenage emotions. His adult perspective allows room for some humor about his younger self.

> For my date, I comb through all the hottest fashion publications of the time to decide what her look would be. I'm in the Sears catalog and Spiegel, JCPenney's. I finally decide that she's going to wear this mermaid dress, and it's going to have some of the material from my suit, because my suit was the base. She would have this pink lace overlay at the top, and it would be great. I couldn't actually draw or sew. So I took my scribble to my seamstress—my friend's mother—and said, "Do you think you can make this?" She said, "Sure, give me about a week or so, and I can put it together once you give me all the fabric and the things you want." I said, "Great." The plan was in motion.
>
> I had no idea that asking my date to accept my design for her senior prom dress was going to be problematic, and Dana was not into it at all. So she broke up with me.

To laugh with a storyteller one minute and then feel your heart swell with empathy for them the next can be a satisfying ride for the listener. If you listen to Phill's story in audio, you can hear the entire audience let out a collective, empathetic "aww" about the breakup. He continues:

> Now, I wasn't necessarily in the closet at sixteen, because I wasn't conscious, per se, that I was gay. But apparently, I was so gay that I wasn't aware that designing my date's prom dress in a white satin with a pink shimmer when it hit the light was essentially my coming-out quinceañera.
>
> For that whole school year where Dana was my girlfriend, it felt great. To just be one of the guys and to feel like I had the things that other guys had, and I could have this future, and maybe I can get married and have this life. It was really powerful, because I hadn't had that feeling before. When she left, it was equally pow-

erful, because it affirmed all the feelings that were starting to brew up in me that I was indeed broken, and I was hurting. But I had about fifty yards of satin, and somebody had to wear it.

KATE ON DISCOVERING NEW PEOPLE AT DINNER: After college, I moved into the attic of a Victorian mansion in Newport, Rhode Island, where I bunked with the other actors who were hired to play the Astor family in the year 1891. We studied Victorian life obsessively, and one of our favorite traditions from that era was the "turning of the table." At formal dinners, the seating was very intentional. Couples who arrived together were never placed next to each other. Guests were expected to speak only to the people seated next to them, turning to the person on their left for one course and the person on their right for the next, back and forth until dessert. By the end of a long meal, the hope was that every guest had started two new friendships (or maybe something more!). It made for exciting evenings. Take a note from Lady Astor at your next dinner party. Save the chatting with your roommate for the Lyft ride home and seek out new stories from a stranger.

SMILE THOUGH YOUR HEART IS ACHING

There's a reason those iconic drama masks show both sides: comedy and tragedy. Laughter is joyous, but it can also break the tension of an emotional or harrowing moment. Say you've just worked up the courage to tell your children that your cancer has returned and the audience is filled with dread thinking about your children being heartbroken. Just as you're about to tell them, a neighborhood dog begins howling at the moon, which inspires other neighborhood dogs to howl too, until there is a crazy chorus of many dogs, and it won't stop for three full minutes and all of you can't stop laughing.

That's a moment of joy in a scene of tragedy. It makes the tragedy more bearable, complicated, and beautiful.

> **DANIEL TURPIN, MOTH STORYTELLER:** Humor is a psychological life raft. Reasoning and rationale only get us so far. You can wrap your mind around actions, or forgive them, or reason them into submission. But I'm not sure you can recover from tragedy without humor.

Sometimes both the teller and the audience need a respite from the pain or suspense, and humor acts as a release valve. These moments can't be conjured. We'd never advise a teller, "During that harrowing chase scene, how about throwing in a joke about pretzels?" Never. But very often, in conversation with a teller about an intense story, they'll share an unexpected detail that will make us laugh.

In "The Good and the Bad," Daniel Turpin describes the aftermath of a frightening altercation with a burglar.

> *I grab the phone, and I dial 911. And I go to the doorway, and I have this surreal moment where I'm watching this man run across my yard, this man that threatened my life and hurt my mother. And I think I can catch him. I'm faster than he is. But I know he has a gun, so I tell the police, I describe what he looks like, what he's wearing, and describe the car he gets into hidden behind the trees. But as I watch him drive away, I make another decision. I go after him. And I jump in my truck, and I tear out of my driveway, and I'm still talking to the police. But then the phone goes dead . . . because it's the landline.*

By including the silly unexpected detail of what happened in the moment, he allows us to feel the relief of laughter after the stress of the situation. The humor is intrinsic to the story—it's truly what happened, and looking back at it, it's just funny. Including this detail also lets us know that despite this intense experience, he and his mother are most likely going to be okay.

A moment to laugh together is like a gift to the listener; it bonds you with the audience. It can be a way of taking care of them and giving them a brief moment of relief in the middle of an emotional scene.

In "The Alpha Wolf," Elizabeth Gilbert gathers at the deathbed of her partner, Rayya, with Rayya's two ex-wives.

> *We came into the bedroom, and Gigi put on sacred music, and Stacey lit a candle, and then the three of us got on the bed, and we wrapped our bodies around her body, and we took turns telling her all the last things that she needed to know if she could still hear us. That we loved her, that she was incredible, what a grand, stellar life that she had lived, that we would never be the same for having loved her and been loved by her, that she had forged our hearts in the furnace of her power, that we would always love her, and that we would never stop telling the world her name. And then it was like this silence descended, and this portal opened from some distant, uncharted part of the universe, and this river of the infinite entered into that space, and we could feel it, that it was taking her very gently from us. And that's when Rayya opened her eyes and said, "What the f*** are you guys doing?" And we're like, "Nothing. Nothing." She's like, "What's going on?" I'm like, "Definitely not a bedside death watch, no." We're wiping sheets of tears from our eyes. She goes, "Babe, why are Stacey and Gigi in our bed?" I'm like, "They're not, they're just . . . dropping off some mail."*

Elizabeth pulls us into this moment in such a deep way that we are almost holding our breath with her. When Rayya busts out with her line, it gives us (and Elizabeth) a little break, allowing us to catch our breath before the final scene of Rayya's inevitable death. Without this, it would be hard to stay in such an intense space for an extended period of time.

FISHING FOR PUNCHLINES CAN BE DEADLY

Humor in storytelling should never feel forced, manipulative, or canned. Are you *in* the moment, or have you *constructed* the moment? The audience can feel the difference.

If you find yourself adding a detail that is simply a joke, that doesn't give us an insight into characters or location or move the story along, you're likely overengineering a moment that the story doesn't need. Even the best comics have to learn this lesson.

> **JENIFER ON WORKING WITH COMEDIAN DION FLYNN:** Even seasoned storytellers who host for The Moth can be tempted to build in too many laughs. Dion Flynn put a bunch of jokes in a story involving his work as a Barack Obama impersonator. I suggested a few to cut, not because they weren't funny, but because there were too many. Some jokes support the story. Others pull people out. At one point, Dion steps away from his story line to do a demonstration of how he learned to do the Obama voice. It was a hilarious *and relevant* stop along the way. But if there are too many funny asides, you'll either let the air out of your story's tires or cause your audience to lose the path. During our live rehearsal for the show, Dion decided to try a joke that I suggested he cut. Crickets. To his credit, right after the joke, he said, "Well, that joke didn't hit. I'm gonna cut that one!" (Which got a laugh.) Seems improbable, but sometimes a story with fewer jokes ends up being funnier.

Comedians have a love/hate relationship with The Moth, because this form challenges them. Professionally funny people are used to measuring their success by the number of laughs they get. It's hard to convince them that their stories would *improve* if they could let go of some of their jokes.

Years ago, in a rehearsal for a Mainstage that happened to include comics and writers, almost *all* of the director's notes for the storytellers were about jokes they should cut. The comedians were putting the emphasis on the jokes *first* and the plot of the story *second*.

> **MIKE BIRBIGLIA, MOTH HOST AND STORYTELLER:** We kill jokes and we leave them on the cutting-room floor, even great jokes that we love, because it has to be about the story. If the jokes can help the story, then it's like the most incredible marriage, but if they can't, it's a strange relationship.

For comedians, there is the added hurdle of learning to love the quiet in the room. It's a big adjustment for people who have honed their craft by tallying laughs per minute.

> **HASAN MINHAJ, MOTH HOST AND STORYTELLER:** For years and years, I was doing stand-up, and it was at The Moth that I learned to appreciate the silence. In comedy, you're focusing on a setup and punch, but at The Moth, I could start talking about other really powerful human emotions: love, pain, regret, humiliation. You can take an audience only as high as you take them low.

A storytelling audience can be just as engaged *silently* together as they are *laughing* together. Both are stunningly intimate. When you learn to tune in to the feeling in the room during the heavier parts of the story, you can intuitively sense it. It's a charged silence. We've come to refer to this as "the sound of the audience leaning in."

HOW NOT TO BREAK YOUR FUNNY BONE

Here are some things to be mindful of when thinking about humor in your story:

- **DON'T STEP ON THE LAUGHS** . . . When you make jokes, the audience will (hopefully!) respond. Give them time to react. Don't race through. If you keep plugging along, without taking a slight pause for the laughs (which people often do when they're nervous), the audience will miss what you are saying. If you keep this up, the audience members will worry that they'll miss more of your story and will actually laugh less to avoid stepping on *your words*.

- **. . . EVEN THE UNEXPECTED LAUGHS** . . . Laughter from the audience can come at any time in your story, and sometimes, getting a laugh where you didn't expect it can be startling. Try to savor the surprise, pause for it, and then keep going.

- **. . . BUT ALSO DON'T BE THROWN IF THE LAUGHS *DON'T* COME.** The line you think is funny might not get a laugh. We've seen storytellers who are telling a repeat story fumble because they get to a certain line or joke and expect a response. And oh, the agony as they pause and wait for a laugh that never comes! Different audiences react to different things, and if you don't get laughter where you're expecting it, never fear—maybe they're hanging on your every word and can't wait to see how it ends. Just stay on track with the next beat of your story. Better to be in the moment every time you tell it and enjoy the genuine response from that night's crowd. Who knows when and where you'll get a reaction? These stories are alive and a little bit different every time you tell them.

TOASTS, WHEN THE ROOM IS ABUZZ—OR JUST BUZZED: Given that toasts are usually given at events like weddings and celebration-of-life parties, the crowd may have had a few drinks. There are also other distractions, like food and noisy silverware, side conversations, a photo booth with props, a clown, a beautiful skyline view of the sunset, and so on. Don't take it personally! You may get tons of laughs and tons of tears, or you may be upstaged by a toddler who has decided at that exact moment she *hates her tights*. No matter what's going on, the subject of your toast is listening. Stay the course and share from the heart. What's most important is that your loved one feels celebrated and seen.

ARE YOU READY TO TELL YOUR STORY?

Part of our job as directors is helping people decide if and when they are emotionally ready to tell their stories. Sometimes it is clear that a story is begging to be told, and that the teller is equipped to do the unearthing necessary to bring it to life. However, turning people's real lives into art can be messy, and sometimes storytellers are *not* ready.

Beyond the question of being emotionally prepared, the pertinent details for a story can be tough to access because the story is still unfolding. It takes time to gain insight into a big life event, whether it's radically changing careers or surviving a tornado. Your perspective is too narrow when you're still in the midst of processing (or living!) the experience. It's important that you let some time pass, especially with a more serious story. We joke that it needs to be at least ten years after a death and five after a divorce, and we're only half kidding (though a psychologist once told us it may be the reverse, because apparently divorce can be more traumatizing than death!).

"DEJA VU, AGAIN": CATHERINE ON WORKING WITH COLE KAZ-DIN: Back in 2006, Cole Kazdin told a story about waking up with amnesia after hitting her head in a bad fall. Her story was engaging, with riveting scenes and intense details, but we struggled to figure out how to land her arc. The night of the show, she was radiant on stage, and her loyal boyfriend, who had seen her through the accident, was beaming at her from the front row. But when we listened back to the audio, something felt slightly off. We couldn't put our finger on it. Here is a moment from her original ending:

> *Eventually, I did recover. My head recovered. I have a slipped disc in my back that is a reminder forever of this accident, but my head is back. I have my childhood memories, I have emotions, and I'm pretty much back to the same person I was before the accident: a vegetarian writer who dates Adam. I wonder, though: Is that who I am in my core?*

Not long after, she and her boyfriend broke up, and she moved to Los Angeles. Eventually Cole and I revisited the story. It turned out that at the time of the accident, Cole and her boyfriend were actually broken up. When she was hurt, he rushed to her side and they got back together. At first things went well, but as her amnesia slowly lifted, things between them became strained once more. They eventually broke up . . . again . . . for the same reasons they'd broken up the first time. Cole actually found this liberating. It meant that some fundamental part of her was still intact after the accident. *This* realization became the new ending to her story.

> *It took about six months for me to recover. My memory just came back slowly over time. And I must have been fully healed, because a few months after that, Adam and I broke up, again. Only this time, I knew it was coming, because we'd done it before. When I got myself back, I realized nothing had changed, but this time, there was something comforting about that, because it meant I finally knew who I was, and it meant I could move forward. Even without my memory, I was still me.*

During the first version, Cole didn't realize it, but she was still living her story. This new, truer ending changed the arc and transformed her perspective.

SCARS VS. WOUNDS

On her public radio show *On Being* (which we love and highly recommend!), Moth storyteller Krista Tippett once asked Nadia Bolz-Weber, a trailblazing Lutheran minister (who is also a Moth storyteller), how she knows a personal anecdote or story is ready to go into one of her sermons. Nadia answered that she always tries to "preach from her scars and not her wounds." The first time we heard it was a eureka moment for us, and the phrase has become part of our vernacular because the same is true in storytelling.

Some stories deal with shocking events and trauma. It's important that the teller has done some healing before they try to share the details. Ed Gavagan was a successful carpenter when he was stabbed and left for dead on the street one night in New York City. His healing was more than physical; his whole life had been disrupted. Many years after the stabbing, in "Whatever Doesn't Kill Me," he said:

> *As I was sitting there, thinking about these feelings of what was happening to me, I realized I could never get back to where I was before. That guy. That business. That whole life was just gone. I lost it. I had never believed that I had lost it. I always thought I was trying to get back to be that guy. And as I thought about it, I realized I gotta do something new. And it felt liberating.*

The perspective Ed describes can come only after you have had the distance you need to process events.

Ophira Eisenberg's story "The Accident" opens with a teenager running a red light, hitting Ophira's mom's car and taking the life of her best friend, Adrienne, who had been sitting next to her. Her story ends years later with the discovery of a letter.

> *So I unlocked one of the drawers, and a letter caught my eye, and it was from Adrienne's dad to my mother. It was written about a week after the car accident, just after the funeral. It had never even*

occurred to me that there was a funeral, because the whole time, I was in operations, and there was all this attention on me. It was the first time I'd ever thought of that.

He wrote that he didn't blame my mom for what happened, that is when God wanted to take Adrienne, and his family prayed for us and my recovery.

I'd never thought of what my mother went through, because she never showed me her pain or vulnerability for one second. I can't imagine the blame she felt, the guilt, the responsibility of taking care of someone else's child, and then it all going horribly wrong. But she showed nothing but love.

I wasn't really the strong one; my parents were the strong ones, because they had carefully led me to this place where I could live like an absolutely normal sixteen-year-old kid. And Adrienne was never gonna be sixteen. It hit me hard, staring at the handwriting of her mourning father. And for the first time, I sat down at that dining room table, and I cried.

Ophira lived through this experience at eight, gained a deeper understanding at sixteen, but told it beautifully in her thirties. Sometimes it takes years to process.

We ask storytellers to go back to a moment, to see it in their mind and share the story from *inside* the memory. Warning: It can be emotionally taxing to revisit traumatizing events or situations. One storyteller who had a particularly challenging childhood would need to take a long nap after she rehearsed her story, just to calm her brain. It can be difficult to relive these intense moments. The choice is always yours.

HOW WILL I KNOW?

You may be wondering: Am I ready? We might never get a chance to work with you (though we hope we might!), but there are some "tells" we've noticed over the years that may lead you to "press pause."

When directing upsetting stories, we pay attention to any signs that a story is still raw for the teller: Their drafts are late and dates to talk are rescheduled last-minute. In extreme cases, the storyteller may get lost in the details of a graphic scene. They are caught in the trauma while exploring the story, and when they stop talking, they might be disoriented. These signs can indicate that they may still be living the story and may not be ready to tell it publicly.

Strong emotions don't preclude you from being able to tell your story; as listeners, we are hungry for that honesty. But an audience has to feel that you are still in command, that you'll be able to get to the next part and ultimately bring us to a satisfying conclusion.

If you are halfway through crafting your story and find yourself overwhelmed with feelings about the events, put the draft away and come back to it in a week. Two weeks. Three weeks. Three months. Does it feel any different?

If your heart rate quickens or you have tears in your eyes in this one part, that's okay! That means you are *in* the story. Let us see and feel that emotion! But if you're still feeling overwhelmed and worried that you'll start crying and won't be able to stop, and your stomach is in knots, that's your body saying no. And remember, it's probably not a "No, *never* tell this" but a "No, not *yet*."

You have to control your story; the story can't control you.

MEG ON A STORY YEARS IN THE MAKING: Jeremy Jennings called the Moth Pitchline and told us about how after being stationed in San Francisco guarding the Golden Gate Bridge, he had been deployed to be a guard at Guantánamo. He was not military police, nor had he been trained in how to work with detainees, and he described how traumatizing and confusing he found the experience. He was conflicted about his duty to serve and the conditions and treatment of the detainees he had witnessed. We talked at length, and I sent him notes on how he might approach telling his story—and then I didn't hear from him for quite a few months. His story stayed with me, but it was clear to me that he just wasn't ready.

Six months later I reached out to ask how he was doing. He apologized for his silence, and I told him I understood that he wasn't ready, and it was okay. He wanted to try again. So after a few phone calls and emails we managed to pull together a first draft and got his story into a pretty solid structure. But he still wasn't ready to actually tell it. The idea of standing up and sharing it with someone other than me was just too much. So we pressed pause again.

JEREMY JENNINGS: I'm not sure why I called the Pitchline. I imagined enjoying the same catharsis that the storytellers on the radio seemed to achieve, and I wanted some of that. The first telling of the story on the Pitchline felt more like a confession of crimes, guilt, and sorrow for what I saw and did in Guantánamo. I didn't think anyone would call me back. I don't think I ever intended to actually tell the story on stage, and when someone did call, it was a bit frightening. It wasn't just that the story was emotionally distressing. I was also deliberately violating the secrecy that the government had imposed upon everything that happened to the people inside that prison. Moving the voice in my head into the telephone was one step, but telling this story to the public was a more risky step in many ways. I might come across as an apologist for war crimes, as a terrorist sympathizer, or trying to make myself look less complicit than I was. I worried that few Americans would sympathize or understand. Paranoia set in, and I even imagined former detainees or al Qaeda or my own government hearing my story and coming after me or my family.

It would be over two years before I found myself flying to NYC for rehearsals. In the intervening time, I had finished a second bachelor's degree, ended a marriage, and started graduate school. I felt more confident about my identity as a veteran and my values. I was still worried about unintended consequences but resolved to tell my story anyway.

MEG: When Jeremy arrived at rehearsal, he was worried about whether he could make it through the story. Between his nerves and emotions, he had a hard time getting the first few lines out, but he persevered. After rehearsal, you could see the relief on his face and a newfound confidence in his body language. When he finally stood on that stage and he shared the experience, you could see a change come over him. He said he felt empowered—so much so that he reprised it for an audience of three thousand a few months later.

If all the pieces of your story are white-hot and charged, you need to take a step back. It is not a show of bravery to tell a story before you are ready. It is actually, *actively,* a disservice to yourself and your lived experience.

Some people may *never* feel like enough time has passed—and that's fine. That's honest.

JENIFER ON WORKING ON A VIETNAM WAR-THEMED SHOW: In 2016, I co-directed a show that was based on stories that explored the Vietnam War. I found an article about a Vietnam veteran in New Jersey named Glenn and invited him to participate. He was an extraordinarily brave man, both in action and in spirit. He'd received two Purple Hearts. In his writing, he fearlessly confronted what he'd witnessed and done in the war and how he felt about it. He wrote back to tell me he was honored to be invited but after thinking about it for a long while, he decided it was best if he didn't. Writing had helped him process many of his feelings, but telling the stories to an audience would be too much. He said his battle with PTSD was daily and while his physical scars had healed, the emotional ones had not.

And right there, Glenn put into practice the maxim "Tell stories from the scars, not the wounds." The night of the show, he wrote to wish us well. And when a *Moth Radio Hour* featuring stories from the show aired, he listened and wrote to say that he was mesmerized and frozen in place from start to finish.

While I was sorry that The Moth's audience didn't get to hear one of Glenn's powerful stories, I'm so grateful that he made his boundaries clear.

By contrast, sometimes sharing an emotional story with an audience can be healing. Constructing the narrative allows the teller to create order in their story rather than feel overwhelmed by the many emotions and details. For some people suffering with PTSD, sharing the story of the traumatic event can help them reshape their own narrative, allowing them to find some level of control over the story. The storyteller proves to themself that they have agency.

In fact, veterans' hospitals and the Association of the United States Army are using storytelling as a way to help treat PTSD. From AUSA.org:

If you are afflicted with PTSD, then telling your story allows the brain to make new connections to that memory. You are not only attaching words to your experience, but you are attaching the feelings and sensory impressions that you felt at the time. And in doing so, the stuck part of the brain can finally stand down. It will realize that the danger is not happening. It can stop firing as if you're in immediate danger.

However, making these connections is not without its challenges. To tell the real story of what happened to you is to relive some of the worst moments of your life. Emotions will be dredged up in unpredictable ways. You might either feel too much emotion or none at all. War often desensitizes its warriors, detaching them from their feelings. But for this type of treatment to be effective, the soldier must connect their emotions about the event with what was seen, smelled, tasted or touched at the time. . . .

The aim is to make sense of what was likely a chaotic experience in which you were helpless. . . . But remember that alleviating PTSD symptoms does not mean you will forget what happened to you. Or forget that you are a different person than you were before. Or forget about what happened to those who died. It just makes it easier for you to live a life that truly honors the memory of your service.

We have worked with many tellers over the years who have suffered PTSD from active military service, surviving a natural disaster, or experiencing violence, and we have witnessed firsthand how the process of building, shaping, and sharing a story can be healing.

"LIFE AFTER DEATH": MEG ON WORKING WITH DAMIEN ECHOLS: Damien spent eighteen years and seventy-eight days on death row in Arkansas for a crime he didn't commit. While I was working with Damien, I began to worry that he was suffering from PTSD but hadn't been given the medical help he needed to diagnose it. He shared his story with me mere months after his release from prison, and at first I thought it was too soon, but he had been processing and living with his trauma for eighteen years and felt compelled to tell us what he had lived through.

The film director Peter Jackson, who had helped secure Damien's release by funding a DNA investigation, had loaned Damien his apartment in downtown New York City, and I went there every day for almost two weeks prior to Damien telling his story live on stage. He insisted on practicing every day, and I could see how important it was to him. The act of telling it over and over was not only preparing him for sharing it in front of an audience, but also seemed to be building him up in some way. And by the time we got to the night where he would share it in New York, he seemed confident—nervous, but confident. I spoke to him the next day, and he said something I will never forget. He thanked me for working with him and said, "After I was finished, I felt lighter somehow, like I had left a piece of the trauma on stage that night." The experience of working with Damien was the first time I truly felt how healing and important storytelling can be.

Storytelling can help people process and heal, but PTSD is a serious condition, and we encourage you to find an organization that is skilled in working with trauma rather than go it alone.

Fundamentally, it's up to you to decide if you are ready to tell a particular story. Be honest with yourself. You may be ready now, in ten years, or you may never be ready—but if and when you *are* ready to share, there will be an audience to listen.

TELLING STORIES ABOUT PEOPLE WHO HAVE DIED

Longtime Moth host Peter Aguero hosted a show in New Bedford, Massachusetts, and after a teller shared a story about losing a loved one, Peter reminded the audience how the simple act of hearing that story brought their memory to life. He then asked the audience of over a thousand people to say the name of someone they had lost who meant the world to them. In unison, a thousand names were said, and then for a moment everyone in the room was silent. We were reminded of our shared human experience, and with it came a deep feeling of empathy for each person in the room.

To tell a story about someone who has died is to conjure them back to life, if only for a few minutes, and allow hundreds or thousands of people to meet them.

> **KATE ON TELLING A STORY ABOUT HER LATE MOTHER:** When I told my story for the first time, I told it for an audience of 2,700 at the Arlene Schnitzer Concert Hall in Portland. And I'd had all these thoughts about what it would feel like. But the thing that I didn't realize until I did it was it was the closest thing to bringing her back. Because I felt like when I told it, for those twelve minutes, all of us thought of her at the same time, and how often do you get to do that? To be in a room with thousands of strangers who, for those moments, are holding your loved one in their thoughts right with you.

But if the story is also about their death, then with every loving detail of their *life* that you include, you also grow closer to telling the details of their *death*. This can feel painful, almost like having a piece of them die once again. You might throw in new detail after new detail to avoid arriving at that painful moment because you can't bear to let your loved one go.

If you're not ready to go through this, the story is not ready for an audience.

ON DEALING WITH EMOTION IN EULOGIES: You rarely, if ever, feel ready to deliver a eulogy. For many people, the thought of breaking down into tears while giving a eulogy fills them with dread, but funerals and memorials are sad occasions that often take place when the grief is still fresh. Focusing on the details can anchor you, but choose them carefully. You may not be ready to revisit some moments, but having something specific to call back to—an afternoon making a pie together, the time you both decided to meet in Penn Station or went skinny dipping in Walden Pond at three A.M.—can help you put one word in front of the other and bring your audience there with you. The experiences that were so special, often more so in hindsight, have another chance to come alive. For a few moments, you're in one intimate space together, one colored by grief, but not exclusively.

It's okay if you cry through some of it. (The people who are at the remembrance service will most likely also be crying.) The advice we give for eulogies is the same we would for a story-teller when they reach a particularly emotional part of their story. If you start to feel the emotions creeping in, pause, take a breath, acknowledge the emotion, and wait until it feels manageable. Don't try to push it back or ignore it, because it will only make it more difficult for you to get the words out. If you know from rehearsing that you always cry at a certain point, then it's absolutely okay for you to give your listeners a little warning: "This part is a little hard for me" or "This is where I'm gonna cry." Acknowledging it gives you the power to face it, and by sharing this with your listener, you let them know you are okay. Unless they have a heart of stone, no one will judge you for feeling, especially when you're talking about someone you have loved and lost.

"FRANNY'S LAST RIDE": CATHERINE ON WORKING WITH MIKE DESTEFANO: In the early aughts, we met the late comedian Mike DeStefano when he was cast in our show at the U.S. Comedy Arts Festival. Mike was a scruffy, no-BS sort of guy who was born and raised in the Bronx. He did not suffer fools gladly, and came across as a bit gruff. But I'd come to learn that he was quite soft on the inside, a deeply generous and empathetic man who had seen tough days and, as a result, had a ton of compassion for his fellow humans.

His story was about his wife, Franny, and breaking her out of hospice to take her on one last motorcycle ride. Franny had died of AIDS, and Mike had never talked about this publicly. We decided to invite him to tell his story in New York City first. We hoped he'd be less nervous there, in front of strangers, than at the festival, where he'd be performing in front of a lot of people from his industry.

He'd been mesmerizing in rehearsal, but when he got on stage, talking about Franny in front of an audience was much more intense than he'd anticipated. The reaction of the audience to the quirky and free-spirited Franny was palpable. He started throwing things into the story that I'd never even heard! I was in the audience, panicking, watching the time run out. At ten minutes, he hadn't even started the main action sequence. Mike later told me that it was joyful to feel an audience fall as deeply in love with Franny as he had, and he leaned into that.

Mike went nearly twenty minutes in that first telling and we were worried he wouldn't be able to pull it off at the festival, but he lovingly begged us to give him another chance. A few months later, he took the stage again, and in just ten minutes he nailed it.

Here, Mike has taken Franny out of hospice to show her his new bike, and she asks him to take her for a ride in spite of her being in a hospital gown with an IV.

> *And then she just put her arm around my belly and started rubbing, and she said, "Can we go on the highway?" And I thought of all that we'd been through and all the suffering. And I said, "Yeah, we could do that." So we got on I-95. And I had it up to eighty. And she was just screaming with happiness. Morphine bag was flapping over her head. And that wind—I always imagined the wind on a bike making you feel free, you know? It's so powerful. And for ten minutes we were normal, and that wind just blew all the death off of us.*

As we mentioned, getting to the moment of the loved one's death can feel almost like having them die once again. Take comfort in the idea of the three deaths, as celebrated in the Mexican tradition of Día de los Muertos:

The first death is the failure of the body.

The second is the burial of the body.

The most definitive death is the third death. This occurs when no one is left to remember us.

Through our stories, we are able to keep the people we love alive long after they leave us.

DIRECTOR'S NOTES

- Punctuate your scenes with emotion. Put yourself back in the moment and describe how you felt both physically and emotionally. Your listener may not relate to a specific situation, but we all know what it feels like to be elated or embarrassed or so nervous your heart races. Emotions connect you to your listener and allow them to experience your story and feel what you were feeling. Remember, stakes aren't possible without emotion.

- A moment to laugh together is like a gift to the listener. It can be used to relieve the tension of a painful or suspenseful moment and can bond you with the audience. It can help illustrate your point of view or deepen our understanding of characters in your story. But the humor in storytelling should never feel forced. Your stories are best told in your authentic voice.

- Are you ready to tell this story? You need distance and perspective to fully process an experience, or chances are you're still living through it. Stories involving trauma or deep upset must be told from a place of healing. Strong feelings do not preclude you from sharing a story, but if you feel you're not in command of your emotions, press pause until you've had a chance to more fully process. It is not a show of bravery to tell a story before you're ready.

CHAPTER 7

STRUCTURING YOUR STORY

The end of a story is like the end of a good meal. We're sated but it doesn't mean that we'll never be hungry again.

—KATE TELLERS

Consider all of the stepping stones you've unearthed and could possibly use in the story you're crafting. What is the best way to *order* these moments? Have you picked the best scene to start with? How will the story unfold from there?

Your story is like a puzzle that can be put together in a hundred ways. We're looking for the optimal way.

We could dissolve into a discussion of all the classic literary structures you could apply, but there is no *one way* to effectively structure a story. The best structure supports the story you want to tell and allows all the parts and elements to flow together seamlessly, without confusing the listener. It should feel organic and authentic, never forced or prescriptive.

When reading, you can revisit a sentence if it didn't make sense the first time. You can linger on it to make sure you understand the meaning. But with live storytelling, the listener can't press rewind, so you have to be clear with the scenes and images you paint.

If your first memory of meeting someone many years ago is a fun scene that gives us a lot of rich background, perhaps you'll want to include that as a flashback somewhere in your story. Or maybe your story is more of a mystery, and telling it in any order other than chronological will spoil the surprise of finding out "whodunnit."

Structuring your story can be a little like playing with the pieces of your puzzle. Don't be afraid to move things around! A story is a living, breathing thing; nothing is permanent. As directors, we find that stories often follow one of the structures below. Pick the structure that supports the journey you want your audience to take.

> **ALISTAIR BANE, MOTH STORYTELLER:** When you tell a story, you have to take your listener somewhere. You can't keep driving around the block.

CHRONOLOGICAL

Often the most compelling structure is one that lets a story unfold for the audience in the order that it happened.

Suzi Ronson's "The Girl from Beckenham" takes us from her teen years growing up in London, learning to style hair at the Evelyn Paget College of Hair and Beauty, to landing her first job at a local salon, where one of her weekly clients, a woman named Mrs. Jones, brags about her musician son, David:

> *I didn't take much notice until one day she mentioned the song "Space Oddity," and I looked at her and I said, " 'Space Oddity,' you know, I've heard that on the radio. Are we talking about David Bowie?" She said, "Yes. I'm his mum."*

Suzi tells her story in chronological order, and we experience the surprise with her: We ride with her as she meets David's wife, Angie; we stand next to her as she meets David to cut his hair; and we share her nerves as she experiments with hair color to create the now-famous signature red hair of Ziggy Stardust.

> *I chopped his hair off, and after I'd finished, his hair wouldn't stand up. It just kind of flopped. And I'm looking at it and I'm kind of panicking, and I can see he's not looking too happy. So I said, "As soon as we tint the hair it's going to change the texture. It's going to look great. I can promise you, it's going to stand up." I was praying I was right. I went and experimented with color, and I found the color, Red Hot Red, with 30 volume peroxide to give a bit of a kick. There were no products in those days. You didn't have gels or fixatives. There was nothing to help me make it stand up. So I used Gard. It was an anti-dandruff treatment that I'd used on the old girls at the salon that set hair like stone. The second he looked at himself in the mirror, with that short red hair, any doubts he had completely disappeared. I mean, Angie and I looked at him in awe. He looked fantastic.*

From there, she takes us on tour with Bowie and his entourage. And she ends by saying:

> *I met so many interesting people throughout that time, you know, and heard so much wonderful music. I'm so grateful for David for taking a chance on me, and taking me on the road with him. My haircut's on British currency now, the Brixton ten-pound note. Who would have thought I could have done that?*

If we knew who Suzi was going to become at the top of the story, we'd miss out on the thrill of meeting David Bowie and her pivotal role in creating that iconic image. By the end, she can hardly believe the turn her life has taken, and we can marvel too, because we experienced it with her beat by beat.

Sometimes a story *wants* to be told step-by-step, especially if it's a little complicated or even a bit of a mystery. For example, if you are Terrance Flynn, and your story, "C'est La Vie," has a big reveal, like, spoiler alert, almost dating a serial killer, you wouldn't start by saying, "In 1985, I narrowly avoided going home with Jeffrey Dahmer. Let me take you back. One night, as a college student in Milwaukee . . ."

Telling it in the order it unfolded might be exactly what builds tension and suspense best.

Bottom line: Don't assume you have to get fancy with your structure. Sometimes the best way is to simply start at the beginning and tell it from there!

TWO CHRONOLOGIES IN TANDEM

Another structure involves cutting back and forth between two stories that unfold simultaneously. Each story has its own tensions and conflicts—though they are often connected to each other—and they eventually resolve together.

Comedian Anthony Griffith worked closely with former Moth executive and artistic director Lea Thau to structure his story, "The Best of Times, the Worst of Times." It charts three appearances he made on *The Tonight Show Starring Johnny Carson,* which coincided with the illness and eventual death of his two-year-old daughter. In the second sentence, Anthony sets up the two threads.

> *In 1990, I took my wife and child to L.A. from Chicago to seek my fame and fortune. And after a couple of weeks, I got two important phone calls. One was from a talent coordinator offering me a chance to do stand-up comedy on* The Tonight Show *with Johnny Carson, and the second call was from my daughter's doctor saying that her cancer had resurfaced.*

Everything we learn about his emotional state is told through both stories.

> *I thought everything was great, because we had the cancer before and we had beat it, so I was sure we'd beat it again. And I was going to be performing for millions of people on* The Tonight Show.

He then takes us through the next few months, moving us through his first appearance and his daughter's illness.

> *A special moment of that night was running into Johnny Carson in the parking lot. And he said, "Hey, you were extremely funny, and I want you to start working on your second set, because I want you back." Now, by the time I got the official call for the second* Tonight Show, *my daughter was admitted to the hospital. And I don't know if you know about cancer, but it's almost like fighting with a gangbanger. You can beat it, but if it comes back, it's coming back with friends, and it's coming to do serious damage.*

As his emotions change and deepen, he keeps us tightly tethered to the two stories.

> *In the evening I would work on my second set, because after all, I'm a clown, and that's my job, to make people laugh. And I was a clown whose medical bills were rising, who was one step from eviction, whose car was one step from being repoed. My comedy is getting biting, and it's getting dark, and it's getting hateful. And the talent coordinator is worried because he's all about the network, and the network is nice, nice, nice. And we started to butt heads, because he wanted nice, and I just wanted to be real, because I was hurting and I wanted everybody to hurt.*

Both stories head toward the conclusion side by side.

> *While I was preparing for the third appearance, the doctor called me into the office, and I knew something was wrong because he was crying, and . . . doctors don't cry. He wouldn't really look at me. And he said, "That's all we can do." So I said, "Okay. How much time does she have?" And he said, "About six weeks."*

And then he brings both stories to their heartbreaking conclusion.

> *When I did my third* Tonight Show, *my daughter had died. I had six applause breaks. No one knew I was mourning. No one knew I could care less about Johnny Carson or* The Tonight Show. *In 1990, I had three appearances on* The Tonight Show. *I had a total of sixteen applause breaks. And I would have given it all up just to share another bag of fries with my two-year-old daughter.*

The tandem telling works well because the two story arcs show us how Anthony's attitude and excitement about his work shift enormously as his daughter's illness progresses. The first arc is deepened by the second arc. Anthony's heartbreak over losing his child is made worse by the fact that he must provide for his family by being funny on stage.

Part of the story's power lies in the fact that two contradictory things can happen at the same time. Anthony explores what happens when your greatest personal success and your greatest personal tragedy coincide. Telling them in tandem illustrates the complexity in a deeper way. We see how over the course of the story he goes from being excited about appearing on *The Tonight Show* to not caring because his grief has blotted out everything else in his life. If the focus of this story had been his daughter and the brave way she faced sickness, then we might not need his comedy career in the background. But the story focuses on how humor and anger lived side by side in him, and so neither of the story lines fully lands without the other.

THE FLASHBACK

Telling your story chronologically is often the most simple and straightforward structural choice, but sometimes it's more effective to mix things up. You might consider using a flashback—a tool used to temporarily pause the story to give the listener information. Sometimes a flashback is vital and integral to the story, but other times it just helps draw the picture.

There are many ways to use a flashback.

THE CLASSIC FLASHBACK

You might be telling your story chronologically but decide, when you reach a compelling moment, to flash back to provide context or allow your listener to linger in the excitement. A flashback can add energy into a more quiet, cerebral part of a story, or it can act as the brakes in a fast-moving one.

In "Treasure Island," Boots Riley is driving across the Bay Bridge between Oakland and San Francisco, in the early 1990s, with his band (The Coup).

> *One morning we were driving back across the bridge. Pam the Funkstress, The Coup's DJ, was driving, and I was sitting in the back with some other folks that had been in the studio. And we realized we left our keyboard player at the studio. And so we needed to turn around, and the only place to turn around on the Bay Bridge is Treasure Island. And at this time Treasure Island wasn't full of condos like it is right now. It was a naval base. So we got off on Treasure Island, made that turn, and started heading back up the hill toward the bridge, when all of a sudden, we hear a siren, and it was the military police stopping us.*
>
> *The cops stopped us and asked us all for our IDs. There were a bunch of us in the car. We all gave them our IDs. They asked Pam for the registration, and I said from the back, "The registration's in the glove compartment." So somebody opens the glove compartment, and a waterfall of bullets come down.*
>
> *Now let me explain how those bullets got there.*

Boots then hangs in this moment of tension and uses it as a place to look back at the historical context of Oakland in the years leading up to this scene. Had Boots started by setting up the facts of the backstory, it would have made for a less compelling and personal beginning. Stopping and recounting how past events have influenced the scene he describes elevates the stakes and tension. We learn about threats white supremacists were making against the

Black community at large, including kill lists that targeted Boots and his band members.

> *White supremacists didn't like us, and we ended up on one of those lists. And it's not a good feeling to know that there are crazy people looking at a list of people that should be killed, and you are one of them. So we bought guns.*
>
> *We also didn't want to get messed with by the police. So we did it all the way legal. We registered them, we went to the shooting range to make sure we knew what we were doing with them, and we transported them legally when we needed to transport them.*
>
> *That meant carrying it in a lockbox while it was unloaded, in the trunk of your car. What I didn't realize before I told somebody to open the glove compartment was that we had recently been to the shooting range, and there was a box of bullets that was open, and they came raining down like a waterfall.*
>
> *And they seemed to be going in slow motion, and I feel like I thought the longest* Oh sh★t *that I could ever think. And in seeming slow motion, the cop pulls out his gun and has it two inches from Pam's head, and says, "Put your hands up! Everybody, put your hands up!"*

At first the bullets are a surprise element that play with perception—the listener questions why they're in the glove compartment and makes assumptions—and then Boots gives us the backstory and explains the context. Now we know what he knows, and when he comes back to that moment and we see that cascade of bullets for a second time, we think *Oh sh★t* too!

Using the flashback plays with the listener's perspective. At the beginning the listener may think and feel one way, but after you flash back and give context, they think, feel, and understand in a new way. The key here is to not take too long to get back to the scene you want to rejoin, or you run the risk of people forgetting the details you described earlier and not making the connection. You want your flashback to flow seamlessly into your story.

THE CLIFFHANGER

While a classic flashback can happen anytime in the story, a cliff-hanger is exclusively used in the beginning. Opening your story with a short scene, or a few lines describing a critical moment, can create drama and tension and introduce the stakes right out of the gate. You can pause the scene and flash back to explain how you got there, leaving your listener hanging (*What happened?!*). Then tell the story chronologically until you return to that edge-of-the-cliff moment you opened with. The unresolved opening keeps everyone invested throughout the story. Again, the trick is to make sure that the scenes connect in a way that's clear to the listener.

In "Home Cooking," Michael Fischer opens with a scene involving a confrontation with his fellow prison inmate.

> *JR looks at me and he says, "Do you realize that I could kill you right now, stash your body under your bunk . . . and just take the pretzels? And nobody would even know?" JR and I are at the end of a hallway and around a corner. We're in a blind spot and we both know it, as far from the guards as we can get.*

He then goes on to tell the story of his relationship with his mother growing up. How he had treated her and how he had taken her love for granted, and how much he regretted that now. Eventually he works his way back to the opening scene.

> *My mom sends me cards, even though I call her on the phone every few days, because she thinks it's good for the officers to see me getting mail. She thinks they'll be nicer to me if they're reminded that in addition to being an inmate, I'm also a human being who has a family. She wants them to know, just as she wants me to know, how much I'm loved. So the only person who's going to eat these pretzels, while I'm still alive, is me.*
>
> *I can tell JR wants to fight about this. He's got his head tilted to one side; his arms are crossed in front of him. He's just waiting*

> *for me to say the wrong thing. But my hands are in my pockets.*
> *I'm scared, but I try to keep my voice steady: "If that's really*
> *where you're at, that you're gonna kill somebody over pretzels,*
> *then I don't know what to tell you, man. They're not for sale."*
>
> *JR stares me down, weighing his options. He stomps off down*
> *the hallway, empty-handed.*

The scene serves as an introduction to the story, and when re-visited near the end, it serves as the climax leading to the resolution.

> *As strange as it sounds, something about hanging on to that bag of*
> *pretzels, come what may, makes me feel just a little bit better. Not*
> *because I like the pretzels all that much anymore; they're actually*
> *too salty for me these days. Not because there won't be some other*
> *guy threatening me over food someday soon, because I'm sure it's*
> *only a matter of time. My mom will never even know the standoff*
> *with JR happened. But at least it's a moment—one small*
> *moment—when I've done the right thing. Something I can build*
> *on. It's a time that I protected the love that she's always shown me*
> *instead of just throwing it away.*

But storyteller beware: The technique of opening with a cliff-hanger gets a bit overused, and not always successfully. We tend to tell stories chronologically, so if you start somewhere other than the natural beginning, you want to make sure you maintain that conversational tone. Otherwise, it can feel theatrical and clumsy rather than organic. It might weigh things down and make it feel longer if it takes more time for us to get into the heart of the story. If the structure feels awkward or complicated when you tell it, then it will probably end up sounding that way to your listener as well.

In an early draft or run-through, a storyteller will often use a cliffhanger to set up their story, only to end up chopping it off later, and suddenly the story feels lighter by starting at the natural, obvious beginning.

Note that the order of a story can take care of your listener. If a story explores a tragic event, and the listener can see it coming, it causes them to sit in painful anticipation. Sometimes that discomfort can serve a story, but often it can be distracting. If your audience is busy dreading, they aren't hearing what you are saying. They are emotionally guarding themselves, and they aren't fully connecting. We've found this especially true in stories dealing with violence or the loss of a child or loved one. It isn't a hard-and-fast rule, but if your story is causing your listener to feel dread, an earlier reveal can help relieve it.

MULTIPLE FLASHBACKS

Instead of *one* flashback as a frame for your story, consider weaving shorter flashbacks throughout. Each flashback can give context and motivation for what is about to happen in the main story.

"PULLING BACK THE TURBAN": JODI POWELL ON WORKING WITH HARJAS SINGH: We centered the story around a pivotal moment for Harjas: the traditional Sikh turban-tying ceremony. The story focuses on his evolving relationship with his turban. We wanted to keep the focus on the ceremony and decided to use flashbacks to give context and support the arc. We began with Harjas waking up on the morning of his thirteenth birthday and then flashed back to him being three years old to show his life and routine up until this moment.

> *This transition from boyhood to a man would be marked by my very own turban-tying ceremony. I was nervous because I didn't know what the turban would feel like but was also excited to follow in the footsteps of my father and grandfather, whom I'd seen meticulously tie their turbans every morning, like it was a part of their bodies. Ever since I was three years old and my hair was long enough to be tied into a bun, a jooda, my mom would sit me down in front of her, my back toward her. She'd oil my hair, then comb*

it, braid it, and then tie it into a bun. Then she'd cover my jooda with a one-foot-by-one-foot square cloth called a patka.

As he prepares for the ceremony, he illustrates his nervousness around donning the turban by flashing back to his memories of the first time he wore his patka to school.

After my grandfather had dropped me off at the bus stop and all the parents had left, some kids came up to me, circling around me like vultures, trying to touch my patka, asking: "Is that an egg on your head?" "No, dude, that's a tomato." "Is that a ball? Can I play with it?" "One kid would try and smack my head. I tried to fight back, but it didn't matter. It was the first time it really sunk in that someone would try to hurt me for how I looked.

Flashbacks in live storytelling can be a bit tricky. You rely on the audience following you and being able to hold on to the different aspects of the story. To help his listeners, Harjas added lines that signaled when we were in the present and when we were in flashback.

I sat down in front of the Guru Granth Sahib, kneeling, as my grandfather started laying down layer after layer of the turban. With each layer that went around my head, I thought back to the times when things became really rough: After 9/11, an anti-turban rhetoric took hold of the world, even in my little town in India.

The day of the ceremony was a linear story base, and by weaving in flashbacks, we were able to hear the advice given by family members, learn the history of the tradition, and get a window into Harjas's ever-changing relationship to his turban leading up to this moment. This is often how we naturally remember things: We have significant moments, and then we go into the catalog of our minds and think, *Where did I first see or think like that?* Much like the central image here—the process of laying down layer after layer of turban—Harjas's perspective has been shaped by accumulating layer after layer of experience, each infused with elements of the past and the present. In the end, he brings us full circle:

> *I decided to wear it to school for the first time, the same place where I had been ridiculed for wearing my patka when I was five. And as I stood in front of the mirror and tied it, I questioned again, "Why can't I just blend in?"* But this time the answer came from within: Why try to blend in when you were born to stand out?

Used skillfully, a flashback can add energy and build up the stakes of a story, introduce important background information, or be used as punctuation to give the listener a deeper understanding. It can act as a reminder that the past and the present live together in every moment.

WHEN DECIDING WHETHER TO USE A FLASHBACK, ASK YOURSELF THESE QUESTIONS:

1. Does the flashback help the story move forward? Will it be more engaging if people sit in suspense for a while? Or is it distracting?
2. Does the flashback add essential details that would otherwise bog the story down at the top?
3. Is the flashback short enough that the listener won't lose track? Does the time jumping back and forth disrupt the flow of the story?

THE CALLBACK AS FRAMING

If you open your story by using a particularly meaningful scene, you can call back to it at the end as a way to frame an entire story— opening with it and then reflecting back can help illustrate how much the journey of the story has changed you and help you land your arc. We see this in Abeny Kucha's "The First Cow."

BEGINNING:

When I first arrived in Portland, Maine, I walked off the plane with my twelve-year-old brother, and my eight-year-old daughter, and my two little boys, four years old and two years old. The woman from social services who met us took us directly to this room with a conveyor belt. I had never seen anything like it before. We stood there in silence, watching the bags, and she asked me, "Do you see your bags?" And I told her I didn't have a bag. Only the plastic bag I was carrying. That's all we had. And she said, "Right. Okay. Well, then, let's go home." And that word, home—I hadn't had a home since my village.

ENDING:

And now, we made it. My children would never walk two hundred miles again. They would never starve again. And they will always be happy, even when I'm not around. Once again, I thought about the last few years. When my daughter graduated from law school, I was so very proud of all my children. Today, I think about that first day in the Portland, Maine, airport when the woman said, "Let's go home." And home means hope to me. Home means I would never, ever run again.

The callback differs from a cliffhanger in that you are not leaving your listener in suspense and then resolving the moment later. Instead, the opening scene is the first step in your story. When Abeny refers back to the opening scene, we are reminded how much she has been through on the long road to finally feeling like she is home. When she repeats the phrase "Let's go home," we feel a depth of meaning that we did not feel at the beginning. The listener has a new, deeper understanding of that very first scene because they have been on the journey through Abeny's story with her.

"MAN AND BEAST": CATHERINE ON WORKING WITH ALAN RAB-INOWITZ: Alan was a big-cat expert, and his story was about convincing the National Assembly of Belize to preserve thousands of acres of land to protect jaguars. When we started working on the story, we began with a scene of him on the floor of the assembly, nervously waiting to give his address. Then we flashed back to when he was a child, unable to speak because of a debilitating stutter. Young Alan had developed a love for animals because, like him, they were unable to speak, and he swore that if he ever learned to talk, he'd become a voice for animals. From there we worked our way back to the scene in the National Assembly.

But we found that the backstory was so moving that it needed a lot of space, and by the time we got back to the National Assembly, the listener would have forgotten where the story began. Understanding his background gives important context to the emotion he felt speaking before the Belize government, because he knew that if his voice shook or stuttered due to nerves, it would undermine his message. So we decided to lose the flashback structure and tell the story in a linear fashion, starting with his childhood, but with a callback of the opening scene at the end. Here is the opening:

> *I was five years old, standing in the old Great Cat House at the Bronx Zoo, staring into the face of an old female jaguar. I remember looking at the bare walls and the bare ceiling, wondering what the animal had done to get itself there. I leaned in a little toward the cage and started whispering something at the jaguar, but my father came over quickly and asked, "What are you doing?" I turned to him to try and explain, but my mouth froze, as I knew it would. Because everything about my young childhood at that time was characterized by the inability to speak.*

This gives listeners a lot of the facts of the story through a scene rather than just listing them off. (That he's a little boy, he has a stutter, but he can talk to animals, adults don't understand him.) Then we end in a similar scene, one in which the healed adult Alan encounters a jaguar in the forest.

> *I knew I should feel frightened, but I didn't. Instinctively I squatted down, and the jaguar sat. I looked into this jaguar's eyes, and I was so clearly reminded of the little boy looking into the face of the sad old jaguar at the Bronx Zoo. But this animal wasn't sad. In this animal's eyes there was strength and power and sureness of purpose. And I also realized as I was looking into his eyes that what I was seeing was a reflection of the way I was feeling too. That little broken boy and that old broken jaguar were now this. Suddenly I felt scared. I stood up and took a step back. The jaguar stood up too, turned, and started to walk off into the forest. After about ten feet, it stopped and turned to look back at me. I looked at the jaguar, and I leaned a little toward it, the way I had at the Bronx Zoo so many years before, and I whispered to it, "It's okay now, it's all going to be okay," and the jaguar turned and was gone.*

By calling back to the earlier jaguar encounter, we are reminded how far Alan has come. The two jaguar encounters serve as bookends and become symbolic of Alan's journey. When he triumphs, getting the land set aside, we cheer with him, because we're also cheering for the little boy Alan. The structure served the arc of the story much better than if he'd started in the present and flashed back.

WHEN A SMALLER STORY CARRIES THE WEIGHT OF A LARGER STORY

Sometimes a story is so overwhelming that it's hard to fathom. Everyone has had their heart broken by the end of a promising relationship—that's something we can all relate to—but when you're telling a story amidst a more harrowing or epic event, it's challenging for a listener to comprehend and relate.

If you have any concern that the main event might be hard to absorb (or isn't particularly relatable), using a smaller story as a frame can help. In Carl Pillitteri's "Fog of Disbelief," he puts a human face on an unfathomable disaster.

"FOG OF DISBELIEF": MEG ON WORKING WITH CARL PILLITTERI: In 2011, Carl was working as a field engineer inside the Reactor Unit 1 turbine building at the Fukushima Daiichi Nuclear Power Station when an earthquake struck. The story of the disaster itself is overwhelming and almost hard for a listener to connect to or imagine. The details and the magnitude of what happened feel chaotic.

We chose to focus on a smaller story Carl shared, about a restaurant where he would regularly dine and his relationship to the owner who would welcome him. He begins the story by describing the restaurant and then reveals where the restaurant is located.

For many years, I have worked along the northeast coast of Japan, and when assigned there, I would frequent this one particular restaurant five, six nights a week. Over the years, I came to grow very fond of the older woman who owned and operated it. She didn't speak any English, and I didn't speak any Japanese, but we shared a friendship just the same. Upon arrival, I would always slide open her door and take a half step in and look at her, as if to say, "Hey, Mom, I'm home," and she would greet me with this warm and welcoming smile, and she was always happy to see me. She knew what I was there for, the same thing every time, her amazing pan-fried chicken dish. She was a motherly figure to me as well. She was always giving me extra things to eat, and just generally a very nice woman. I would stop there so often after work just to rest and relax, yet I never knew her name or the name of her restaurant. We all referred to her fondly as the Chicken Lady. Her restaurant was located just south of the Fukushima Daiichi nuclear generating station, where in 2011 I was working as a field engineer.

When he introduces the location, the context is suddenly changed.

Carl then takes us through the story of the terrifying and now famous events of that day. Nine months later, when Carl is finally allowed to go back to Fukushima and to his apartment, he stops by the restaurant first to check in on the owner.

I returned to the exclusion zone on December 3, and after several checkpoints, I was given protective clothing from head to toe again, not to go to work, but to enter the community and neighborhood where I lived. And I asked my escort to take me to the restaurant first, and when I pulled her door open this time, I was tearing cobwebs with it, and that was unsettling to me, because it was obviously clear that no one had opened that door in nine months. And it just made me wonder and worry more about what had happened to her.

This leads him on a search to find the owner. He's not just hoping she survived; *we* are hoping she survived.

That night I reached out to The Japan Times, *and asked them if they could help me find her. Is she with family, is she going to be okay, can I help her? And eventually they did find her, and they told me her name. For the first time, I learned her name. And it was Owada. Owada is her family name, Mrs. Owada-san. And they told me the name of her restaurant was Ikoi, and they told me that Ikoi in Japanese means rest, relax, and relief. And I'm thinking, what a wonderful name for a little place. I used to stop there so often after work to rest and relax. And now I had this relief, you know, in knowing that this disaster didn't take her, that she was alive. And then finally, on February 19, 2012, Mrs. Owada-san sends me a letter. "I have escaped from the disasters and have been doing fine every day. Pillitteri-san, please take care*

*of yourself. I know your work must be important. I hope you enjoy
a happy life like you seemed to have when you came to my restaurant. Although I won't be seeing you, I will always pray for the
best for you. Arigato gozaimasu."*

By using the story of Mrs. Owada-san, Carl is able to illustrate
life before and after the tragic event—how his relationship with
this woman changed, and how their lives were both changed forever. The frame allows the listener to feel a personal connection to
this historic disaster and Carl's experience. Mrs. Owada-san was
also a *unique* part of Carl's experience. Others telling a story about
Fukushima may not have had Mrs. Owada-san in their lives.

As a storyteller, you should constantly ask yourself: What was
unique to my experience? Why am I the only person who can tell
this story? How can I best deliver my story to an audience who may
not have lived through the same thing?

Often when you're telling a story about an event, especially a
tragic event, it can quickly become a recounting of a series of things
that happened. The dreaded *and then and then and then.* By finding
a smaller detail or story within the larger events—a narrative
thread—you are able to give the story an arc instead.

MEG ON EULOGIES: When I was contemplating the eulogy I was
asked to give at my grandfather's funeral, I was flooded with
memories and stories I might share. I didn't know what I would
say when I had a lifetime to choose from, and then on top of it,
factor in the deep sadness I was feeling—it all felt overwhelming.
My grandfather was such an optimistic and caring man, and I
wanted my words to reflect that. I thought about my relationship with him, and I kept coming back to the word *grateful.* I felt
incredibly grateful for having him in my life, for everything he
taught me and did for me. I loved how he adored my grand-

mother and took pride in his family. And so I started thinking about that word. I remembered being a little girl and driving in a car with my grandfather and how he was explaining to me why it's important to always be grateful—for big things and little things. I don't remember how the conversation started. (I am pretty sure I was probably being a spoiled rotten child!) I think the fact that my grandfather lived through the Great Depression inspired his deep appreciation of things. So I used that conversation as a way into the eulogy and talked about all the things I knew my grandfather was grateful for—and gradually worked it back to my deep appreciation and gratitude for having been loved by him. I focused on that feeling of gratitude, and it made it easier for me to organize all the many thoughts and memories I was trying to wrangle.

If you're called upon to give a eulogy for someone, try to ground it in specific and idiosyncratic details that show us the depth of their character, their kindness, or their spicy side: "He always saw me move my ball on the golf course and never said a word," "She told people she only watched documentaries, but I know she was hooked on *The Real Housewives*." It helps give people a sense of the unique space that person's life took up in the world.

CHOOSING A UNIQUE LENS

While Carl Pillitteri used a smaller story to help us grasp the depth of his experience, sometimes viewing your story through a unique lens, such as a small detail or distinct perspective, is what makes it easier for your listener to relate. Not everyone will know what it's like to experience homelessness, but we all know what it felt like to be a child. Sharing a story from that perspective grounds us in a relatable context.

"A BRATZ LIFE": MOTH DIRECTOR JODI POWELL ON WORKING WITH TALAYA MOORE: Growing up, Talaya lived for a time in NYC housing shelters. When we were first discussing her story, she told me about these Bratz dolls that she loved as a nine-year-old. Her descriptions of them were so lifelike they dominated the story, and she recalled every detail: the color of their eyes, their boots, their assigned characteristics. And that's when I thought that this was not just compelling but also empowering. I realized the story could be told through the eyes of a nine-year-old, with her main characters being these larger-than-life dolls.

My obsession with Bratz began when I was eight years old and I was gifted one for my birthday. So, Bratz are dolls, kind of like Barbies, but better. They didn't have these unrealistic dimensions. Instead, they stood about ten inches tall with these huge heads, full lips, curvy physique, and they had the coolest makeup. And also, they had these glittery punk-rock boots that I loved. I knew I was hooked, and I wanted more, but I could not ask my mom for more, because we were homeless. We had been homeless for over a year, and she had bigger worries, like if she had enough money for train fare or food, what borough we would end up sleeping in, and if I had a clean uniform for school. So I knew that if I wanted these dolls, I would have to get them myself.

Throughout the story, the Bratz dolls give a glimpse into her childhood experience navigating the shelter system with her mother: They become a sort of mirror in which we get closer to understanding Talaya. We see how her bond deepens especially with the doll that is most representative of her, Sasha.

Sasha was beautiful. She was Black, and I was Black. She was gorgeous. She had this long, dark brown hair, and her clothes were the best out of all the Bratz. And in the pamphlet that she came with, they told me things about her, like how she wanted her own urban clothing line, how she wanted to be a music producer, she had two parents and her own room. She just seemed like she had it all, and I wanted that. I had this carry case where I could keep only one Bratz doll, and I always chose to put Sasha in it. Inside it was blue velvet and a spot just for Sasha, and on the other side was her wardrobe, where I kept all her clothes neatly stacked. It was like her room, and sometimes I would pretend that it was my room. And for a second, I felt like the other third-graders in my class: I have a room and a closet full of clothes. It was me and Sasha's world.

One day, when Talaya comes back from school, she discovers that her Bratz dolls are missing. She is thrown into a panic and immediately grabs her mother's phone and calls the police. The police arrive, but they tell her there is nothing they can do.

One of the officers bent over and said, "I'm sure they'll turn up. They're just dolls." Just dolls? They were more than just dolls to me. They were my family, especially Sasha. She was my role model, my ride or die, my best friend. She was the first to know about my crush on Adolphus Butts in the third grade and how he looked like milk chocolate. She also was there with me that night where I slept in my coat and my shoes in this nasty motel, and I held her tight the whole night. She was also there when I wanted to jump in the bed with my mom but there wasn't enough space. That night, before bed, I was at the top bunk, and I just kept looking at the dresser, and it was empty. And I felt empty. I went to bed with my pillow wet, and I woke up with my pillow wet. And my mom asked me what I wanted for breakfast, but I didn't have an appetite.

Spoiler alert: Talaya is eventually reunited with her dolls.

I was holding Sasha, and I realized that when they were gone, that was the first time I actually really felt homeless. And having them back, I felt whole again. And that's when I realized that

Sasha was . . . she was there for me. These dolls were there for me. Everyone has someone or something that may get them through the day or even a year, and for me, for nine-year-old me, it was Sasha. It was this Black plastic professional businesswoman who doubled as a superstar in my eyes. And she was a constant reminder that, in a world filled with uncertainty, there could be a happily ever after.

Rather than tell us about her overarching experiences of being without a home, Talaya was able to focus on what it felt like as a nine-year-old, and the dolls were the vehicle for this. They gave the story a framing that was surprising, original, and relatable.

THE BETTER TO TELL YOU WITH

Structure can sometimes feel abstract—perhaps because the best structures often seem invisible and natural—so let's put everything we've discussed to use. Most of us know the story of Little Red Riding Hood. Let's pretend for a moment that this is a true story.

THE ONE SENTENCE OF THE STORY COULD BE: After a trip through the woods to visit her grandmother, Little Red Riding Hood learns the importance of listening to her mother.

THE NARRATIVE STEPPING STONES ARE:

- Little Red Riding Hood's mother asks her to take a basket of cake and wine to her grandmother who is not feeling well, and instructs her not to stray from the path in the woods.
- On her way, she meets a wolf. She tells him she is on her way to visit her grandmother.
- The wolf suggests she step off the path to pick flowers for her grandmother (thus buying him time to run ahead to her grandmother's house).

- When Little Red Riding Hood arrives, she sees that the door is open and nervously calls out for her grandmother, but there is no answer.
- She goes to her grandmother's bed and sees her lying there looking very strange.
- Red Riding Hood questions "Grandma," thinking her enormous eyes, hands, and mouth look strange until . . . finally . . .
- The wolf eats her up (brutal!) and falls asleep.
- Little Red Riding Hood and her grandmother are rescued when a hunter finds the sleeping wolf and cuts him open.
- And Little Red Riding Hood vows to always listen to her mother and never stray from the path in the woods ever again!

The story is told chronologically, but it also could have been told:

- Starting with a cliffhanger of Red Riding Hood arriving at her grandmother's house, finding the door opened and coming face-to-face with the wolf in her grandmother's bed, then flashing back and telling the story chronologically, working back to this moment.
- It could begin with Red Riding Hood wandering off the path to pick flowers in the forest and then flashing back to a scene of her mother asking her to take a basket to her grandmother but not to stray from the path.
- It could even be told from a different point of view—e.g., from inside the wolf!

Choose a shape for your story that will be most compelling and *least confusing* for your audience. Try a few on for size before you decide. A thoughtful structure gives you the road map you need to be calm and confident in the telling of your story. You know the route, you're on your way.

DIRECTOR'S NOTES

- How will you order the moments and scenes you've identified? Which structure will you choose? Pick the one that feels organic and best supports the story. Forcing the story into a complicated structure will make it feel overworked and will be harder for you to tell.

- Would it be better to let the story unfold for the listener the way it unfolded for you? Would telling it another way spoil the surprise or the mystery? If so, then telling it chronologically is probably your best bet!

- Flashbacks can support critical moments and change the listener's perspective within the story. Use a classic flashback to temporarily pause a story and add necessary information. Choose a cliffhanger to add tension and create drama to give the story a running start. Or use multiple flashbacks to give backstory and illustrate motivations. Sometimes flashbacks are vital, but other times they simply help you draw a picture of a moment. Be careful to ensure your flashbacks support your story—you never want to risk confusing your listener!

- Near the end of your story, you can call back to the very first scene to create continuity and help you land the arc. (Sometimes the arc comes full circle!)

- When dealing with traumatic, epic, or historic events, try to find a smaller, personal story to use as a frame or narrative thread. This helps ground the listener and allows them to relate to a story that might otherwise be hard to fathom.

CHAPTER 8

BEGINNINGS AND ENDINGS

Takeoff and landing are considered the most dangerous parts of a flight. And so it goes with stories.

—JENIFER HIXSON

Entrances and exits are deceptively simple, but they can be the parts of your story you have to work the hardest to articulate. We can't stress enough how vital your first and last lines are. They define your story's parameters and are the story version of hello and good-bye.

You most likely wouldn't choose to meet your partner's parents for the first time in a bathrobe. Similarly, you want the opening of your story to be presentable, fully clothed, best foot forward. Good-memorable. As the saying goes, you have only one chance to make a first impression.

Same with your exit. When you end your story, you need to leave the audience feeling resolved, like they understand where you've taken them. The central question of the story has been answered; a different you has now been revealed. The change is evident. There probably won't be a Q and A to tie up any loose ends. You want your ending to feel like you mean it.

Over the years, Moth storytellers have handled their entrances and exits in some memorable ways.

Ari Handel, "Don't Fall in Love with Your Monkey"

BEGINNING:

"Don't fall in love with your monkey," my adviser warned me, but I didn't listen. There are some things you have to learn for yourself.

ENDING:

I wrote a thesis, and the thesis is 364 pages long and is filled with facts and data and graphs and theories. But the most significant page for me is the first one, which says simply: "Dedicated to the memory of Santiago."

With his first sentence, Ari takes us right into the heart of the story's conflict (his adviser's warning not to get emotionally attached to his lab monkey). The last sentence ends the story with Ari so emotionally invested that he dedicates his doctoral thesis to his monkey, Santiago.

It's helpful to think of the beginning and the ending as a launchpad and landing pad (or the first and last stone in your path of stepping stones). You unpack the memories, you weigh the importance of each one. You contemplate *why* you revisit and care about these memories and you start to understand how they've changed you, how they've made you who you are. Finding the very beginning and end can often "crack it"—and make clear to you, the teller, the *why* of the story.

Dante Jackson, "The Prom"

BEGINNING:

Back in middle school, I wasn't really the type of kid to let myself have any fun. I was afraid that if I let myself have fun, I would

end up being judged, and I don't like being judged. So eighth grade
rolls around, and prom is coming up . . .

ENDING:

And I'm busting moves I never thought were possible for me, and
I wasn't aware of this until I took the time to look around and I
was in that little circle they made—and everybody was like,
"Ayyy! Go Dante, go Dante!" And it turns out that was one of
the best nights of my life. My life up until that point was like I
was locked in a dark room, but I decided to unlock the door, and I
took a step out, and I learned how to dance.

As you dig into what the experience means to you, start to think specifically about examples, short scenes, or details that are reflective of the larger idea you're exploring. Is there a scene that takes us into who and where you were at the beginning of your story? And is there one that shows us where you have landed at the end? Crafting these scenes can help crystallize exactly what *this* telling of the story is about, since many events in our lives can hold multiple story-worthy elements.

Barbara Collins Bowie, "The Freedom Riders and Me"

BEGINNING:

My brother and I were born and raised in Jackson, Mississippi,
during Jim Crow. In 1961, my brother got involved with Martin
Luther King and the civil rights movement. He became a Free-
dom Rider. At that time I had no idea what a Freedom Rider was.

ENDING:

I realized why my brother and the Freedom Riders were challeng-
ing the Colored Only *and* White Only *signs, why they were*
riding the buses, and why we were doing sit-ins and protests. Be-
cause this was our struggle, this was our fight. This movement was
about equality and freedom. This was a fight for life and death.

As in Ari's story, Barbara's first and last lines parallel each other. She includes very specific details in her opening sentence, establishing the central question of the story. She ends with those very same details, only now she's in a completely different place.

Having these details come back is satisfying for the audience. Specificity is important throughout a story, but relating the end of the story to the beginning reminds the listener of where we have all, collectively, just come from. The end is set up in the beginning and the beginning informs the end. There's a narrative balance.

In Kate Braestrup's "The House of Mourning," a chaplain well versed in adult tragedy is confronted with whether her practices will apply to a five-year-old child.

Kate Braestrup: "The House of Mourning"

BEGINNING:

Nina's mother came up to me, and she said, "I have a problem. Nina, my daughter, wants to visit her cousin Andy." I looked over and Nina was hanging by her knees from the swing in her back yard. Her hair was kind of sweeping the ground. I said, "How old is Nina again?" She said, "Five."

I should probably mention that Andy was dead.

ENDING:

Nina walks right up to the dais where Andy's little body lay, covered with his quilt his mom had made him when he was a baby. And she walks all the way around the dais touching him, making sure he's all there. She smooths the hair back from his brow, and she sings to him. She puts his Fisher Price telescope in his hand so that he can see anything he wants to see from heaven. And then she said, "I'm ready to go, but he's not gonna be getting up, so I have to tuck him in." So she walks around the dais again, tucking him in very carefully, and then she says, "I love you, Andy Dandy, goodbye."

You can trust a human being with grief, even a small human being. I tell the other game wardens, "Walk fearlessly into the house of mourning, for grief is only love that has come against its oldest challenge. And after all these mortal years, love knows how to handle it." I don't need to have confidence. I certainly don't need to have to feign confidence anymore in that because I have Nina. And with her parent's permission, so do you.

Kate's beginning and ending show us that even young children have the capacity to face the complexity of death.

Faith Salie, "What I Wore to My Divorce"

BEGINNING:

The night before I flew to my divorce, I was standing alone in my bra and underwear and basic black pumps, trying on dress after dress.

ENDING:

I wish I could go back and tell that motherless, partnerless, child-less woman, standing in front of a rented mirror, trying on dress after dress for her divorce, that what seems to fit you now may not suit you at all a season hence, and you'll outgrow old favorites and slip effortlessly into something new.

Faith ends with a callback to the first scene but concludes by addressing her change in perspective.

Musih Tedji Xaviere, "Unwritten Rules"

BEGINNING:

Growing up in Cameroon, all I ever wanted to be was a writer. My parents' plan was for me to become an accountant and then get married, in that order, but being a writer was my dream.

ENDING:

My parents still don't get it, but recently they stumbled across positive reviews of my novel and they seemed proud. . . . The rules and traditions are changing. Slowly but surely, more women writers have a chance.

Xaviere sets up her parents' rules regarding what she must become, and by the end, we understand that she has literally written her own story. She has become what she always wanted to be, and her parents have come around. With this ending, Xaviere lands her own arc, and her parents' arc too.

If takeoff is seamless and you know where you're going, the story can feel like it's telling itself. Storytellers report that the story is the most fun once it has reached altitude, meaning the essential facts have been communicated and the landing spot is in sight. Being prepared makes all of it so much more enjoyable!

AND . . . ACTION!

Storytellers use the first few sentences or the opening scene to set the stage and the tone of the story. In film terms, this usually includes an establishing shot (i.e., the big landscape view that sets you in the middle of the environment you need to know).

> *Every family has secrets. In my family, the secret was me. I was secret because I was Black. These days, you'd say I was biracial. But in the fifties, when you were born, there was no biracial. You were either born Black or you were born white. End of story.*
> —June Cross, "Secret Daughter"

> *When I was fifteen years old, I lived for a while in a mausoleum in the back of a cemetery in New Rochelle, New York. And when people find that out, they often ask me if it was creepy. And it really wasn't. I didn't find it particularly creepy.*
> —George Dawes Green, "Coming of Age in a Mausoleum"

Beginning the story by describing an active moment or scene hooks us in, sets us up, and brings us along! It can . . .

Drop us into a place and time:

There was a hard knock at the door in the middle of the night. I saw three men in military uniforms. One of them, the KGB major, handed me a warrant for my arrest.

—Victor Levenstein, "Surviving Comrade Stalin"

I was standing on the roof of the New York Times *building in* Times Square. *I was on the roof because I'm an elevator mechanic, and that's where the elevator machine rooms are. I was drinking a cup of coffee and watching the traffic below, and I heard the phone ring, and when I answered it, it was my mother and she said, "Are you okay?" I said, "I'm fine. Sorry I haven't called. Are you okay?" She said, "I'm okay." She said, "A plane hit the World Trade Center."*

—Nancy Mahl, "Miss Larchmont Returns"

It's 1943. Nice, France. It's in the middle of the war. The Germans have just invaded the town. I'm seven years old. I'm standing on the platform of a train with my mother. A very tall man with a long black robe approaches us, and my mother gives me to him. I don't remember how we said goodbye, but I never saw her again.

—Flora Hogman, "My Name, Embroidered"

It was an early spring day in 1975, and my two younger brothers and I were waiting in a cargo airplane to go to America. We were with about fifty other orphans, mostly babies and young children.

—Jason Trieu, "Operation BabyLift"

Or introduce us to the most important players in the story:

In August of 1998, I was trying to give birth, and it was well attended. I had a nurse, two midwives, my boyfriend at the time (who was not the father), my foster brother, and two women who were also awaiting the birth of their first child, who also happened to be my child.

—Carly Johnstone, "A Perfect Circle"

I was walking down the street in New York City, in the East Village, and it was a glorious day, and the sun was bright, and I had the love of my life on my arm, and she was dying. Really dying.

—Elizabeth Gilbert, "The Alpha Wolf"

Or drop us right in the heart of the stakes:

I reached over and secretly undid my seatbelt. And when his foot hit the brake at the red light, I flung open the door, and I ran.

—Jenifer Hixson, "Where There's Smoke"

I was on an ambulance stretcher, as all of the screams from the people trying to save my life faded away.

—Carol Seppilu, "Outrunning the Dark"

It's March 2013. Two A.M. Results are trickling in, and with each announcement, my heart stops. It's been a tough year running a rigorous campaign in my bid to become the next member of the county assembly in Embakasi Central, Kenya.

—Bina Maseno, "Citizen Bina"

I'm at Mesa Grill, right here in New York City. I was editor in chief of Vibe *magazine, and I was feeling pretty good about myself. I'd moved up in the journalism world. I was able to afford $250 pumps. I'm enjoying myself. And what I didn't realize is that in a few short moments, platinum recording artist and Grammy-nominated emcee Foxy Brown was gonna come in there and threaten to beat my ass.*

—Danyel Smith, "Foxy"

Choose the details carefully, because the audience may tune out if it's too much work to stay with you. You want the audience to think, *What happened next?*, not *Why am I hearing this? What does this have to do with anything?*

There is no need to start by telling us what the story is about or do any setup ("I'm gonna tell you the story about the day I became a man"). If we know the end, we're less likely to lean in and listen to the details of your story. Let us wonder what happens. Let us learn what the story is about *with you* so that we are in sync. This shared experience is one of the most beautiful things about storytelling. Please don't take it away from us! If you tell it well (and we know that you can!), we will be deeply invested.

COMING IN FOR A LANDING

One of the most challenging parts of storytelling is the ending. (We hate seeing things come to an end!) Those final moments are so precious and can make or break the story. A great ending can take the listener's breath away and leave them speechless or fill them with a giddy delight that causes them to high-five the person sitting next to them! A bad ending can leave them questioning why they just spent their time emotionally investing in something that wound up having no point.

The creative team at The Moth reviews every story told on our stages, and there are times we think (with love), *Ack! They fumbled the ending!* Usually this is because the story left us hanging, or it finished in a way that had no relation to the beginning. You want to leave the listener feeling satisfied and grounded; you don't want to yank them off the ride before it has ended or have them meandering in circles, begging for it to stop.

EARNED ENDINGS

A beautiful ending makes us feel the power and potential of the story and puts everything in perspective. Sometimes it's so moving we almost forget that we didn't love the rest of the story. Those are the stories we feel inspired to rework with the ending in mind. We ask: "How can we build the story so that it is worthy of that ending?"

LARRY ROSEN, MOTH DIRECTOR: Imagine hearing a complex story about the troubled relationships in someone's family. The story concludes with a beautiful scene in which the storyteller's uncle tells him how proud he is, they embrace, they both cry, and the storyteller says, "This is all I ever needed." And you think to yourself: *It's an emotional ending, but something's off. Why am I not feeling it?* As you think back through the story, you realize the storyteller never mentioned wanting or seeking the approval of his uncle. He may have told us other things about the uncle—his stinginess, perhaps even his coldness—but nothing about the missing approval or why it was important to him. Without that context, the end can feel *unearned,* leaving audiences skeptical of everything they've just heard.

The events of a story can pose a question that is answered when the story concludes. Your story may have a well-crafted answer (ending), but it will only really "click" if we understand the question!

The ending is the last thing we hear, and it has the potential to sour the entire story. A bad ending—one that's confusing, glib, arrogant, indifferent, or manipulative—can even make the audience angry.

STATE YOUR CHANGE

Endings are often rooted in the change you experienced: Who were you at the beginning of the story versus who are you now? How did this story and these events leave you feeling different about yourself or the world around you?

It took us eighteen years from the day that we arrived here for me to be granted an American citizenship. On January 29, 2009, I was sworn in as an American citizen, and I pledged allegiance to my new homeland. And it is through my children, my two-year-old son and my unborn child in my womb, that I will make sure that this gratitude that overflows in my heart every single day will continue to live on long after I am gone.

May God always bless our America.

—Dori Samadzai Bonner, "A New Home"

I went from someone who couldn't even admit he had a crush on someone to asking a girl out to prom with my ukulele, having my first kiss, and more important than that, establishing a really special connection with someone I like. I just kept thinking, I did it.

—David Lepelstat, "Let It Go"

When the police arrived—and the police department was there, because I'm a pretty noted figure in my city—they offered not only counseling but to relocate me if I needed that to happen. Despite my kids' fears or even my own, that intruder had given me a gift. For the first time in my life, I knew that I'd been tested, and not only survived but prevailed. And I'm now ninety-seven, still living alone.

—Betty Reid Soskin, "The Test"

STICK IT!

Over the years, we've witnessed storytellers get to the end of an amazing story, and then end in a weak place by saying something like, "Well, I guess that's my story" and wandering off stage, effectively taking the air out of the whole experience. The best stories feature endings that are succinct and strong—the storytelling equivalent of a mic drop.

Use your last line to land us somewhere special and unique to you; don't waste it on a broad concept. For example, don't say, "So that's my story about heartbreak." Instead, try, "She hurt me so badly that some days, when I woke up, it was all I could taste for hours. But she taught me how to love."

We often say that by knowing your last line you can dismount with certainty. This isn't the Olympics, but you still want to stick that landing.

> *Because that night I realized an important lesson—that sometimes the most horrible night, the most horrible day, could change on a dime, when there's a knock on the door. And music and joy arrives.*
>
> —Taylor Negron, "California Gothic"

> *After a while, my home attendant and my sister left me alone with my boyfriend. I won't go into details, but I will tell you this: It was the best New Year's Eve I ever had. And I want people to know that even though I have a disability, I can still move. I understood that someone could see me for the woman that I am, and not just my disability.*
>
> —Janice Bartley, "Italian Stallion"

> *The week we separate, they tear down my family home of twenty-five years, and my Jeep gets stolen. I have this keychain with three keys on it—one to the house I don't live in anymore, one to my family home that's been torn down, and one to my Jeep that's been stolen. God is banging on my hood. So I toss the keys, head to art school, and join my tribe.*
>
> —Tricia Rose Burt, "How to Draw a Nekkid Man"

If you can't figure out the ending, don't worry—it isn't always immediately clear. Your ending requires reflection, sorting through all the possibilities, sitting with the events to figure out what they mean to you. If you can't find a satisfying ending, sometimes you need to look back at the beginning, because a key to your resolution may be there.

> **TOASTS:** When it's your turn to take the "stage," do it with confidence, share what you've prepared, and then know how you'll exit. Who do you give the floor to, where does the mic go, and, most important, what's your last line? Remember, you want to leave them "wanting more" rather than checking their watches. And if all else fails, say, "Cheers!"

ENDINGS TO AVOID

As directors, we know that telling a story can be both thrilling and tiring. People often want to rush to end a story—or they're so relieved to be done that they subconsciously fall into a "Hollywood ending" template. Here are a few kinds of story resolutions to steer clear of.

THE PERFECT BOW

We don't recommend you end your story ambiguously, but this is not to say you have to tie it up in a bow. The *happily ever after* thing can work, but not often. Sometimes if a story is too pat, or "neat" at the end, it can seem false. The ending can dilute the deeper aspects or negate the importance of the story you shared. Many stories end in a messy and perhaps still-complicated place. Try to resist the urge to make things too perfect.

The last lines of Hasan Minhaj's story "Prom" are a great example of how everything isn't picture-perfect at the end, but we still feel satisfied:

> *There are days where I feel like I can forgive Bethany, and there are days where I feel like I can't. I'm working on it. But I'm gonna try to be brave. I'm gonna be brave for me and Dad.*

THE "NOT CLEARED FOR LANDING"

Storytellers can sometimes struggle with where to end. They circle their ending like they're circling a drain, which can exhaust the listener. They include half a dozen sentences, and each one could be a last line on its own. They say the same thing several different ways—or they'll be unsure and offer up several options as possible ends (But wait! Which is it?). Or they reach the end and then tack on a joke for a laugh.

Take this (made-up) ending:

> *I still can't dance. At the end of the wedding, my mom took me out onto the dance floor and we just stood still and talked while Fleet Foxes played. Just like always, she met me where I was and let me be the awkward goof that I am. I hope I can be that for other people in my life; I hope I can be that for my partner. We are partners for life, in our own special dance. Seeing the way my mom opened her arms to my partner made me love her more. She has always put family first. Family, whether blood or chosen, has always mattered most. She was my first family, and now we are one more. My mom was my first dance, my best dance, and she is still my first call. Hey Siri, call Mom.*

There's so much love in this ending! But what is the story about? The big events in our lives can be full of emotional arcs—sometimes homing in on the ending can help you choose the story that you want to tell.

THE "FABLE TIME WITH AESOP"

In this Moth style of storytelling, you don't need to announce *the moral of the story*. Even though stories can be "teachable moments," they should never feel that way. No need to tell the listener what they should think or take away from the story. Instead, keep it in your experience. How it changed you. How it made *you* feel.

Note the last line from Monte Montepare's "Nowhere to Run."

This experience was going to present me with my own personal demons in their most aggressive forms. And if I tried to run or hide from them, they were going to kill me. If I was going to survive, I was going to need to be brave, learn how to stand my ground and look them right in the eye.

His ending is grounded in how his experience changed him—it isn't a moral for us all to live by, but his own personal revelation about the direction he intends to take moving forward.

THE "READER, I MARRIED HIM"

Leaping forward in time is also a pitfall. For example, the story is about a tragically awkward courtship that seems doomed, but then the last line is, "And we've been married for twenty-four years now." It's cute—the audience will usually clap—but it feels gimmicky, and we sort of consider that cheating.

SATISFYING ENDINGS

The best endings are true to life. They should make your listener feel, understand, or relate to something without you having to tell them what that something is. All the steps in your story should lead to an ending that answers any questions you may have raised along the way. Here are a few things to keep in mind when considering how to close your story in a satisfying way for your listener.

THE STORY STOPS HERE

Sometimes the logical ending for your story may not be true in the present. For instance, it's okay to stop your story of adopting a feral cat on the day you brought it home even if, in the years since, your daughter developed an allergy and you had to find the cat a new family.

Have you seen an EKG of a heartbeat? It's no coincidence that one heartbeat is also what a story arc looks like, and the end of one heartbeat leads to another, just like stories do. The end of one story will become the very beginning of your next.

GROUNDING UNCERTAINTY IN TRUTH

Often the storyteller isn't sure how one part of their story might end, like in the case of Cynthia Riggs, who told an epic love story about a man from her past reaching out to her after sixty-plus years. She reveals that she met Howie as a young adult sorting plankton in a university lab, and they bonded by writing secret cryptograms on paper towels that they would pass back and forth. And lo and behold, sixty-two years later, he sent her a package—when she was eighty-one and he was ninety—that included all of those paper towel cryptograms from sixty-plus years ago, wrapped in archival plastic, with a new note on top, in code. When she deciphered the note, it read:

I have never stopped loving you. Howard

Cynthia told us that at the time, her children were adults and she was a mystery novelist; she was happy with her independent life. She also let the audience in on her romantic past, for context.

> *Now, you need to know a little something about my background. I wasn't totally off men, but I was a little uncomfortable, because I'd been married for twenty-five years to a very brilliant but very abusive husband, and though we were divorced for thirty-five years, for twenty of those years he had stalked me, so I was not comfortable opening any doors to any kind of intimacy. But these paper towels . . .*

This cryptogram from Howie led to months of letter writing and a slowly but steadily developing romance, as they discovered how similar their decades apart had been.

When she ended her story the first time, she hadn't seen Howie since their work together in the marine biology lab sixty-plus years ago. She had no idea what the future held, but she was able to land her story in truth. She told us she had just purchased her airplane ticket, and she'd be on her way to meet him in just a few days!

Cynthia ends with a decision to *take action* and try it, and see if this relationship with Howie will deepen, which is a far cry from where she started the story. Even though, at the time the story ends, they haven't met again, she is able to put a period at the end of the story. The resolution is satisfying, while still being full of possibilities.

> *Howie has changed my life. I had been pretty much closed up, but he gave me some very gentle warmth. He also introduced me to a kind of a calm love that I had never thought of before. He introduced me to a sweet passion—you'd be surprised what you can do in letters and codes—but most of all, the thing that has really affected me a lot is that he gave me back a sense of great self-worth. And with that, I hope you can all find a Howie or his equivalent.*

AAAND . . . SCENE

Similar to beginning in the action, *ending* in the action, or in an active scene, can help to amplify the emotion, as these storytellers demonstrate.

> *Over the blazing fire, I spotted Mama. She had tears in her eyes as she listened. My heart quivered with joy. I might have lost my book battle with her, but I had won the war. No, we had won the war together. Our books have been burned, but not our story, not our hope. That was when I knew my college dream would come true, even though it still seemed dangerous and impossible.*
> —Wang Ping, "The Book War"

> *So here she was, six months after the amputation, and right there in the middle of the street fair, she hikes up her jeans leg to show me her cool new leg. And it's pink, and it's tattooed with the characters of* High School Musical 3, *replete with red-sequined Mary Janes on her feet. And she was proud of it. She was proud of herself. And the marvelous thing was that this six-year-old understood something that it took me twentysomething years to get,*

but that we both did discover—that when we can celebrate and truly own what it is that makes us different, we're able to find the source of our greatest creative power.

—Aimee Mullins, "A Work in Progress"

We pack the apple cake in the bag. As we enter the hospital, it's cold and it smells like medicine. But as we get to my grandfather's room, everyone's surrounding him and creating some warmth, and I try to discreetly hide the bag behind my back, but my grandmother sees, and she goes, "What do you have there, Luna?" And I hand her the bag, and she pulls out the apple cake, and then she tells my grandfather, "Look, Luna made apple cake." He looks down at the cake, and then he looks back up at me, and he smiles. And I just feel this rush of memories flowing back to him, of every time we've made apple cake together. And even though he was in the hospital, it felt like we had made it together once again.

—Luna Azcurrain, "Abuelos, Apples & Me"

We looked at our daughters playing on the porch. And I looked him in the eyes, and I said, "Take care of that little girl. And if you need anything, give me a call. Anything."

—Shannon Cason, "Downstairs Neighbors"

I'm acting. With Anthony Hopkins. Outside the van, Jonathan Demme watches with pleasure. For those few moments, we three are the party.

—Josh Broder, "Cut"

I asked my father to join me on the Pakistan Day parade. I was not a little girl anymore, and I was in uniform. I saw a little girl looking at me, at my shining boots, gold buttons, and my blue uniform, and dreaming dreams to do the impossible. With tears in my eyes, I stood under the shining spring sun, shoulder to shoulder with my father, and saluted the passing parade.

—Quratulain Fatima, "The Sky Is the Limit"

THE RAPID WRAP-UP

Ending in summation also makes for a satisfying landing. This does not mean ending in a moral; instead, articulate how *you*, the storyteller, have changed.

> *I'd like to think that I changed the way she thought about people of color—that we weren't whatever it was that those people were teaching her, and that she might reconsider the prejudices that she had. As for myself, I got a job that gave me something to do every day, which I desperately needed. I had left Indiana to change the world, and I didn't. I couldn't. But I realized that even if I couldn't change the world, I could change a little piece of the world that I was in, and that was enough for me.*
>
> —Stephanie Summerville, "Life Support"

> *Out there in the cold, I realized something. It took one man to alienate me and make me feel like I completely didn't belong. But then seventeen amazing nerds let me know that I did! And I knew right then that these were my people, Boston was my city, and I wasn't leaving the U.S. anytime soon.*
>
> —Ali Al Abdullatif, "The Patriots Game"

> *I aced that interview and got the job. That was the day I got in touch with my other side. She doesn't make many appearances. She's available on an as-needed basis. I call her my Quiet Fire.*
>
> —Phyllis Bowdwin, "Quiet Fire"

> *It's not like I went back to school and I was all of a sudden this Indian girl who ate Indian food at lunch and listened to Indian music and wore Indian clothes and spoke in Hindi. But I began to realize that I didn't have to pretend to be someone I wasn't, and I began picking up pieces of myself that I'd let fall.*
>
> —Saya Shamdasani, "Priceless Mangos"

My marriage died, but I lived on. I hope both of my kids grow up to be wonderful people. The types of people who bring so much joy to everyone around them that their absence would be a tragedy, because that's the type of person that Henry was. He died twenty-four years ago, and it's still fresh, but I'm no longer miserable. In fact, I'm well on my way to becoming the happiest person I know. And I think that fact would have made him happy. He also doesn't visit me in my dreams anymore. And I can finally admit that I'm comfortable with never seeing his face ever again, in my dreams or otherwise, because at the end of the day, what will an old man like me have to say to his fourteen-year-old friend that hasn't been said already.

—Kemp Powers, "The Past Wasn't Done with Me"

And in the end, the only thing that I could do for her in those last harrowing hours was nothing. Was nothing. Except to surrender to my powerlessness and to have to let her go, and to have to watch her go, and she went down swinging and battling to the last awful breath. And it was brutal. And it was beautiful. And she was brave. And I howled like a wolf when she was gone. And I will never stop telling the world her name.

—Elizabeth Gilbert, "The Alpha Wolf"

In Baghdad I was weak, and I couldn't belong to an organization or an entity to help me stay and defend my city. But in America I'm strong, and today I am a sergeant in the Army National Guard, because I can belong to an organization that can prepare me to defend my adopted country and do my part as a citizen. Because I know how it feels living under terrorism, and I don't want to ever experience that again.

—Abbas Mousa, "Leaving Baghdad"

When the main event is over, and we have the answer we need to resolve the story and complete your arc, you have only a few sentences to go. Choose a last line that your audience will remember, the thought that you want to reverberate with them well after you leave the stage.

CALLS TO ACTION AS A TOOL FOR ADVOCACY: Moth stories often end on a note of personal reflection, but if your goal is to use your story to move people to invest in change, tap into the emotion, land your arc—but at the end, add a call to action. "And this is exactly why you need to vote in the county election this Tuesday! Stand up and be counted!"

DIRECTOR'S NOTES

- Choose the opening and closing points of your story. Knowing where you begin and where you end will help you plot your course and define your arc. Beginning in the action of a scene can drop us into a moment in time and introduce us to key people in the story as well as the stakes. Always end in a place that is satisfying for the listener and unique to your overall experience.

- **UNSATISFYING ENDINGS . . .**

  - Feel too pat, perfect, or matchy-matchy.

  - Are undefined or unresolved. (Never leave the audience wondering, *What happened?*)

  - Tell the listener what to think. (No moral of the story is necessary. Tell us instead what you think and feel.)

- **STRONG ENDINGS . . .**

  - Come to a definite stop without meandering. (You want to *land* your ending!)

  - Are rooted in the change you experienced.

  - Answer the central question or conflict of a story.

PART 3

TELLING YOUR STORY

CHAPTER 9

FROM PAGE TO STAGE

There's nothing quite like sitting shoulder to shoulder in a room full of people who are all quiet, spellbound, and listening with you. To me, it's magic.

—CHLOE SALMON, MOTH DIRECTOR

In 2004, on a very cold night in January, The Moth produced a show at a theater in rural Massachusetts. It was one of our very first shows outside of New York City. The audience was small, and the room was (literally and figuratively) a bit cold. Mark Katz, a long-time Moth favorite, told a story about being a speechwriter for Bill Clinton. He began his story, but not long after, he stopped. He seemed to have forgotten his place. He tried to start but stopped again. Mark finally said, "I'm sorry" and left the stage. Gasp. Record scratch. Everyone froze. No one was sure what to do—this had only happened one time before. But eventually everyone took a breath and we moved on to the next story.

After intermission, Mark came back on stage and jokingly said, "So as I was saying . . ." and finished the story beautifully. He went on to tell it in a few more shows, and always nailed it.

So what happened on that cold Massachusetts night? Mark

knew the story by heart, but he was so caught up in remembering the words and saying them in a particular order that when he forgot a word, he lost his place.

> **MARK KATZ:** Here's what I remember from before I blacked out: I walked onto that stage very excited to tell my story. Too excited. I didn't just want to tell my story that night; I wanted to tell the hell out of my story. But something went haywire. I struggled to recall my opening line and then two sentences in, I honestly forgot what story I was there to tell. Offstage prompting from The Moth producers failed to register with my stalling brain. The sequence of events recounted above is entirely accurate: The room was stunned and eerily silent as I mumbled "I'm sorry" and stumbled off stage.
>
> After The Moth team determined that I was not unwell but had merely experienced every storyteller's worst nightmare, they cleared me to return to the stage after intermission.
>
> This time, instead of relying on the room, I took my emotional energy from the narrative unfolding. In effect, I retreated to the interior of my mind where I imagined myself in the setting of my story—in this case, a small hotel holding room where I was wearing a tuxedo, holding an egg timer, and engaged in a terrifying encounter with the president of the United States! By the time my story was over, I had told it as well as I had first set out to. At least, in my mind, anyway.

Delivering a story on stage takes practice, preparation, and yes, a little courage. In this chapter, we offer tips on how to keep your cool, amp up your confidence, and tamp down your nerves.

MEMORIZATION VS. FAMILIARIZATION

Many people fear getting on stage and forgetting their story—as in, *completely* forgetting—and standing in terrifying silence while an audience watches them wither inside. The anxiety is understand-able, and we also understand why people think that committing a story to memory is the best way to avoid a mind freeze on stage. But in the twenty-five years we've been directing stories, only a handful of storytellers have *totally blanked* on stage, and always—always!—they were the ones who relied heavily on word-for-word memorization.

Think back to learning the alphabet. Almost all of us remem-bered our letters by singing the little song. Have you ever caught yourself in an alphabetizing task needing to sing the whole thing, or a section of it, in order to determine if the *P* goes before the *T*? That's why you shouldn't memorize your story. On stage, you can't go back to the start and speed through to find where you are in the sequence.

People feel the need to know their story word for word because they are afraid of leaving something important out, but this isn't an acting monologue. No one in the audience will fault you for drop-ping a line; only you know what happens next. When you tell a story, you want to be able to really *tell* it, not recite it. If you mem-orize, you aren't remembering your story as it happened, you're recalling what you *wrote down* and you're less present in the room. You risk losing the connection with the listener.

Many of us have been taught to be a formalized version of our-selves when "presenting." To tell a great story, you'll have to let some of that go. While it may seem counterintuitive to prepare in order to be more casual, it is the key to your confidence on stage. Stick with the voice of the real you—the backyard-in-jeans you, as opposed to the suit, tie, and Spanx you.

When preparing, you can organize your thoughts in a few differ-ent ways. Some people think on paper, so they like to write out their entire story before they say it out loud. Others prefer to just write out bullet points that serve as a guide. (Think of your stepping stones!) Some folks never write anything down at all. There is no *right way*! And yes, we know—this is a how-to book, and we're tell-ing you there is no right way! But it's the truth! Think of the text as your road map—you don't need to memorize every street, you just need to know where you're going. Of course, there will be certain turns of phrase that you love and will repeat the same way every time, but you don't need to remember each and every word. You just need to *familiarize* yourself with the general course of your story.

That said, a warning: If you choose to write it out, it can be hard to get off the page. You run the risk of falling in love with the way you wrote it, and the breakup will be messy! But if you are one of those people whose process includes the written word, we suggest you boil the draft down to bullet points *before* you begin practicing.

This "cheat sheet" can help you distill the major scenes of your story into short sentences or phrases. Try doing it with just ten bullets. While you rehearse, you can glance down to find your place if you get lost. Eventually, tell the story with the cheat sheet facedown on the table and only turn it over if you're truly lost. And finally, tell it with no cheat sheet at all! Look Ma, no hands!

Also, remember that regardless of your method, what's on the page is just a *representation* of the path your story takes. Sometimes, in the energy of telling it, you'll throw in some new detail that popped into your brain in the moment, and it will be the best part of the story. Give yourself the freedom to just tell it.

Moth stories are conversational and involve an exchange between you and your audience. Their physical presence and responses will affect the way you tell your story. It's okay to react to the unexpected laugh from row three. And you'll only seem more human when you pause and say, "Wait, I forgot to tell you the garage door opener was broken!"

These stories are alive. To some degree, stories are never "done." They are *supposed* to be a little different every time you tell them. The story will be pushed or pulled a little based on how your day is going, whether your pants are too tight, if you're slightly distracted with worry that your parking meter might run out mid-story . . .

"CENTS OF LUCK": SARAH ON WORKING WITH FLASH ROSEN-BERG: Flash Rosenberg is a visual artist who was working on a bittersweet story about never hearing the words "I love you" from her father. Together, we crafted the story for weeks leading up to the Mainstage. It was clear from the considerable time she'd invested that this story meant a lot to her. But on the day of the rehearsal at The Moth's office, surrounded by a few staff and the other storytellers cast in the show, Flash was almost in tears. She could barely remember the order of the story at all. She started with her setup of being a quirky creator, and a bit about her relationship with her father growing up, but then she stopped and jumped to the end of the story and stopped again. She kept saying, "I can't remember what I wrote" and she asked to reference printed notes. At this point, with only a day to go before the show, we were all worried. Our hearts broke for her. We knew she had crafted a unique and lovely story; it just wouldn't come out. And during one very long pause, fellow cast member (and style icon) Simon Doonan popped up and said, "Flash! You are an artist. Why don't you DRAW your outline?" And we gasped. That was it! And that's exactly what she did. In the end, this artist needed to *draw* her story outline in order to remember it. Once she had the visuals and could hop from image to image in her mind, she was confident and ready to take the stage. And in the end, art saved the day, and the story was a success.

We know we just told you that it's best to never memorize. But there's one exception to this rule. The only things we suggest you memorize—and we stress, *the only things*—are the first and last lines of your story. Knowing your first line allows you to start strong out of the gate. Most people are quite nervous when taking the stage. When you know your first line, it can help you push through the nerves and anchor your story. Yes, the first thirty seconds will probably be scary, but don't forget, you crafted that strong opening. By the time you're on your third sentence, the story will be driving itself—over hill and dale. Your last line is in sight! There's no stopping for tolls or gas. You're on your way.

Flash Rosenberg's hand-drawn outline for "Cents of Luck"

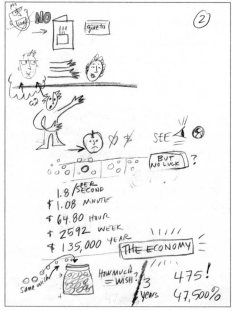

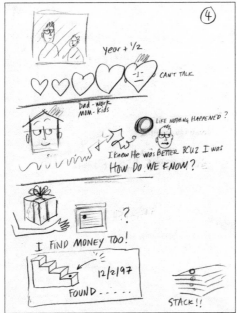

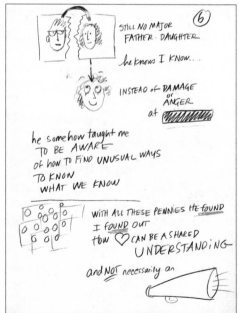

USING A STORY TO OPEN A PRESENTATION AT WORK: Bill Robinson's daughter brought him to the Chicago Moth StorySLAM as a Father's Day gift. Bill had always been drawn to stories, but after his night at The Moth (where he actually got on stage and was ranked third in the competition!), he decided to use stories to open his presentation to the board of a professional association as their new VP of membership. This group was so risk averse that he had to send them his PowerPoint slides of data twenty-eight days in advance to review, but in the three presentations he gave, he always surprised them with a personal story at the top—like one about trusting his gut and boldly ignoring GPS directions. The tactic was effective; Bill raised $15 million for his new initiative. He says, "Stories change where people's heads are in the room, and I wanted everyone to make decisions from their hearts."

SAY IT OUT LOUD

These stories are built to be shared, and now's the time to test your wings! You have an almost fully baked draft of the story, either written in bullet points or up in your brain. The next step is to tell it out loud to yourself—the words must leave your lips whether you tell it into a mirror, out of a window, or to your cat or houseplant. In this first telling, you're listening to see if there are edits or additions that might help enhance the structure of the story.

When you run your story for the first time, most often it will get longer, because you're remembering your way through it. That is okay! It's part of the process. Bushwhack your way from the first line to the last in roughly the right order. We sometimes jokingly refer to this as the "free to flop" version, because the point isn't to tell it perfectly. You just need to get it out of your mouth. As you get more comfortable telling it, you will become more efficient with your words. This is your opportunity to try things—see what works and what feels honest to you, and edit out the rest!

If you need to sneak a peek at your notes, that's okay, but this is your opportunity to take a leap off the page. The majority of first drafts are overwritten, so the first time you tell it, you will probably find some redundancies, some sections that feel long and thick. There may be some phrases that sound unnatural when spoken. You may even decide to record yourself and listen back. Take note of any parts that feel awkward, extraneous, unnecessary, or repetitive. You might stop and start and forget where you are at times. Honestly, it might feel bumpy, but this is an essential step in the process. Throughout this chapter, we'll highlight some other pitfalls to look out for on the road to smoothing out your story.

STORIES EVERYWHERE: You never know when you'll hear the story that will alter the trajectory of your life. Be open to stories in all places. Commutes really can take you where you need to go.

JENNIFER BIRMINGHAM, FROM "THREE THINGS":

I jumped into the cab, and the driver was chuckling in the front seat. He told me that he had witnessed the kiss and it looked really good. I said, "No, it was not good, it was awkward," and I told him the story of how this had been my first first date in fifteen years and it was all too much. The driver introduced himself as Pablo and told me that he himself had been on a sabbatical from dating, and then he told me all his theories on dating as he drove me home to Harlem. When we got to my building, he turned off the meter and we talked for another forty-five minutes, all the while holding hands between that little window. And I wish I could tell you this was the

> night I fell in love with Pablo, the wise man of the New York City taxi fleet. It wasn't, but it really did feel like the universe put Pablo in my path to make it a little easier for me to move forward.

IT'S ALL IN THE TIMING

Moran Cerf, a professor and neuroscientist, has told stories on the Mainstage, and he's probably the *fastest* talker ever to appear at The Moth. In an interview for *The Moth Radio Hour,* Moran said, "I don't worry about the time limit. . . . If it's running too long, I'll just talk faster."

We love Moran, but we don't recommend a fast-talking workaround if you don't naturally speak that way. Better to edit the story down to the most essential beats than require us to wear a seatbelt in order to listen. We want to hear every word!

While Moran fits hundreds of words into a minute, many-time Moth storyteller Edgar Oliver is the opposite. He speaks . . . so . . . slowly. As a result, the number of actual words Edgar utters in one of his stories is far below average.

Here is what Moran managed to get in during the *first minute* of his Mainstage story, "The Dream Recording Machine":

> *So I'm a neuroscientist, and I do research on people. We don't get a lot of fame doing that, but I actually, I can tell you a story about how I did somehow end up being famous for that. So in my research, I'm working with patients undergoing brain surgery, and we tried to do all kinds of things to help them, but we also do research with these patients. And one of the things I did in the last couple of years was a study where we took patients who are undergoing brain surgery, and they put electrodes deep inside their brain during surgery to help them for clinical reasons. But we also did something where we told*

them, "We're going to show you pictures and see how your brain looks when you see those pictures. And we can have a map of your brain when you see those pictures. And then we can basically know how your brain looks when you think of those things." So the patient could sit in bed and think about the Eiffel Tower. We would see a pattern that they organized from before, and we would picture, we would project a picture of the Eiffel Tower in front of their eyes. So patients would basically sit in bed . . .

Two hundred fifteen words in his first minute!

Now compare that with the first minute of Edgar's story "The Apron Strings of Savannah":

Mother used to always say to us, "Savannah is a trap. It'll try to imprison you. Even if you manage to get away, it'll find a way to drag you back." Mother also used to say, "Beware of other people. They won't understand you. We're different. We're artists." So all throughout my childhood, it was just the three of us—Mother, Helen, and me. And then there was the world as though we were lost in it. We were like three lost children, Mother, Helen, and me. No one ever made it into . . .

Just ninety-two. Less than half the words of Moran!

We are not suggesting you speed up like Moran (few could pull off a story at this speed) or slow it down like Edgar! Just tell your story at the pace you'd use to talk with friends over dinner. See how long it takes so you get an understanding of your natural cadence. Later, consider the time frame you've been given and make edits from there.

"STANDING UP": SARAH ON WORKING WITH ED KOCH: In preparation for a Mainstage more than a decade ago, Meg and I traveled to Mayor Ed Koch's New York City office. The former mayor kindly greeted us. He looked to be seven feet tall, much taller than I had imagined, and his desk was huge, to match his frame. Meg and I must have looked like elves staring up at him. Mayor Koch wasted no time, and launched into his rehearsed story, but—uh oh!—it's an entirely different story than the one he pitched for the show. My eyes were wide, and I'm taking notes and at the end, he says, "I've timed it. It's two minutes. What do you think?" After a beat or two and fast diplomatic consideration, I say, "Well, Mr. Mayor, I liked that story! And it would be perfect if we told two-minute stories at The Moth, but with all due respect—we don't. We tell ten-minute stories at The Moth." And he looked off for a few seconds of thought, and then nodded and said, "I'll give you six. But that's it." The night he took the Moth stage to tell "Standing Up"—his story about World War II—he opened with: "When I first thought about this, I thought I would tell a funny story. I know two. But they don't make ten minutes, so instead, I'll tell a serious story." And yes, for the record, his story clocked in at 5:29.

Though you probably won't have a timekeeper gently playing the violin to tell you it's time to wrap it up, you generally have an idea of an appropriate time range you're aiming for. Believe it or not, it's completely possible for you to tell the same story in two minutes, five minutes, or ten minutes, depending on which details you feel are crucial to understanding what the story is ultimately about.

It's hard for most people to gauge how long they've been talking. A storyteller who is practicing a ten- to twelve-minute story will often be surprised when their first telling is twenty-six minutes long. They will say, "But it didn't feel that long!" If you have to meet a certain time frame and you're running long, we advise you to make friends with your timer. While you're telling it, try to find places where you can tighten things up. Can you say something more simply, using fewer words? Can two sentences be pulled into one? Maybe you don't need that extra description—one is enough! If you run it with your timer a few times, you'll start to become more efficient with your words. It's important to *feel* the time so you can bring your story into the right range.

Another tip for hitting your allotted time limit is to break up your story into parts. How much time will you give to your beginning, middle, and end? Think of your time frame as a budget. If you have only ten minutes to tell your story, how are you choosing to *spend* that time? For example, do you choose to give two minutes to the setup, five-ish to the middle, and three to the end? Spend wisely! If you take eight minutes for the setup, you'll have only two minutes left for the heart of the story. Not enough! In a ten-minute story, your stakes should be established in the first few minutes. You'll need the remaining time to round out the arc of the story and come to a conclusion. Practice hitting your marks by editing yourself to get there. Then go back and put it all together!

We often use the term *critical choices* to describe the editing process. Pruning makes stories stronger—cut off some of those leggy branches, and you'll end up with more beautiful roses. Edit out anything that might take the story off course.

SKÅL, À VOTRE SANTÉ, PROST, CHEERS! In the sixteenth century, people would put small pieces of toast in the bottom of their wineglass (to improve the taste of wine). It was customary to drink down to the toast when honoring someone. It was also the custom to throw the glass into the fireplace! These days, thankfully, lifting a glass and saying a few words will suffice. When called upon to make a toast, one to two minutes (maybe three, tops!) is considered appropriate. Short and sweet is the way to go. (The Gettysburg Address was around three minutes long—and it changed a nation.) We recommend that stories in other social settings come in under three minutes as well. Open up the floor so others can share too.

You can revisit your *one sentence*. If a detail or scene feels out of place, ask yourself if it supports your one-sentence summary. Does it relate to what the story is ultimately about for you? Does it move the story forward? Is the overall story arc clear?

It's often better to err on the shorter side when practicing, because your adrenaline combined with the energy of an audience and their reactions (especially if your story is humorous!) will always make your story expand slightly.

TENSES

Editing The Moth's anthologies allowed us to fully articulate one of the major differences between the written word and the spoken word: the use of tense.

Generally, when you write, you choose a tense and stick to it. But when we transcribed the words that the storytellers actually *spoke,* it became obvious how many of our best storytellers switched tenses frequently throughout their stories. It wasn't usually noticeable in audio or live, but when we read them on the page, it jumped out. Our former editor suggested that we "just pick a tense and stick with it," which seemed reasonable, since that's the way we're taught to write. We tried it, but were surprised to find it crushed the "liveness" and immediacy right out of the stories. We lost the storytellers' natural voices and the feeling of being present in the room with them.

In live storytelling, you have more freedom to play with tenses than you do on the page. In general, when people talk, they jump back and forth between tenses. Most people do this naturally, so don't get too caught up in overthinking it. But as a storyteller, you can use tense deliberately, as a tool to help define or shape moments in your story.

Looking at Carl Pillitteri's story again, he describes the moment he is working in Reactor Unit 1 at the Fukushima power plant when an earthquake hits. He begins his description in the past tense (*technically,* for our fellow grammar nerds, past continuous).

And we were squeezing each other with every jolt that this thing's throwing at us. And we were huddled up, you know, three grown

> men like three little boys, and I began to pray earnestly aloud for all
> of us. And it appeared that the Japanese boy on my left was pray-
> ing in Japanese, and we were standing just yards in front of this
> massive turbine and generator which was spinning at 1,500 rpm
> being driven by the steam coming right off the Unit 1 reactor.

But then, at one of the most heightened moments, he drops
into present tense.

> And it was at 100 percent power, and the sounds that began to
> come out of this turbine catch my attention, and I start to realize
> that it sounds like it wants to come apart, and it's going to explode,
> and it's going to pepper us against the walls. As if to galvanize and
> confirm my fears, I hear my American co-worker from afar in
> complete darkness scream, "It's gonna blow. It's gonna blow."

Like Carl, many great storytellers play with tense to draw the
audience in. They might start out in the past tense, but then switch to
the present tense at a crucial moment of drama so we're *right there with
them.* The present tense can be used like a zoom lens in film, bringing
you right into the heart of the action and indicating to the audience
that *this part is important,* so they should pay special attention.

Another example of this is Journey Jamison, who was just sixteen years old when she told her story "Theory of Change":

> **[STARTING IN THE PAST TENSE]** *And I never imagined going
> outside and putting myself in danger to help anybody. But it turns
> out that I didn't have to, because seconds later* **[NOW SHE
> SWITCHES TO THE PRESENT]**, *my back door flies open and a
> young man, nineteen years old, comes in holding his neck. It's
> bleeding. And he's just saying over and over again, "I've been shot!
> Can you help me? Can you help me?" And I just say: "Yes!"*

A bleeding man enters the room with her, she switches to the
present tense, and we are there with them.

Be mindful that tinkering too much with something as natural as tense can make your listener feel manipulated. A good rule of thumb when thinking about tense is that your story should sound like it would if you were sharing it with a friend. Starting off in the present tense can feel too dramatic—more "one-person show" than intimately sharing a story. It might feel bold to start in present tense, but it can change the dynamic with the listener and it creates a subtle distance. A person starting a story by saying, "I'm standing in the middle of a war-torn city" might sound like the aural equivalent of someone doing a "reenactment" of a scene. There's a real risk that the audience will see you as more of a performer, and judge you accordingly.

Also, starting in the present tense can sometimes lead to confusion. When a man in his forties begins a story by declaring, "I am six years old and it's my first day of kindergarten," the brain of the listener automatically questions this statement. Of course, after a moment, they catch up to the device, but that's it—it's a device, and that device can be off-putting. And when that happens in the *first sentence,* you have to win the listener back.

This can be especially confusing for the listener if, say, the story-teller looks like they're in their twenties and they start with, "I'm seventeen years old." The listener is left thinking, *Are you? You look a little older . . .* It can take them a beat to catch up, and during that beat they're distracted and may miss the next five things you say. Better to just say, "I was seventeen years old." In this case, using past tense will help your listener feel more present.

As you tell your story, remember that you will likely change tenses naturally. You don't need to comb through for consistency— let your tenses live!

REPETITION CREATES A SPOTLIGHT

If something is important to the story, shine more light on it! Repetition can show the listener where to look. They don't have words on a page to refer to, so sometimes you have to find another way to underscore an important detail. If a point is particularly critical, dedicate a few sentences to it, to ensure the audience hears it. You can even slow down saying it, to signal: *Hey, you don't want to miss this!* Or simply repeat the detail for effect.

> *I spent 10,000 hours practicing—10,000 hours!*

> *At the end of the road we saw a dead body—a dead body!*

Repetition can be another way of saying, "Did you hear that?" This is especially good when one detail is important to understanding the entire story. If the audience misses it the first time, they will be lost later on—so make sure they don't miss it!

In "Eye Spy," Michaela Murphy uses repetition to make sure the audience absorbs a critical detail that's crucial to understanding the story: the moment when she discovers her uncle Al has a glass eye.

> *And then my uncle Al, who never, ever played with us, ever, comes into the water to play chicken fights with us. And he puts his daughter, my cousin Eileen, up on his shoulders, and then I get up on my cousin Kevin's shoulders and we're having chicken fights, and it's like actual family fun for a moment. And we're, like, you know, hitting each other, falling in the water.*
>
> *And then I take my foot and I accidentally kick the side of my uncle Al's head really, really hard, and his eyeball pops out of his head, falls into the water, and sinks.*
>
> *It pops out of his head, and it sinks.*

FLOWERY LANGUAGE

Tempting as it may be, there is no need to use big words and flowery language in your stories. Talk like you talk, not like you write. It will make you a better storyteller, and it just might help you see your writing in a new way.

ADAM GOPNIK, *NEW YORKER* STAFF WRITER AND MOTH STORY-TELLER: I sensed in myself that I had become, in some ways (and doubtless still am in every way), an unduly fancy writer. That is, that the sort of curlicues and ornamentations of erudition had begun to drown out my ability to simply tell a tale about what had happened. But I think writing is a business of perfection. You want every sentence to glow and shine, and have its own little balance and structure and charm. A story's not like that. A story can tolerate a lot of rough stuff in the course of its being relayed, as long as what's being related is significant. You can't write that way. Readers are not forgiving of imperfection. But don't you think listeners are totally unforgiving of insincerity?

The one thing that will make an audience turn on storytellers is if they seem to be performing or disconnecting emotionally in some way.

Either find the poetry in straightforward speech, or skip the poetry and say things in a more direct way.

RAY CHRISTIAN, MOTH STORYTELLER: Be genuinely and authentically you. Whatever that is. However flawed. However different. The more fabricated you try to be, the less poignant your story feels to the audience. It may sound perfect, but unless it's delivered from your heart, with all the intensity you felt in the moment, it doesn't *feel* perfect, and that's when the magic happens.

SALTY LANGUAGE

Stories should always sound like you, but if your everyday patter sounds like a scene from a Quentin Tarantino film, consider the audience. Some people seem to curse more when they're nervous. It can be jarring, and f-bombs are not something the audience gets used to. Are you willing to lose listeners? If not, can you tone down *some* of the cursing? The age-old notion of a well-placed f★★★ is a good rule of thumb. There are times when it seems nothing else will do! Don't diminish the power of the word by using it like punctuation.

> **JENIFER:** My grandmother once and only once said "damn it" in my presence. She was on her knees scrubbing our kitchen floor, and I passed through with muddy boots for a fourth time. I can still feel that "damn" in my stomach. I was scorched. She meant business, and she pulled out the big guns. I felt the power of language.

Consider Jon Bennett's story "Curses!," about a father who absolutely never uses profanity and is eternally correcting those around him with his puritanical "There's no need for that language!" Later, when the father is faced with a situation *so* extreme that he lets out a curse, the audience falls apart with delight. Good curse.

An entirely un-prudish man from Louisiana once mentioned that every time someone drops an f-bomb in casual conversation, it feels like he's been slapped in the face. Maybe you intentionally want to slap people in the face with your curse. Great, but you might only get to slap them once before they recoil/tune out/shut down/disengage. If you want to reach people far and wide, maybe there is another word you could use. You can also suggest a curse without actually saying it. (What the . . . do I mean by that?)

In Sheila Calloway's story "True Justice," she describes a moment of intense frustration where she lost her cool and let a few choice words fly. Instead of telling us exactly what she said, she phrases it like this:

> *I knew in my heart of hearts that this judge would never give this kid expungable probation. And the frustration just grew in me. And the more I talked to the DA about it, the more smug he seemed to be, and he would answer me, "Well, he did the crime, he's gotta do*

the time." And he kept saying that over and over and over to me. And it just built inside of me, the anger was so deep, that all of a sudden I snapped, and I immediately put down my files and I pointed my finger in his face and I said, you don't know what justice is, you are blah, blah, blah, blah, blah, bleep, bleep, bleep, *blah, blah, blah, blah, blah,* BLEEP, BLEEP, BLEEP, BLEEP, BLEEP, BLEEP, BLAH, BLAH. *Now, mind you, this was a courtroom full of people. There were attorneys, my supervisor, my poor client, all watching this. But at that moment I didn't care who was watching. All I thought was,* This is not right; this is not fair.

THINGS TO BE MINDFUL OF WHEN PRACTICING YOUR STORY OUT LOUD:

- **STAND UP!** It's important to stand when you practice telling your story—there is an immediacy to standing, and it actually engages the brain in a different way. Scientists at Texas A&M studied three hundred students using standing desks and found their cognitive engagement went up by 12 percent. Turns out the old adage that we think better on our feet is true.

- **TRY YOUR STORY WITHOUT A NET.** "I'm so nervous, I need notes!" We understand you'll want to use them in the beginning, but as you practice more and more, you should eventually try doing it without the notes, even if you don't feel quite ready. Better to see where you get tripped up and smooth out the bumps. Using notes gives you a false sense of security (plus, stories are always shorter with notes, so you won't have an honest running time).

- **AT THIS POINT, YOUR STORY MIGHT NOT EVEN MAKE COMPLETE SENSE. DO NOT FRET!** When you first separate yourself from the page, you may find that you have finished a section and don't know where to go next. This could mean that you don't have all of your stepping stones in place. And now you know! This is a good time to step back and think about what the key moments are in the story that connect each beat to the next and give it its larger shape.

- **PAY ATTENTION TO WHERE YOU LOSE YOUR PLACE:** If, as you're telling the story in draft form, you lose your place or zone out, it means something isn't working, either structurally or emotionally. Can you reorder? What's the greater truth? What's a very *simple* way to say it? Maybe the detail you keep forgetting isn't necessary! Your subconscious can be a great editor. If you continue to get lost, maybe you're trying too many fancy tricks with your structure. Go back to a chronological telling and see how that feels.

- *ZHUZH* **THE STAKES.** If you find your story is falling a little flat, or after telling it, you think *So what?,* you may need to "punch up" or, as we like to say, *zhuzh* the stakes! What is the moment of tension? Do you need to build on it or turn up the heat? What did you stand to lose, and is that clear in the setup? Is there something for your listener to invest in? You can tell us you want to stay dry in the rain, but once we know you're wearing your sister's brand-new suede boots . . . without her permission . . . the stakes of the rain are amplified.

- **LISTEN FOR WHAT DOESN'T FEEL AUTHENTIC TO YOUR OWN VOICE.** Are there places in the story where you falter or where it doesn't sound like how you speak? Change it! As you get to know yourself as a storyteller, you'll probably discover phrases or rhythms that are natural to you.

- **ISOLATE AND PRACTICE THE END OF YOUR STORY.** The beginning of your story tends to be rehearsed more frequently, because you start it in the shower or on your commute, but then your phone rings or you have to swerve to avoid a cat. You ask, "Where was I?" and then you start at the top again! Be sure to spend some time finessing and going over how you'll land the story. Start at the fifty-yard line and make your way to the end zone.

- **IF YOU'RE FINDING IT HARD TO LET GO OF THE WORDS YOU'VE WRITTEN, PRACTICE TELLING THE STORY USING ALL DIFFERENT WORDS.** It will take you a little longer, but it will show you that you know your story, and there is no one right way to tell it, as long as the meaning is there.

TELLING IT TO OTHER PEOPLE

Storytellers are often worried that if they tell the story again and again in practice, it will get stale. And it's true that there may be a point when the story starts to feel a little flat. But we sometimes tell a storyteller that they have to get "better-worse" before they can get "better-better" again, meaning it's okay to practice it to the point of it feeling a little tired to you. The story is getting into your system. That's why the piano teacher makes you do the scales, so when the improv solo comes, you can reach for any note and be sure that you'll hit it. It will come alive again the second you tell it to a group of people, and it's only through repetition that you can get to know your story well enough to be truly comfortable telling it in front of others. The more you have the beats down, the more you can play with it and feel at ease responding to the reactions of your listeners.

And now comes a moment of vulnerability: telling it to another person. Cue the nerves! But if the end goal is to tell this story to a group of people, whether as part of a work talk or as a wedding toast, it helps to tell it to a friend first. An audience of one friend is "fresh ears," and can give you much-needed feedback. (And if that is still too much, you can even record yourself telling it and listen back.) Informal is ideal here! Think of this like a rough draft.

You've heard "practice makes perfect," and the closest thing to a "perfect" story is when the teller is confident, prepared, and in the moment on stage. Stories should *feel* off the cuff, but they should not *be* off the cuff, as you've likely surmised.

NOTES ON DELIVERY

One of the last things we focus on in rehearsal is delivery. While we don't want you to *perform* your story, there are certain things you have to be mindful of in order to tell it well.

- **REMEMBER THAT YOU KNOW YOUR STORY BETTER THAN ANYONE ELSE.** If you lose your place, don't panic, just take a breath. If you mix something up, cop to it, jump back, and add in a detail. People will only love you more. *You* lived this. Just think, *What's the next thing that happened in the story, chronologically?* Continue there. And then, if you get to a part that you forgot to set up? Just tell us what you forgot to tell us!

- **IT'S GOOD TO TAKE A BREATH BEFORE YOU SPEAK.** Take the moment in. Remember, your listener is choosing to be there. They want to hear *you* share your story. They are looking up at you with an open heart and mind. There's no need to feel rushed.

- **SPEAKING OF FEELING RUSHED, CONSIDER THE SPEED OF EACH SECTION OF YOUR STORY.** Stories can feel bland if they're told at the same pace all the way through. Don't give every moment in the story the same weight! A story is like a song; it has variance. It's not a metronome, simply keeping the beat. In places that are serious or dramatic, or that include a lot of integral information, you might want to slow down. But of course if there's a moment in your story where things are chaotic or exciting, you might pick up the pace.

- **SILENCE CAN BE JUST AS IMPORTANT AS THE WORDS YOU SAY.** There is a rhythm to how you deliver your story, and a few pauses throughout are essential. A breath punctuates the story and can let the audience know what is most important. A pause after a *huge* plot point can also help the audience *take in* what just happened. If something is a big deal, put a little space around it to give it extra weight! When we write, we create paragraphs to group ideas. When we speak, we create paragraphs with our voices by pausing. Taking a beat can signal to a listener that we are changing gears or changing scenes. If you pause before you flash back or jump ahead, it gives the listener a chance to stay with you.

- **ACTING IS A DIFFERENT ART FORM.** Sometimes if the person is "acting" the story out, it can be distracting. Gesticulating is perfectly fine—we are not storytelling robots—but a full-body reenactment of the story is a different art form. Moth-style storytelling is more like "live documentary" than long-form physical comedy, acting, or mime. If you aren't someone who typically talks with your hands, don't start now.

- **WHEN SHARING DIALOGUE, PUT THE "I SAID," "SHE SAID," ETC., BEFORE THE QUOTE.** This is what we do when we speak naturally. It's the opposite of how we often write, so when storytellers try to do it in the reverse order, they tend to sound very written. And once you establish who is talking, you can also drop the "he said"/"she said"/"they said" altogether.

  Notice how these lines differ:

  "How old is Nina?" I said.
  "Five," she said.

  But if you switch it up . . .

  I said, "How old is Nina?"
  "Five."

  . . . it flows well. This will make your story sound more natural.

- **USE THE PERSONAL "I" INSTEAD OF THE COLLECTIVE "YOU."** Sometimes tellers get a case of the "yous." Keep the story rooted in your own experience instead of generalizing. To generalize is to subconsciously step away from the bigger feelings—it can create distance for the audience, too, and take them out of the story. Compare these two versions of Kiri Bear's "A Natural Mother." Here's how she could have told it:

As a parent, you always consider that what your kids think about you doesn't matter. Your job is to show up, to love them. What they do is completely up to them. But you find out how much they love you.

Here's how she actually told it:

As a parent, I'd always considered what he thought about me didn't matter. My job is to show up, to love him. What he does is completely up to him. But I found out how much my son loves me because the thought of never seeing me again was devastating.

- **USE THE PERSONAL "I" INSTEAD OF THE COLLECTIVE "WE":** Using "I" instead of "we" language keeps the story personal. What is true for *you* might not be true for "all microbiologists" or "all Angelenos" or "all the single ladies." Your story is an opportunity to speak exclusively for yourself.
- *SEE* **THE MEMORIES.** If you're describing a specific moment in time, especially one that is seared into your brain, try to go back to the memory, or as we like to say, "drop into the moment." See it in your mind as you're telling it. A new detail may suddenly flood back and make your description that much richer! You might find yourself experiencing the emotion of the moment, which will in turn influence your delivery.
- **BE CAREFUL NOT TO OVERHYPE A MOMENT.** Avoid saying things like "And then the most amazing thing happened" or "And then she said the most hilarious thing." Often when you set something up as being the *most* anything, it somehow falls flat. The listener is like, *That's not THAT amazing. It's not THAT hilarious.* It comes down to human nature. People don't really like to be told what to think. When you set something up like this, the listener instantly goes, *I'll be the judge of that!* If you drop the declaration and just say the

actual thing, nine times out of ten your listener will think it's the most hilarious or amazing thing!

- **NO SPOILERS!** Resist the urge to tell us what will happen before it happens. Often people will throw in a sentence like "And then something happened that would change my life forever." This is like telling us the end of the story before you get there. It might feel dramatic to you, but it can actually kill the energy of the moment. Before that moment happened, no one told you it would change your life forever; try to recount it the way it unfolded for you so your audience can experience the same element of surprise or suspense you did.

- **BEWARE OF FILLER WORDS.**
  - **"YOU SEE?"** People often have a phrase or word they pause on while they're preparing for their next sentence. *Um* and *like* are the most common. It's good to be aware if you're doing this, because after the twentieth *like, right?* or *literally,* it can become a bit tedious and ultimately fatigue the listener.
  - **"YOU KNOW?"** No, we do not know. We may be familiar with the themes or circumstances of your story, but we do not know your story. That is why we're listening. Also avoid these phrases:

    > *As you can imagine . . .* Can we?
    > *It goes without saying . . .* Does it?
    > *You understand . . .* Do I?

    Typically, tellers don't even realize they're dropping these phrases. Stay aware, and you can lift them right out.
  - **"SO . . ."** If we had a nickel for every time a storyteller opened their story by saying, "SOOO," we would have . . . a huge pile of nickels. Starting with *so* is another thing that people aren't aware that they're doing. Some storytellers default to this as a way to claim the space and share their voice without committing any word, thought, or emotion to the room. But rest as-

sured, the audience is on your side. Instead, just take a minute and center yourself. Know your first line, and deliver it confidently. You will be *so* great.

- **DON'T PRACTICE TOO CLOSE TO SHOWTIME.** We find that if you've rehearsed too recently, it's easy to leave something out in the actual telling because you'll think you've already said it (because you did . . . a few hours before!).

DIFFERENCES IN STORYTELLING CULTURE: The Moth teaches personal storytelling workshops for people all around the world. Everyone is welcome. One workshop of twelve people may have folks from twelve different countries and many different religious faiths. (At times, we've even had participants from warring countries in the same storytelling group.) Respect is of utmost importance. Over the years, we've learned that storytelling in other cultures can be very different from Moth-style storytelling.

In one workshop, a doctor crafted a story about a harrowing experience at the start of her medical career. In early drafts, she shared the backstory of growing up as the eldest child in a privileged and supportive Ethiopian family. She tells her father she wants to be a nurse, and he says, "Why don't you become a doctor?" She then details her path to medicine. The story builds to one stark scene on her first day of rounds in the local hospital. She enters a ward through swinging doors to find dozens of women in cascading states of distress, all in critical care because of unsafe abortions. She had never seen something like this; she had never known that some women in her own community resorted to terminating unwanted pregnancies in secret, risking death.

As she rehearsed the story in The Moth workshop, she unexpectedly switched from "I" to the collective "we" once she entered the hospital ward. She described the scene vividly, but it was told from the perspective of *all* the new doctors, rather than from her own individual experience. To our ears, we had lost the singularity of her character.

When we mentioned this, she said that in her culture, using "I" is considered showy. Garish. People do not tell stories about themselves. She said to shine a light on the self, as opposed to the community as a whole, was thought to be narcissistic. But she decided to try a personal lens for this story *just as an exercise* in the workshop to explore her own perspective and motivation.

Moth-style storytelling is one of *many ways* to tell a moving story. After workshops, we encourage participants to take the tools that feel most helpful for their future storytelling. While reading this book, use what aids you and discard what doesn't. Share stories that only you can tell, and share them in a way that is authentic and true to you.

ON MAKING SPACE FOR STORIES OF PEOPLE WHO HAVE DIED:
Casseroles and flowers are nice, but sometimes the most meaningful thing you can do for a grieving friend is to make space for them to share their stories about a loved one they lost. Asking broadly for stories might feel overwhelming, so instead start small—ask about a tradition, a memorable meal, or what made them laugh. You'll allow them to spend time outside of their grief and may inspire a memory that adds brightness to their mourning. Let the stories build upon each other. Your friend may be comforted by hearing stories from other people who loved their loved one.

KATE: My mother's birthday is always hard for me, so last year I texted my high school friends and asked them to share a memory of her. The day was punctuated with short memories: her excellent hummus, her obsession with Sérgio Mendes's *Brasileiro* album. My favorite? One friend said that she was the first adult he came out to. It made the day for me.

DIRECTOR'S NOTES

- When you say your story out loud for the first time, it will be long, because you're remembering your way through it. That's okay! As you tell it, listen to how you've structured and ordered your pieces. Is everything in the right place? Does it all flow together?

- Listen for where you might make edits. Are there phrases that are redundant or too many details that might cause confusion? Is there a spot you trip up on every single time that you just need to let go? Is there something you say in two sentences that could be said in one? The more you tell it, the more efficient and comfortable you will become with your words.

- There is no need to rush to the end. Savor certain moments and accelerate when the story calls for it. Lean into the quiet and more thoughtful moments, and enjoy the laughs when they come!

- Remember, your story is alive! It will be different every time you tell it. Your tenses may switch up or a detail might spring to mind as you remember the moments you're describing. This is not a recitation.

- Find a trusted ear to listen to a run-through of your story. Ask them the same questions you asked yourself. Is there anything confusing or distracting? Were there points in the story that felt superfluous? (Were you tuning out during that part about the goat?) Did they need more info about anything to better understand? If nothing else, a run-through with a trusted listener will help you build your confidence.

CHAPTER 10

ALL THE WORLD'S A STAGE

Years ago, we produced a Mainstage in Detroit. The stage manager at the theater kept asking me how many towels we needed. He was stressed. He was holding a few white hand towels and was eager to know how many more he should find. I told him: no towels. Then the supervisor came. He said, "We have fifty towels. Will you need more?" I thanked him and said no, The Moth only needs a single standing microphone. Our setup is so simple, he was shocked. (Turns out the Insane Clown Posse played that stage regularly and needed towels because their lively shows generated a lot of sweat.) But there are no towels at The Moth. You may sweat a bit during the telling of your Moth story, but in twenty-five years, no one has ever needed a towel!

—SARAH AUSTIN JENNESS

The Moth Mainstages have been held all over the world, in places as wide-ranging as the iconic Sydney Opera House, Golden Gate Park in San Francisco, New York's Lincoln Center, an amphitheater in Tajikistan, a cave in Stockholm, the Kenya National Theatre in Nairobi, and on the floor of the United Nations.

The storytellers sit in the first row of the audience and the host calls them up to the stage individually. They share their stories, center stage, and then return to their seats. This reminds us that the storytellers are not performing their stories—they're *sharing* their personal experience. There is no fourth wall. The storytellers are not "them," with "us" in the audience. It's only *us*. We're all together. Anyone in the audience *could be* telling a story.

Often people will say, "Oh, I couldn't tell a story at The Moth, I'm not a performer." Even just the idea of being in the spotlight is terrifying for some people. You may worry that you will forget what you're going to say, or that you'll say the "wrong" thing, or that no one in the room will care. But working through these fears will allow you to be comfortable enough to connect with the audience.

Other first-person theater forms, such as cabaret and solo shows, often feature people "playing" themselves in a heightened sense. Production elements like music, props, and lighting cues might add to the theatricality of one person's true story shared on stage. This can be magical, transportive, moving—all the things we love about live theater—but these forms are not what we aspire to at The Moth. We don't want you to "play" you. We want to meet you. The real you! No pancake makeup, dance moves, or deep curtain bows required.

Moth shows, and personal storytelling shows of all sorts, attract an audience who want to be transported. How often do you get to hear fully formed stories from the hearts of strangers? Sometimes the stories will overlap with the audience's experience, other times they might not. How often do you have the chance to walk for ten minutes in someone else's shoes? Or have your long-held beliefs challenged?

Compelling storytellers create an intimacy that can make a room feel small just by their ability to make individual connections. When you share a story with 3,000 people, you want the listener to forget the other 2,999 people in the room and feel like you're sharing the story with only them. Maybe you're just telling your story to two or three people. The same rule applies.

ABBAS MOUSA, MOTH STORYTELLER: Do not worry about having the perfect words or worry about your stage performance. You're not acting in a play. Do not wonder whether your story is good enough, or what others might think. Storytelling is a lot more than this. Your story is unique, just like other stories are, so focus on reliving that experience or event, and translate your feeling into words. That's what gives the best delivery to your story, and that's what the audience wishes to see.

At The Moth, our setup is deceptively simple: We always have one mic, kept on the stand. The microphone grounds the storyteller. The single storyteller on stage grounds the audience. No props, no set, no PowerPoint graphics, no light changes. There are no production elements to lean on, and that's on purpose. We want the tellers and their stories to speak for themselves.

Our number one stage rule: Don't touch the mic. Fussing with the microphone or gripping the stand for dear life is distracting and can mess with the audio. Unlike a stand-up comic, Moth storytellers can't walk off their hot, anxious, happy feelings with the mic. You have to express whatever you are feeling *through* your story. Nowhere to run. Nowhere to hide!

We've noticed that people who handle the mic with ease or rock it back and forth are perceived as pros. The audience thinks, *Oh, this is a performance* or worse yet, *He's going to try to sell me a vacuum cleaner at the end.* When you invite the audience into the world of your story, it's important that they feel the story is coming from your heart and not part of a routine.

Back in the day, we made an exception for our storyteller Darryl "DMC" McDaniels, the rapper who founded and fronted Run-DMC. But after he told his first story, he told us that he'd rather leave the mic on the stand like everyone else. And ever since then, we like to say that if Darryl McDaniels can leave the mic on the stand, everyone else can too!

Our tellers disarm with their honesty and vulnerability. Can you imagine a place where Darryl McDaniels doesn't take the mic off the stand, John Turturro doesn't transform into a character, Christian McBride leaves his bass at home, Teller of Penn and Teller actually talks, or Molly Ringwald doesn't personify our teenage angst? It's The Moth.

You may not aspire to ever stand on a Moth stage; maybe you're reading this book to learn to tell stories at work or at dinner parties. Wherever you plan to tell your stories, we suggest you go it alone: no bells, no whistles. Just you. Straight up.

NERVES

At The Moth, we ask people, many of whom have never practiced public speaking, to go onto a stage in front of hundreds (or thousands!) of people and share pieces of their lives. They do so with no podium, notes, or special effects, and trust that the facts of their life, intentionally woven together, will engage a room full of strangers. It has all the pressure of a first date that is also being recorded at broadcast quality. It's like the most profound revelations of therapy, but with the potential for applause.

By now you've read many pages about the power and exhilaration of sharing your story, but for so many of us, it is fraught with fear.

Nerves often arise when people worry about screwing up their story. But we have good news: The only way to really fail is to think *there is only* one right way *to tell your story*. You have all the answers. You are the only person who can tell it with authority!

DAN KENNEDY, MOTH HOST AND STORYTELLER: Even if a little part of the story didn't go exactly the way you wanted it to, you realize the audience was always on your side, from the moment you got on that stage, because you are them, and they are you, and you were all in it together.

MICHELLE JALOWSKI, MOTH DIRECTOR: One of my favorite things about this work is how much it reminds me that everyone is just a person, which is very humbling and also confidence-inspiring. Every single person I've worked with—including seasoned hosts and professional actors, musicians, and performers—gets nervous about getting up on stage and telling a Moth story. It's a leveling platform, and I love that about it so much. It's a constant reminder that everyone is a flawed human being, trying to figure it all out as they go along. As long as you're willing to be vulnerable, you can tell a compelling story.

Remember: It's natural to be nervous! Nerves are good; they mean you care.

SHERMAN "O.T." POWELL, MOTH STORYTELLER: When I get on stage, I block out the audience so I don't have the jitters. My batteries get charged once I get into the rhythm of the story, and once I have the rhythm, I'm HOME, whether there are two people in the audience or two thousand.

SO WHAT DO I *DO* WITH MY NERVES?

During the rehearsal for a show that featured a blues musician, a celebrated journalist, a passionate pâtissier, and a famous actress, Jeremy Jennings stood at the front of the room preparing to share his story. The story explored his conflicted emotions around his deployment as a prison guard at Guantánamo. Jeremy became overwhelmed by nerves and found it difficult to get through his first few lines.

JEREMY JENNINGS: I was literally choked by a panic attack. I could feel all of the eyes in that small room on me, and I couldn't get the words out as I tried to breathe. Kathleen Turner, a veteran actress and star of movies from my childhood, sat there unfazed and immediately suggested that I "shake it out! Go ahead, just shake it out!" I start jumping around, waving my arms and making strange noises. Her unflappable expectation that I was going to tell the story, that I couldn't just run away, helped get me through. I managed to push on, and I told the story, but it was rough. I ran into Kathleen in the elevator afterward, and she said nothing about my meltdown, just treated me like another colleague.

The night of the show, it was still difficult to get through the story, but the response from the audience was amazing. At intermission, so many people came and shook my hand and thanked me. I was overwhelmed with kindness and support. A few people even leaned in, with tears in their eyes, to share personal experiences similar to my own, and they were grateful to know they weren't alone. It was liberating, and reframed how I saw myself in my own story.

Okay, so everyone gets nervous! If you don't have Kathleen Turner at your disposal, how do you get through the nerves?

SHANNON CASON, MOTH HOST AND STORYTELLER: The anticipation to go on stage is nerve-racking. I actually hate the feeling and would rather be doing anything else. I think, *Why am I doing this? I could be eating pizza instead. I could be doing anything besides going on stage to tell a crowd about the deep, terrible, and funny things that happened in my life.* Then I get a flash: *I'm doing what I'm meant to do.* I tell myself that someone in this audience needs to hear this story. And at that same time, I need to tell this story for them . . . and for myself. I have to find a reason. Some or ANY reason beyond just being in front of a crowd to talk about me—if that was the case, I'd just go eat pizza instead.

PRESHOW NERVES

To deal with nerves, some people have preshow rituals. They may listen to music before going on. They eat a special food, or they don't eat at all. Some people have one glass of wine or a shot of whiskey (note: one).

Some people exercise to use up all their pent-up energy, while others find ways to be still and get out of their heads—like getting a massage or catching an early matinee. Kate's preshow ritual is to get a manicure. It keeps her away from screens or useless busy work. The plus? When she talks with her hands on stage, they look *good*.

You may not be totally confident, but try to tap into your courage! In her story "The Spy Who Loved Me," Noreen Riols reminds us that "courage isn't the absence of fear, it's the willingness—the guts, if you like—to face the fear." You're going to be nervous, so just accept it and put a positive spin on it. Really, what's the worst that can happen? Remind yourself you can do this! Maybe you come up with a personal mantra to build yourself up.

SIMON DOONAN, MOTH STORYTELLER: While trawling The Strand bookstore one rainy afternoon, I stumbled upon a biography of Judy Garland . . . and voilá! There it was. The antidote to my anxious cringing. Here's the deal: Judy, back in the day, had a unique way of battling stage fright. As she walked from her dressing room, she would repeat, out loud and proud, a helpful little mantra. It went as follows: "F★★★ 'em. F★★★ 'em. F★★★ 'em."

It was Judy's way of refusing to be intimidated by an audience. She reduced her fear of failure by big-upping herself. By the time she reached the stage and opened her legendary pipes, she had lost all fear and negativity, and was ready to love her audience, to share her gifts, and to connect.

Maybe mantras aren't your thing and you prefer to don your headphones and block out the world around you. Many storytellers will listen to a track of music to set their mood.

DANUSIA TREVINO, MOTH STORYTELLER: The day of the show, I usually need a lot of quiet time by myself. I listen to music, often

Bach, to take down any defenses. Once I get to the theater, I find myself needing to listen to something that would open me up further and bring joy to me. For some reason a song by Arcade Fire, "The Suburbs," has become my go-to. I put my earphones on and dance to it about fifteen minutes before I tell my story. Not only does it take the nervousness out, but it also makes me feel so happy to be alive.

PETER AGUERO, MOTH HOST AND STORYTELLER: While dressing for the show, I always try to listen to "That Old Black Hole" by Dr. Dog. I'm usually dressed by the time I hit the line "Who am I to tell the truth? I don't even know what it is. I don't know how to say it, but I know that I can show you." That whole passage pretty well sums up my intent for the evening.

When in doubt, do a power pose: hands on hips, feet apart, and chin in the air. It's a little trick to make you feel invincible.

ONSTAGE NERVES

Sometimes when that adrenaline kicks in on stage, your nerves take over. Your body defies you, and no amount of power posing or positive affirmations will control it. Here are some tips to keep in mind:

- **NO ONE KNOWS IF YOU MESSED UP.** Remember, as you're telling your story, the audience will have no idea where you're heading. Only *you* will know if your story is progressing in the way you prepared it. Don't be worried if you reorder things or have a momentary blank. Just think: *What happened next?* Storytelling is a journey for you *and* for the audience.
- **HAVE WATER ON HAND FOR A MOUTH OF SAND.** It's surprising how quickly someone's mouth can go dry when they're nervous. Sometimes it can get so dry that they have trouble

speaking. Water is your friend. Set it discreetly somewhere close where you can grab it. Your audience will far prefer you pausing for a sip rather than muscling through with cotton mouth.

- **GIVE YOURSELF A HELPING HAND.** We get asked a lot, "What should I do with my hands?" The standing mic centers and grounds the teller on the stage. If you don't have a mic, find another way to feel grounded: Plant your feet, stand up straight. Do what feels natural to you. If you tend to talk with your hands, that's fine! But fidgeting can be distracting. And no need to cross your arms for protection—you're among friends. Whatever you do, please don't put your hands deep in your pockets and jingle your spare change around. The microphone picks that up . . . we learned the hard way.

- **BRACE YOURSELF.** When taking the stage in front of a packed house, the lights are usually so bright you can only see a row or two of faces in the front. Usually in the first few minutes of telling your story, the silence of the audience intently listening is loud. But the first time you hear the audience respond with a laugh or gasp, you'll be reminded that you're standing in front of upward of a thousand people, and it can throw you off. You might suddenly become distracted by your nerves all over again and risk losing your train of thought. Even if your audience is small, the first time you hear them respond can be a little surprising, but try to stay focused, breathe through it, and push on!

- **IT'S OKAY IF YOU SHAKE, RATTLE, AND ROLL.** Sometimes a storyteller is visibly shaking—hands trembling, knees knocking. We've seen some of the most confident people, some who have done downright heroic things, appear terrified on stage when they begin their story. But when they get going, and often when they hear the first response from the audience, they settle in and the nerves calm. Sometimes a storyteller will simply call attention to it. They will quite literally say, "Wow, my hands are shaking" or even just "I'm a little nervous." When storytellers do this, the audience will often give them a little cheer or break into encouraging applause and remind them that they are on their side. Just the thing the teller needs to keep going!

NERVES IN A BUSINESS PRESENTATION: If you're in a professional situation where you're *not* comfortable drawing attention to your nerves—say you're using a story to open a pitch for new business or a board presentation—you'll want to eliminate the chances that they'll become obvious. If you have notes, read them from a screen, since paper notes in your hand might shake with you. If you feel your voice trembling, pause and take a deep breath before you speak again. You may not be able to outwardly acknowledge your nerves, but a moment of silence can steady you. If you're worried about your knees shaking, especially if you'll be on a raised stage where your knees are at your audience's eye level, fashion can be your friend! Cover those knees and wear something loose.

DYLAN PARK, MOTH STORYTELLER: When I stepped onto the stage to share my story for the first time in front of 1,200 people at Lincoln Center in New York, my mouth was bone-dry, and I remember gripping a water bottle so tightly that it could've burst. In the dozen or so Moth Mainstage shows I did all over the country following that night, I always carried a bottle of water with me onto the stage. If I was ever feeling overwhelmed or too emotional, taking a quick sip was a good way to reset myself.

Catherine has her own preshow ritual. She goes to each storyteller she's directed and reminds them that they have worked hard. They know their story inside and out. It's their story. They *can't* get the lines wrong. In fact, there *is* no wrong. All they need to do now is to *please have fun on stage.*

We know this may sound obvious, but sometimes storytellers get so nervous they forget to enjoy the experience. This saddens us. We promise, the first minute of telling your story is usually the scariest, but once you get a few lines in, you will feel the audience is with you.

> **PHYLLIS BOWDWIN, MOTH STORYTELLER:** When I step out on that stage, facing an audience of ten or ten thousand, stage fright and nervousness fade away, because I have what I need: I have my truth. I let go, lose myself, open my mouth, and let my story flow.

And remember, most audiences will be on your side. People want to see other people do well! And we may be biased, but we believe Moth audiences are the best in the world! We hear this again and again from our storytellers.

> **BLISS BROYARD, MOTH STORYTELLER:** When I'm at a show listening to a Moth story, I always get the feeling that my fellow audience members and I are holding hands underneath the table— all of us collectively invested in the teller's fate.

> **KATE ON NERVES BEFORE A BUSINESS PRESENTATION:** A lot of the time when I give a keynote or business presentation, I am part of a highly produced series of events that have been planned down to the minute. I'll take the stage after a Power-Point on Q3 earnings and before a departmental awards ceremony. The production team will have my slides loaded and strap a mic to me way too early so I can spend thirty minutes hoping no one is listening to my heart beat. When they count down to

me on stage, there is no turning back. What helps me is to remember that the presentation is finite. I will go on stage, and even if it raises the roof, there are three presentations scheduled after mine. So I remind myself that it's thirty or forty minutes, and whatever happens, I'll most likely walk off of the stage alive. How lucky am I? It keeps the stakes in perspective and helps me show up as my best self.

EMOTION ON STAGE

If your story deals with anything emotional, chances are you will *feel* it when you share it with other people in a way you didn't when you practiced by yourself. Your voice may get wobbly, and tears might appear. That's not a bad thing. You want to be present and feeling the emotions around the events that you're sharing!

There have been so many occasions when we have seen a storyteller share their story and suddenly become overwhelmed by the very emotion they're describing. They have told their story to us, one-on-one, multiple times without incident. But there is something about being vulnerable in front of other people, being heard and feeling the connection, that brings the emotion out. You might feel out of control and exposed, but the most communal moments in stories can come from this space.

TIG NOTARO, MOTH STORYTELLER: My story for The Moth ended up making me cry. And it's so funny to me that I found myself that touching that I made myself cry. The story was very fresh and hard for me to tell, and so it was very emotional. And that's very different from my comedy. I had never done that before, gotten on stage and just said, "Here's a story to tell." And it wasn't really funny . . . but I enjoyed it. I liked the feeling of the pressure being off to be hilarious through the whole thing. There were natural moments and beats where I got laughs and I just rested in *Okay, well, they're just listening to this part.* And then there were about two or three times where I almost started crying. So it was uncomfortable, in that I had a little bit of stress, where I didn't want to have a breakdown. And I remember Sarah telling me, "It's okay. It's a safe place if you want to cry." And I was saying, "I believe you, but I really don't want to start crying." And then it was making me laugh to think: What if I really abused that and sat down and had a cry on the stage that night, to where everyone was so uncomfortable and didn't know when to interrupt and be like, "Okay, that's enough crying."

So many times a storyteller has said, "The last thing I want to do is cry." If you do feel your emotions creeping in—you're getting choked up or your eyes fill with tears—fighting the emotion will only make it worse. It's important that you remember to breathe! If you try to push those emotions down, you will get *more* choked up. Just take a breath, feel the emotion—and then, once you're ready, carry on.

People are often afraid to show their emotions, but these feelings signal exactly what is important to you. Your audience will lean in, not judge you. They will understand that this story matters to you. There is beauty in the emotion!

WHO IS YOUR AUDIENCE?

The audience plays an important role in the art of storytelling. It's a conversation, a give-and-take. You, the teller, feed off the energy of the audience as they [insert reactions here]. This relationship between the teller and audience is a crucial part. It's less in your control than other elements of storytelling, but aspects of this relationship are still important for you to consider. Some audiences may have a similar common denominator, like a room full of pediatricians at a medical convention, a Pride Club gathering on a college campus, or a table of dinner guests at a political fundraiser. Some audiences may be more diverse in identity and experience—and there may be instances where you'll be surprised by who is sitting in those seats in front of you. You may not know what part of your experience overlaps with theirs or if this is something they're hearing about for the first time.

There is power in telling your story to those who can relate wholly; there is power in telling your story to those who cannot relate; and there is ultimate power in choosing which story to tell to whom.

In 2015, we produced a private show in which three Dominican Sisters shared their stories with their community. Despite the common Catholic faith of everyone in the room, this event did not feel like Mass. In fact, the tellers volleyed with the audience, gasping and laughing together at familiar details. One teller, Sister Mary Navarre, surprised herself by adding a spontaneous line. She remembers, "When the audience began to laugh and clap and join in, I knew it was going to be okay. I felt free to improvise, which led me, in the middle of my story, to make the rather shocking remark (for a sister): 'Can I say *pissed*?' That remark has been quoted and making the rounds ever since." Later, while describing the lessons she learned in Catholic school, she asked the question, "Why did God make you?" As she continued, the audience called out, "To know, love, and serve Him in this world," in the way that someone else might sing out lyrics at Madison Square Garden. By the end of the evening, the room was electric; hundreds of people with a shared faith were hooting and stomping their feet in community.

If your audience doesn't have a similar background or vocation, you may have to add context to avoid possible confusion. Before you take the stage, you will want to consider whether the audience is familiar with elements of your story. Are there important details you need to provide? Words you need to define? Geography we need to orient ourselves?

If you're a scientist speaking to a group of residents at a town hall, you will lose the technical lingo in order to make your story more accessible to the nonscientists in the room. If you know that the majority of the people might not relate to your particular experience, you might acknowledge that by adding in a bit more context in order to draw them in closer. If you're from New Orleans and your grandfather had a jazz funeral, you might need to give more detail for people who aren't familiar with life in the Big Easy.

Being aware of what your audience needs to "technically" know is different from what ideologies or experiences your audience brings into the room. Sharing a story with people whose lives you presume have been different from your own can be exciting—but in some cases can feel daunting. It does not come without risk.

DAME WILBURN, MOTH HOST AND STORYTELLER: If you're lucky, you will have the chance to speak to an audience that is *not* in your comfort zone. We all like to talk about how humans are one big family, but, like most families, we don't always get along.

In 2018, The Moth asked me to host a show at the National Cowboy Poetry Gathering in Elko, Nevada. As a Black woman from Detroit, this did not seem a natural fit. The out-of-town storytellers agreed with me.

Now, the sight of hundreds of pickup trucks in a theater parking lot may be normal for a lot of folks, but for those of us with darker skin and/or immigration-status issues, it was a reminder of how out of place we felt, so far away from home, surrounded by people who seem so different. Nestor Gomez shared that he was fearful that his story would not be received well once they realized it was about crossing the border undocumented. This feeling of being outsiders was amplified when a local photographer touched our First Nations storyteller Bobby Wilson's braid. I watched Bobby's eyes widen, and then he calmed. It was clear no harm was meant; the slight was more a lack of awareness than malice.

The Cowboy Poetry Gathering is famous, and one of the most well-known poets was doing a reading at the same time as our show. We all figured that our audience would be small. But when I walked on stage, the house was packed and the applause was thunderous. In an instant, the doubts went away. I started with my greetings, and we got going.

Nestor drew the audience in as he shared his memories of crossing the border into the United States.

> *I heard a noise far in the distance. At first I thought,* Oh, it's gonna rain, it's probably thunder, *but then I realized that it wasn't thunder; those were helicopters. I was only fifteen years old, and I had never seen helicopters in my life before, so I got really excited, and I started to try to look at the helicopters, and the coyote grabbed me and threw me on the ground and told me,* "This is no time for sightseeing."
>
> —"Undocumented Journey"

At a time when we felt the nation being torn apart with issues around immigration, the room was silent. It was a story of love and courage and terror. After he was done, the applause was some of the loudest of the night. No one seemed to be mad or ready to turn him in; they listened. It was a reminder of what The Moth means. It is an opportunity for us to prove that we are one family. That we can and must sit in a dark and quiet room—a boardroom, a living room, any room we can get to—and listen to each other's stories. That wasn't the first time I was uncomfortable, and the Lord willing, it won't be the last.

NESTOR GOMEZ: I half expected them to start booing once they realized that my story was about crossing the border undocumented. But in spite of my fear, I knew that I had to share my story, and help give voice to those that face the same undocumented issues that I did.

An invitation to share a story with a group whose experience varies greatly from your own can bring a different set of pressures and considerations. The responsibility of being the only person representing a community or culture can feel overwhelming. You might find yourself questioning the intent of the group inviting you to speak. Will they hear the story you are trying to tell, or will it instead feed a narrative they are looking to perpetuate?

When Frimet Goldberger worked on her story "My Knight in Shining Sidecurls," about leaving her Hasidic community, she was conscious that it could be used against a group of people who were already the subject of criticism and attack. It was important for her to be respectful. She didn't intend her story to be an indictment; it was more of an exploration of her own experience of leaving the only way of life she had ever known. While her lifestyle and the way she practiced her faith had changed, her love and respect for her family and community had not.

FRIMET GOLDBERGER: Rabbi Abraham Joshua Heschel, the famous twentieth-century rabbi, philosopher, and theologian who marched from Selma to Alabama with Martin Luther King, Jr., once said, "Wise criticism begins with self-criticism." At this point in my journey, I ask myself: What am I accomplishing by telling this story, and whom am I hurting in the process of this telling? If the answer is not immediately clear, I will sit on it. When I drafted my story, I did so knowing that my family members wouldn't be in the audience, but that nagging voice that they might someday hear it after it's aired still gnawed at me—and to this day! And maybe it's my own self-doubt, or perhaps I am conscientious of the pain my story could inadvertently inflict on others, namely a community that is already heavily marginalized. Of course, that does not negate the realities of the grimy underbelly within, but I always wonder whether people are capable of holding conflicting truths and understanding nuance. As I grow up and start ticking off the awkward thirty-five-to-forty-four age-group box, I realize that no society is immune to problems—that in leaving the community, which I *had to* and don't regret, I traded one set of problems for another. My sisters are happier than I am in a life I could not live. So where does that leave my story? In an uncomfortable space of multiple, conflicting realities.

Frimet carefully considered the details that were most important to her story, while respecting the many truths that lived in tandem, and consciously sidestepped details she felt could feed stereotypes.

Sometimes a storyteller will take the stage and be surprised, or even caught off guard, by who is in the audience—but you may intentionally *choose* to take on the challenge of sharing a story with an audience whose experience might not overlap with yours.

SUZANNE RUST, MOTH SENIOR CURATORIAL PRODUCER: Damon Young, an African American writer, shared a very complex, multilayered story about race and the power of the N-word on stage at The Moth. And while I hate to spoil the ending for those who haven't heard it, his story brings up so many important issues for us all to reflect on.

Damon had grown up hearing stories about family and friends getting into fights with someone who had called them the N-word. The teller always came out as the conquering hero with a wild tale to tell, a sort of rite of passage. Damon himself wanted such an "honor." He wanted that cred, but it never came. No one ever called him the word.

Eventually, while he's still a young man, he gets his wish. While he's standing waiting at a bus stop, a guy in a pickup truck leans out of the window, hurls the word at him, and then drives off, leaving Damon without his moment of victory, without the fight, without a story. Damon is stunned. Suddenly, he breaks out into an ugly laugh and has an epiphany.

I just realized how ridiculous it had been for me to want this to happen, to want this terrible, awful thing to happen, and to assign any level of my racial identity or my Blackness to how white people treated me. And that's the last time I did it.

As curator, I had reached out to Damon to see if he wanted to tell a story. When he came back with the idea for *this* story, I'm not going to lie . . . as an African American woman who has a deep problem with the word, I was a little shaken up. I loved the story, but *should we do this?* Several discussions took place in the office, and feelings were mixed among staffers of all races. Several of my colleagues shared my fear, not so much because of the story itself, but because it would be told to a primarily white audience. We worried that this intricate and powerful story would fall on ears that would have difficulty navigating and appreciating it. But Damon's story speaks truth about race, identity, and power in this country. It felt like the right story to tell for our times, and Damon was convinced that *this* was the story he wanted to tell. He told us:

> *This story was the center of my book* What Doesn't Kill You Makes You Blacker *because it is an irreverent, uncomfortable, transparent, and (occasionally) hilarious dive into some of the genuine absurdities of existing while Black in America. Part of this story's draw to me is the uniqueness of it and the anxiety I had—and still have—in sharing it. These are the same rationales that went into me choosing this for The Moth. Also, I knew that sharing this in front of a predominantly white crowd of hundreds would be uncomfortable for me too, so this became a bit of a per-sonal challenge to see if I could pull it off and hit each of the notes the way I wished to.*

The night of the show, when Damon shared his story "Fight-ing Words," as he guessed, the audience was primarily white. As I sat there with them, I could sense that many people weren't sure how to react. There was some awkward laughter, people shifting in their seats, and I wished that in the crowd there had been more people who could have personally related to Damon's story—he would have gotten a much different reaction.

CJ Hunt, our host that night, was able to give Damon's story the supportive landing that it deserved.

I feel so seen by that story. I've waited my whole life to be called the same. I just loved your story. The way you capture the absurdity of having violence be part of your identity and a rite of passage, I think is resonant to anyone who is Black. And, I imagine, partly resonant to any of those who have an oppressed identity, this wild way where you need a confrontation to see yourself. And I also love the story because it makes me think about a theme that has been running through the stories tonight about what it means to know who you are without depending on seeing a reflection of yourself in other people. I just want to say thank you again. That's all.

I was grateful for CJ that night. Stories are universal. Everyone can benefit from hearing a good story and perhaps learn something from it, but learning isn't the same as relating. Stories like Damon's, and many others we have shared on Moth stages, can land very differently on the ears of a white person versus a Black or brown person. This is also true for stories from Asian, Latinx, Indigenous, or LGBTQ people or tellers with disabilities. It's great to share and enlighten others, but it's both comforting and empowering to see some people in the crowd who are nodding their heads in agreement, laughing in the right spots, and mouthing the word, "Yes!"

Regardless of whether people relate fully or not at all, they bring their own opinions, interpretations, and explanations to a story. People hear stories through the lens of their own experience. And no matter how much you practice or how clearly a detail is explained, you will come across people who will infer something counter to what you meant.

On many stages around the United States, Samuel James shared his story "The Little Pink General Lee," which is about coming to understand his white maternal grandmother's relationship to both him and his father. In the story, he said:

She was a loving grandmother, there was no doubt about that. It's absolutely true. But she was also a cruel person who would ma-

nipulate her own grandchild in order to make his father suffer for their race. Both things are true.

After one show, several people came up to him to say how his experience mirrored theirs, but after another show months later, several people came up to him and said how great it was he had forgiven his grandmother. Nowhere in the story had he said this—this idea had been projected onto his story by the audience.

SAMUEL JAMES, MOTH STORYTELLER: Most storytellers don't think of their stories as works of art. But they are. And like any form of art, once you put it out there, it's the audience's to interpret. Some people will relate, and some people will hear something they may not have considered before. But there are some people who won't get it. People said they loved my story, but they didn't always hear it. There is nothing I can do, but I keep telling it and concentrate on the people who do relate.

People might not fully relate to or interpret a story the way it was intended the first time they hear it, but stories live on. Certain elements of a story might stick with a listener. They might find themselves understanding a story differently after experiencing or witnessing some new event. It might even inspire them to listen again. The potential impact of a story is not limited to the moment it is told; it is long-term.

Tell your true story where and when you are comfortable. Our only note: It is a disservice to yourself to change your story (and your lived experience) based on what you think the audience wants to hear. An honest story told to a group of people who have not lived through the same experience can create a lasting ripple effect. Discomfort is a catalyst for change—but you decide which spaces are right for you. One person's no-fly zone is another person's empowerment.

DIRECTOR'S NOTES

- The first minute of telling your story is usually the scariest, but once you settle in and feel the audience, it will get easier.

- Nerves are normal and expected. It's how you manage them that counts!

  - Find a way to pump yourself up or calm yourself down, whether it's quiet affirmations and a cup of tea or blasting ABBA in your headphones before the big moment. Whatever works for you!

  - Before you begin, find a way to ground yourself. Plant your feet, stand up straight, take a deep breath. Don't rush to the start; it will throw you off balance!

  - Don't be afraid if your nerves show—they only mean you care.

  - Acknowledging your nerves to the audience is okay—it will only endear you to them. Trust and know that people want to hear from you, because who's better than you?

  - Water is your friend—have it handy. There is nothing worse than suffering through a dry mouth, for both you and your listeners!

- If your story deals with an emotional subject, you will likely feel the emotion the first time you tell it to other people. Running your story with someone beforehand will show you where the emotions might creep in so they don't catch you by surprise. If you need to, stop, take a breath, and feel the emotion. Don't try to hold it back—you will only get more choked up.

- Consider whether there are elements of your story that might need more context so your listener can understand and follow along. Technical, experiential, and cultural details may need more explanation, depending on whom you're addressing.

- Honor your lived experience and never base your story on what you think an audience wants to hear. Remember that where and when you tell your story is entirely up to you.

PART 4

THE POWER OF STORY

CHAPTER 11

THE RIPPLE EFFECT

Stories weave us together as human beings. And yes, they can be a tool of power. True power. That's why it's more important than ever to hear more stories from more kinds of people, especially those who have been and are usually silenced.

—CARMEN RITA WONG, MOTH STORYTELLER

Once you've developed a story, what can you do with it? As events unfold in our daily lives, much is out of our control, but in processing and telling our stories, we are powerful decision makers. The act of telling a story can feel triumphant. Sharing a story of celebration in which the problem is solved, the home team wins, and your mom says you can keep the dog, can be as much fun for you, the teller, as it is for the listener. But even a story where you get kicked in the teeth, dumped, or duped feels better when you're in charge of the telling. Hindsight, oversight, and command of the situation means it has all been processed, digested, and reconstituted. Owning it feels *good*. But stories are meant to be shared and can also bring about significant change in those who listen.

STORIES IN SCHOOL

Adolescence is unforgettable, whether you loved it (some people) or found it excruciatingly awkward (most people). Our teenage years are some of the most transformational in life: so many firsts! Consider how your life would be different if *you* had shared stories with fellow students in your high school. If you'd had the courage to talk about the things that really mattered to you. Imagine if teachers had more of an opportunity to listen to students' stories, or share their own.

For decades, The Moth has worked with high school students and educators to provide space for young people's voices and use storytelling workshops in schools to build community.

One spring afternoon, high school students who had been participating for weeks in a Moth workshop at The Beacon School prepared to tell their stories on stage in the school's black box theater. Aleeza Kazmi was nervous as she watched the room fill with an audience of her peers. The crowd was restless; students were whispering in the back. She stepped out on stage and began her story with a memory from elementary school, when the students were asked to draw a self-portrait to be hung on the classroom wall.

> *I started drawing so slowly, going around my lips and my eyes, and was coloring in all one direction. And I was watching as the oil pastel melted into the paper and my face came alive, and I colored inside of the lines. And when I looked down, it was like I was looking into a mirror. This girl I had just drawn is exactly how I see myself. And I felt my teacher over my shoulder. She loved it when people drew well, and so I was getting ready for her to praise me, to say, "Aleeza, that is the most beautiful self-portrait I have ever seen. I'm gonna hang it above my desk so everyone who comes in can see it." And instead, the teacher says, "Aleeza, that's not your color." And I'm confused by this, because I don't understand how colors can belong to people. But before I can find a way to ask*

her, she's gone to the oil pastel box and started looking for it. And she doesn't find the color that she's looking for, and so she goes to the crayon bin. Now, every school had this infamous crayon bin that had bits and pieces of wrapped-up and gross crayons that had been rolling around forever. My teacher is rummaging through it, and she reaches in and she pulls out this little nub of a brown crayon. And she hands it to me. And I'm still really confused by all of this, but I noticed my friends are staring at me and my heart is beating really fast, and I want this to be over.

Aleeza goes on to explain how this memory stayed with her and the question of identity lingered with her throughout elementary and into middle school. After she told her story, she said she was able to forget about the audience (because the lights were so bright she couldn't see them from stage!) and just shared the story from her heart.

On the first day of sixth grade, this one kid comes up to me and says, "What race are you?" And I had never been blatantly asked this question before, and so I didn't have a prepared answer. I thought back to that teacher and that brown crayon, so I told him, "I'm brown." And he gets this confused look on his face and he says, "What do you mean you're brown? Brown isn't a race." And I couldn't believe it. I couldn't believe that I had finally said, "I'm brown," and it still wasn't enough. And then the little six-year-old girl deep inside of me gets really angry. And I said, "You know what? If I say I'm brown, then that's it. I'm brown."

At this point, the room was quiet and she closed with:

And today, if you ask me to draw a self-portrait, I'd draw a confident young woman who's proud of her Afghan and Pakistani heritage, who is a proud American. And I would find the most beautiful, soft oil pastel to color in my face. No one would have to tell me to pick it up, and it would be my first choice.

After five minutes, it was over. Aleeza told us she felt a rush of adrenaline from being vulnerable in that way on stage. A few weeks after the show, a student she did not know well approached her on her way to class. Aleeza told us:

> She was one of the few other brown kids in my school. She told me that she saw the show and loved my story, and felt really connected to it. I realized that even though I couldn't see the audience, they could see me. Like, really see me. And for the first time, I understood the true impact that sharing our stories can have: It can bring people together and make them feel truly seen.

It is rare in life—but particularly in the life of a young person—to be listened to uninterrupted for five minutes. By sharing a personal story, students claim their agency. They share these lived experiences *themselves* without interference. The result? Young people tell us they have greater confidence, greater control, and a richer sense of belonging.

What happens to adults when they stop and listen to young people—and vice versa? Sharing stories between teachers and students breaks down barriers, invites a greater understanding, and *dismantles the hierarchy*. Educators who "walk the walk" as storytellers experience the vulnerability of sharing a story. Oftentimes they'll tell stories from when they were a young person; it's a chance to just remember what it's like to be in the shoes of their students.

Telling a story gives teachers a deeper sense of what they're asking of their students. One teacher told us how frustrated she gets with her high schoolers when they say, "I don't have anything to write about!" But when it came time to brainstorm ideas for her own story, she had the same experience. The process gave her a better understanding and empathy for her students.

Neema Avashia, an educator and Moth alumna, has been a civics teacher in Boston for years. At The Moth, Neema crafted a story about the senseless death of Angel, one of her beloved students, who happened to be a graffiti artist. In the story, she and two of her former students register their sorrow in what Neema calls "the ultimate act of grievance"—they graffiti the side of a building together, with a tag in Angel's honor.

> One of my students says, "I've been carrying this can of spray paint around all week. I don't know what to do." I say, "I think I know. I think we need to go tag something." I'm not just a civics teacher during the day, I'm a civics geek at night. My students know I don't drive more than five miles above the speed limit. I just am pretty square. So this student is like, "You're a civics teacher. You're not supposed to do this." What they didn't know is that for the previous eight months, I had been trying to meet with city leaders, with the superintendent, with street workers, with anyone I could get to listen to the fact that in Boston last year, sixteen young people under the age of nineteen were killed. And of that, four were my students. I was doing all of this advocacy, and it wasn't doing anything, and it also wasn't helping me. I didn't come away feeling better. Then there was this spray can. I was like, "Well, nothing else has worked. Being a civics teacher and using those strategies hasn't accomplished anything." So we went behind the school, and we basically took turns tagging. In Boston, when young people are killed, their friends in the community create a hashtag. So we tagged #Angel'sWorld and the students said, "Angel would f***ing love this." And then, "Oh, sorry, actually, I forgot that you were my teacher for a second." And right then, that hierarchy between teacher and student, it just flattened, and we were just mourning, and we were trying to figure out how to connect with Angel, and how to connect with each other. So we took our pictures, some with me in them, some without me in them, and I said, "You better not post pictures with me in them. That could get me fired." Because at the end of the day, I'm still their civics teacher.

We grow up being *told* who we are. In school, we are taught how to communicate, and we worry about "right" and "wrong" answers. When young people are invited to work on their personal stories, they are in charge; they decide what stories they want to tell, how they want to tell them, and *if* they want to share them with an audience.

Often when we ask young people to share their stories, we hear: "But nothing has happened to me!" That doubt is compounded when the teller has been habitually dismissed because of their age. If it matters to you, it will matter to your audience. We will care if you care. You can tell a story about anything, in your own voice and with your style of expression. That permission can be very freeing.

A FEW EXERCISES TO USE IN THE CLASSROOM (WITH STUDENTS OF ANY AGE!):

- **"I USED TO_____ BUT NOW I_____."** Take a few minutes to brainstorm one-sentence stories that tell us one way you are different now from who you once were. Any change will do! Big or small.
- **"THE OBJECT EXERCISE"** is a take on show-and-tell. Think of an object that has meaning for you. Tell us what the object is, how it came into your life, and why it is important to you. What would it mean if you lost it? This is always a rich brainstorm that helps us talk about *stakes*.
- **"LIFE WEB"** is a way to generate story seeds quickly. Write your name in the middle of a piece of paper, then draw spokes extending from it. On each spoke, write something that's important to you: people, places, activities, and so on. What is a moment or memory that comes up when you think about a person/place/thing that is important to you? Use these ideas to inspire your story.

A NOTE TO PARENTS: Try pulling these out during your next long drive. Maybe start with one of your own to break the ice, and your kids might follow suit.

The Moth's high school curriculum—a resource for brainstorming and story crafting—is available for free online, for educators around the world.

STORIES AT WORK

Sometimes a quick catch-up by the copier can be a breath of fresh air between spreadsheets. But beyond our human need to socialize or shake out the sales data, stories have a practical impact at work too. They bring meaning to the transactional and amplify culture, tying employees back to each other and their work. Storytelling is an empathetic communication tool that can elevate the effect that organizations have internally and in the world.

BRING YOUR "I" TO T-E-A-M

For years, the notion of "team-building" at work was often met with eye rolls. *Please, not another trust fall/ropes course/corn maze.* However, data proves that organizations are better when their people feel connected to each other. According to *Forbes* magazine, "teams who score in the top 20 percent in engagement realize a 41 percent reduction in absenteeism, and 59 percent less turnover. Engaged employees show up every day with passion, purpose, presence, and energy."

Most organizations are not set up for focused listening. They prioritize efficiency, multitasking, and results. Personal storytelling gives colleagues a way out of the superficial interactions that can happen during the awkward wait for the microwave.

Some people know very little about the co-workers they regularly pass in the hallway. You can rightfully assume some similarities with your colleagues: similar education in technical fields, similar politics in a social justice nonprofit. And maybe you noted that their Google profile photo is a cat in a dress.

Creating a space for individuals to share their personal stories and respond to their colleagues' can transform the internal dynamic of your organization. And because it requires vulnerability and some time, it's likely that it won't happen without intentionally making the space for it.

In our MothWorks program, where we lead workshops and host private events in business settings, the pressure is high for participants. They are being asked, for their job, to be vulnerable in front of their boss or their boss's boss, with the knowledge that they will immediately be given notes by a stranger from a nonprofit arts organization whose logo is a bug. Very often this means that the first-draft stories that we hear are safer—simpler, with lower stakes.

KATE ON LEADING A MOTHWORKS WORKSHOP: During a session with a global communications company, a man stood and told a short story about how, at the end of his senior year of college, he and his buddies threw all of their mattresses out of their dorm and then leaped onto them from the second-story window, screaming, "I'm alive!" It was clearly a story he'd told at bars a hundred times for a few laughs. In the first telling, it seemed like he wanted to be the type of guy who would throw furniture and bodies out of windows. But in his breakout group, colleagues who had never heard this story challenged him to think more deeply about his stakes. He landed on this: The event occurred on the day that his friends were getting offer letters for their first jobs. From the day that he entered college, he felt like he was out of his league, and on this day, he was the only person he knew without a plan for after graduation. He felt terrible and worthless. Now "I'm alive!" wasn't just about being a goof with senioritis. He was yelling it to remind himself that he was, at least, that.

In one short breakout session, using personal storytelling, his colleagues helped him discover a deeper truth about his life, and in turn deepened their understanding of the person who they interact with every day.

Stories beget stories. We find that if one person shares a story of getting kicked out of the marching band in high school, another teller might identify a rebellious thread in their own story. Subthemes emerge organically. The energy shifts.

Stories break us out of our professional identities. After a recent workshop at a large tech company, a participant wrote:

Six of us all work in different parts of [the tech company]—sales, customer success, product, engineering, marketing, and data science. We would not have known each other, and now, we are connected by each other's defining life moments. I felt seen and known, and I feel I see and know my coworkers as beautiful, unique individuals, rather than "yet another standard tech person."

A FEW STORYTELLING PROMPTS TO USE AT WORK: Instead of kicking off a meeting by reading the agenda that everyone has in front of them, why not start it with a story from a colleague? Give one lucky volunteer a prompt (and a time limit) to inspire what they'll share.

Prompts can tie to . . .

- The work: *Tell us about a time you realized this work was important to you.*
- The theme of the meeting (for example, expanding into new markets): *Tell us about a time you knew you had to leave home.*
- Company values (for example, acting with integrity): *Tell us about a time you had to stand up for what's right.*

You'll be surprised at what you'll learn in three minutes, and how the mindset of the room can shift and tee up more empathetic and impactful conversations. Draw from a hat to see who goes next!

BUILDING AN INTERNAL CULTURE

We were invited to host a workshop to celebrate a software company's Great Manager Award recipients. One participant, Alexandra K., shared a story that was surprisingly vulnerable. She told us that a few years earlier, her team had issued a complaint about her management style. Confronted by this, she was deeply ashamed. Fortunately, her manager didn't "write her off," and she enrolled in a comprehensive 360 review process to get to the bottom of what was going on and fix it properly. That, in part, was why being acknowledged as a great manager meant so much to her now.

Alexandra said, "It was hard to share this story, making eye contact with leaders across my business who I respect and who I have worked closely with, and just hoping knowing this about me isn't going to change things. But then toward the end, when I could see people's reactions and feel the release of all the pressure, it was actually empowering to own the story."

After the workshop, she was inspired to keep sharing it. "I've actually found myself revisiting it with my team, especially as we come up on reviews and promotion cycles or career-growth conversations. It just reminds us that we're all human beings. And I think it's helped them really appreciate when I say, 'I'm here for you' or 'This didn't go as we planned, and that's okay. Let's not dwell on what we could have done differently. Let's talk about what we're going to do next time.' It's not just lip service, because there's a whole personal narrative behind that, that they have lived with me and that they have seen play out positively for me."

But her story didn't stop there. She says, "When I think about my impact on company culture, I think about the multiplier effect of story. What I do affects the eleven people that report to me, but then it reaches out to their circles—the blast radius of this change is powerful." She shares her story of failing forward as part of their new-hire onboarding presentation to hundreds of people monthly. "People reach out to me all the time saying, 'That story was validation that I made the right choice to join this company.' The culture of our company is why people uproot their lives, change industries, leave a fancy title on the table. We have to communicate our culture to them on their first day, and this story does that."

MAKING DATA IN PRESENTATIONS MEMORABLE

Recently we had a global media agency approach us after they lost a pitch to a competitor. They handed us the deck they used— seventy-five pages, mostly data. It was clear that they needed to make their information more compelling. We often get calls from people who simply cannot live through one more PowerPoint dense with data ("assault by information" is a phrase we hear again and again). Even in the most technical lines of work, every person in the room is a human with a heart and mind, and those hearts and minds are bored. To be truly called to action—to be swayed to sign off on an idea, increase a budget, change the way they do their day-to-day—people need to know *why* they are doing it.

Sometimes your stories are closer than you think! We worked with a tech company who was struggling to tell the story of how cutting-edge and sensitive their experiments were. They were so proud of their data and they wanted to share *all* of it—which made their communication, frankly, tedious. But then, over lunch, one of them mentioned that they have to schedule experiments around a train station over two miles away, because vibrations from the arrivals and departures were picked up by their highly sensitive equipment. We all looked at each other and said, "That's it! That's your story!" That the work they did was so precise that a *commuter train two miles away* would affect their results. Years later, we still remember that story; the data was supplemental. Cognitive psychologist Jerome Bruner is credited with saying, "We are twenty-two times more likely to remember a fact when it has been wrapped in a story."

When using storytelling to communicate data . . .

- **START THE DATA PRESENTATION WITH A STORY.** Open with a story to set up the "why" before you share your data findings. For example, Moth storyteller Lindiwe Majele Sibanda starts her agricultural research presentations with a short story of growing up on her grandmother's farm in Zimbabwe and the hope that their harvest would feed the whole village.

- **DROP DATA IN THROUGHOUT ONE LONGER STORY.** Use one story as the spine of your entire presentation and pause to share critical data points.

- **USE A STORY AT ANY POINT WITHIN THE PRESENTATION TO ILLUMINATE A CRITICAL DATA POINT.** Your story is a way to pause and give space to information that is crucial for your audience to understand.

STORIES WITH FAMILY

Photographs are moments frozen in time, while stories are living and breathing. What if instead of family photo albums, we had family *story* albums? A place where you could hear the stories of your ancestors? Which would you rather hold in your lap? Through stories, you can conjure facets of your loved ones' lives, their joys, and their sorrows. You probably know a few treasured family stories—how your parents met, what everyone did on the day you were born—but don't you wish you knew more? Many say that our ancestors' stories tell us who they are and, by extension, who we are.

A comfortable rhythm can develop with people who are a part of your everyday. We assume we know how others feel, or that they know how we feel. Stories help you underline the significant feelings that can get left unsaid. They're a chance to stop and say it, whatever "it" is. This type of sharing can take an ordinary day and make it an occasion.

Ellie Lee decided to share "A Kind of Wisdom" with her family.

It was a story about finally recognizing what her father had done for their community in Boston's Chinatown.

ELLIE LEE, MOTH STORYTELLER: When I first played the story for my parents, they cried. My dad is not a very emotional person, so it was incredible to have that magical moment together. It's one thing to tell someone you love them. It's another to be able to convey that in a story, to express other depths of meaning, emotion, and connection. Perhaps he thought all his hard work and sacrifice was something he did without much acknowledgment because that's what's expected as a parent. He was really surprised and touched that I chose to use the space that The Moth provided me to honor him, and to show the world how much I loved him.

Stories can also help us connect with a family member who is far away.

CATHERINE: When I was still a baby, my dad was drafted into the Vietnam War. With him away so long, and me so young, he was worried that his only child wouldn't know him when he got home. So Mama had an 8 x 11 picture of him printed and framed. She sat it on the floor in a corner of the living room, so it'd be at eye level for me. Every day she sat me in front of the picture and would point at it, and say, "Daddy, daddy, that's your *daddy*." She told me stories about him, even though I was too young to understand. She realized the talking calmed *her* down and helped her stay connected to him. Her only other contact with him was the occasional letter. When Daddy came home, he flew into Maxwell Air Force Base in Montgomery, Alabama. In those days, you'd walk down the stairs of the plane right onto the runway, and your loved ones could meet you on the tarmac. The way Mama tells it, as she approached the plane, she saw my father come down the stairs, and I broke away from her and ran toward him yelling, "Daddy, Daddy, Daddy!"

ENCOURAGING OLDER GENERATIONS TO SHARE THEIR STORIES

When storyteller Tomi Reichental's grandson was studying the Holocaust in grade school, he told his teacher that his grandfather was a survivor. She in turn invited Tomi to speak to her class. A shy man, he never discussed his experience of being a prisoner at Bergen-Belsen as a six-year-old boy. The memories were too painful. But because he had never really talked to his grandson about his experience during the Holocaust, he decided it was something he needed to do. After he spoke to the classroom, something shifted in Tomi, and the importance of bearing witness became a driving force. In the years since that day in the classroom, Tomi has become an active member of the Holocaust Education Trust in Ireland, where he lives. He broke his silence only after being asked to share his story by his grandson.

Our loved ones' stories might hold keys to the past—whether they were eyewitnesses to history or they're the only one who really knows why your two great-uncles stopped speaking, setting off a family feud that has lasted to this day. Perhaps you have always wondered why your great-grandmother was so good at the tango. Have you asked her? Encouraging loved ones to share their stories helps us to know them better, but also allows us to keep a piece of them with us after they are gone. What may seem mundane to them may be thrilling to you. (*Whaaat, you worked in a munitions factory during World War II? You mean like Rosie the Riveter??*) Unbeknownst to you, every older person you know has had love affairs, work dramas, wild times, and crushing disappointments they may not have shared with you. Are there stories that went over your head at Thanksgiving when you were younger that you want to hear again? Now is the time to ask!

SARAH: My grandpa Jack was in the throes of dementia when I recorded him talking about his life. He had no short-term memory left, but with the help of photographs, my grandmother and I were shocked and delighted to know that his long-term memory was still intact. With each black-and-white photo we revealed to him, he was transported. He told us of his lake vacations in the summer as an only child; Jerry, his beloved hound and companion; and his doting parents. "My father was an insurance salesman. He cared so much about his few clients, he kept visiting and asking if they were all right and if they needed *more* insurance. They didn't need more insurance. He needed more clients." The photographs lit up not only detailed memories from the past but also his dry sense of humor that we worried had vanished.

Photos and musical recordings can unlock buried memories and long-lost stories for all. They are an easy gateway into the past.

For those of you who want to give a nudge to the older generations (or even old friends, your sister, that teacher you've kept in touch with all these years later), here are some prompts to get you going. Grab your phone, a pen, anything you can use to record them.

- What is the story that everyone tells about you?
- Which memory still makes you laugh?
- In the movie of your life, what are some scenes that you'll never forget?
- Tell us about your first kiss. Your first love? Your first heartbreak?
- What is the greatest challenge that you've overcome?
- When have you felt certainty in your relationships, a choice you've made, or your work?
- Tell me about a moment of regret.
- What were your favorite moments from growing up?
- Do you remember when ____?
- What is something that you want to be remembered for?
- Tell me about a risk you wish you'd taken.
- What was it like the first time you set foot in the city you now call home?
- Tell us about a time you were proud of yourself.
- Tell me about the one who got away.
- What was it like when we first met? What happened?

- Tell us about the first time you hosted a family meal.
- Tell me about your favorite holiday memory.
- When has someone saved you with a great piece of advice?
- When did you share something you kept secret for a long time?
- How do you want your story to end?
- What is an object you hold dear? How did you come to have it?
- What was a typical day like when you were three, thirteen, thirty-three, ninety-three . . . ?
- When did you realize you were good at [thing that they're good at]?
- Tell us about a moment that you felt extraordinarily jealous.
- If you could relive one day of your life, what day would it be?
- Tell me about a time you felt homesick.

A TIP ON RECORDING PEOPLE: Sometimes they get shy when they know they are on camera. Recording in audio can be much less intimidating than a video camera. Most smartphones now have a voice memo setting, or you can point a video camera away and just capture the audio. You may find your loved ones will quickly forget about the recorder as you go along!

IN REMEMBRANCE

Conjuring memories can feel like tiny visits from the person you've lost. Sometimes the process of gathering stories—connecting to loved ones and reaching out to those who would otherwise be strangers—can add dimension to the person that you knew. The stories create a prism that enables you to view their life.

MICHELLE JALOWSKI, MOTH DIRECTOR: When my dad died, I felt untethered, like my connection to the world was severed somehow. I really wanted to gather my community around me to commemorate him in a way that felt both mournful and joyful. The problem was, most of my friends didn't really know my dad—he was a pretty insular guy. So I had to think of how to celebrate him in a way that was bigger than him—that was about him and his place in my life, but also his legacy, that of all fathers, and the patrilineal lines that we all descend from.

On a warm July night, I invited about twenty-five people to gather in a corner of my yard. I started with a short eulogy for my dad—just a few things to get a taste of who he was. He was a trend-setter, always on to some new thing way before it was officially trendy, like big sunglasses and track suits, and cellphones way before they were ubiquitous. He was cool—handsome and charming, he was often a favorite at family events. But sometimes too cool, and there was definitely some toxic masculinity involved in our relationship that had always been difficult to negotiate. But I always knew that he loved me. I called him Aba, the Hebrew word for dad, and I always knew how much he loved being an aba. My sister and I were the most important people to him—we know for sure because his passwords to things were often some combination of our names. When I was done, I acknowledged how hard it can be to honor our fathers—that often, the relationships are complex. I invited people to share stories about their own fathers and what they've inherited from them. It was quiet for just a moment before the first person spoke. People shared beautiful reminiscences about their dads—the love of music and appreciation of art that their dad always modeled for them, the sense of adventure their father imbued in everything he did. The time he flipped off a racist and made a joke, letting my friend know that racists deserved the finger and also that it's okay, and often important, to laugh about hard things sometimes. There were also some less fond memories—of stubbornness inherited and anger passed down.

One by one, almost everyone shared something with the group. Hearing the commonalities in so many of our experiences made me feel more connected—to them, and to my father and to their fathers. By the end of the night, the feeling of being untethered and unwhole had abated somewhat, and I felt grateful for community, friendship, and storytelling.

Telling these stories is also a way to make sure precious memories of beloved family members get passed on to future generations. Telling and retelling family stories helps cement them in our collective memories.

SUZANNE RUST, SENIOR CURATORIAL PRODUCER: My mother, Edna Rust, died when I was just twenty-two, and my father, Art Rust, Jr., when I was in my forties. Losing them left a huge hole in my life, but their stories keep them around. I am forever weaving stories about my parents into conversations, and my children, Julian and Sofia—who never got the chance to meet my wonderful mother—often toss her stories back to me, and through them, they have a pretty good idea about her. They know that when she was a teen, she was invited to tour Europe with Katherine Dunham's dance troupe, but that her mother said, "No, there will be no hoochie-coochie dancers in the family!" They remember how she met my father at a dance at the Savoy Ballroom in Harlem, and how he sauntered over to her with his address book out, even though she was with a date. They know that before my mother wrote books with my father, she was an adored elementary school teacher. I still occasionally have her former students see my name in print and reach out to me asking if I'm her daughter, and share sweet stories about her.

They know that their grandfather loved playing stickball on St. Nicholas Avenue in Harlem and how he cried when his beloved "bat" Betsy accidentally fell into a sewer. They've heard the story of how he and his cousin Irving hated summer camp so much that they tried to hitchhike their way over seventy miles back to Manhattan but were picked up on the highway by a state trooper. They understand that despite the racism that he endured, their grandfather grew up to be one of the first Black sportscasters in the country with his own radio show. They comprehend that he was beloved by many, because once people find out who their grandfather was, they share a story about listening to him on the radio or meeting him in person, and what that meant to them.

Talking about my parents is like sprinkling a little handful of fairy dust that brings them back to life for a few moments. I'm a big believer in celebrating my parents' birthdays every year. I make their favorite meal and pour them a drink (vodka and tonic for her, rum and Coke for him), but really, it's just another excuse to talk about them and have a good laugh or a cry and repeat our favorite stories about them. Usually both. It is a ritual so normalized in my family that my daughter assumed everyone did it.

For me, the best stories help capture the essence of a person: What made them laugh? What got them riled up? They offer a glimpse into what made them tick. They add color and vibrancy to the picture of someone who is no longer physically here, and they keep their memory alive.

I'd like to think that when I'm gone (hopefully a long time from now!), my kids will remember my birthday, have a cocktail, and share their favorite stories about me. That's how I'd like to stick around.

STORIES IN THE WORLD

The year 1982 was the first time a U.S. president (Ronald Reagan) invited notable, but not necessarily famous, people to the State of the Union address. During the speech, he'd call them out and tell little stories about their situations, their personal successes, or their needs. This practice was adopted by all the presidents going forward because it makes for effective, impactful communication. It's one thing to say, "My policies help people" or "We are in dire need of a new initiative," but the human stories tell it large. A story exemplifies what has been accomplished or what needs doing far better than any statistics.

Presidents tell personal stories about others because they are the most direct and critical path to the human heart and mind. What was once "other" in the audience's mind now becomes familiar and recognized. Story is the tool that helps us see *behind* the too-complicated (or too-sensitive) issues.

Leaders from Ruth Bader Ginsburg to Malala Yousafzai, from Martin Luther King, Jr., to Greta Thunberg, from Mahatma Gandhi to Colin Kaepernick, have all harnessed the power of their personal stories to amplify the shared experience of a larger community, a nation, or a people—all as a means of calling people to action and driving monumental change.

Moth stories have been told on the floor of the United Nations, in front of presidents, and to members of Parliament. They've been told on buses and trains, matatus and rickshaws, in line at the grocery store, and behind podiums to present the findings of elaborate (and complicated) research studies. They've been told on elevators, on family farms, to strangers, straphangers, and lawmakers. And what have all these scenarios shown us? Well-told stories have the power to make significant change on a global scale.

SARAH LEE NAKINTU, MOTH STORYTELLER: I told my story to the European Parliament in Brussels, Belgium—and they committed to considering a new budget for more investment in sexual and reproductive health for youths, and access to services that will enable them to make informed decisions about their lives.

Not all of us will bear the mantle of history, or even have the opportunity to run for student council, but strong storytelling skills can (and will!) transform individuals, build communities, and change worlds, however big or small.

ADELLE ONYANGO: The Moth helped me confront aspects of grieving my mother, and it showed me the power of storytelling— a power that I then decided to use to amplify Africans' stories. I built my podcast, *Legally Clueless,* to give Africans agency over their stories and to help us learn about each other through storytelling.

STORIES IN COMMUNITY

In 2008, The Moth was asked by the U.S. State Department to direct a storytelling show in Dushanbe, Tajikistan. As the show began, our team and state department contact looked out at the crowd nervously. Half the audience was wearing Western clothing and the other half traditional Tajik tunics and dresses with colorful headscarves. It had been ten years since their civil war had ended, but few people ever talked about the war. Music professor Anoid Latipovna Rakhmatyllaeva stepped onto a delicate old wooden stage covered in gorgeous carpets and shared her story about raising her children by herself during the war because her husband had been kidnapped and forced into the army. She told of nervously standing down soldiers with machine guns and machetes to prevent them from destroying the instruments at the college. She decided to play the *Moonlight* Sonata for the soldiers, and they were transfixed and agreed to leave in peace. At the end, Anoid had the entire crowd raise their voices together and recite a famous Tajik poem about how the people will go on. Later, over dinner, Anoid and her friends and family said the past ten years had passed in silence. No one in the community felt they could talk openly about what they had experienced. To tell her true story, and be heard by the audience, felt like a breakthrough.

Telling our stories and listening to the stories of other people reminds us that we're in this together. We are all making our way through a world that is sometimes joyful, oftentimes embarrassing, and never, ever perfect.

STORIES FOR ADVOCACY

Some storytellers endeavor to use their voice for advocacy and raise awareness around global health and human rights. People want to stand up and be heard, and use story as a tool to deliberately change the world to be healthier and more equitable. Stories reframe our worldviews. They debunk preconceived notions and challenge long-held traditional beliefs.

We met Nkem Osian through our work with Voices of Periods, a storytelling initiative launched by HealthyWomen and Myovant Sciences whose mission is to elevate conversations about menstrual health. Nkem was raised in a Nigerian household where talking about anything "below the belt" was taboo. For years she hid her heavy bleeding. One day at church, her sister looked over and noticed that Nkem's gums were white. She was rushed to the hospital, where her doctor took her vitals and told her they were "not conducive to life." She was diagnosed with fibroids, which she only then learned her mother also lives with. Despite her mother's objections, she shares this story now as part of her work advocating for funding and research, and says, "It's really liberating. Why keep this struggle to myself when I can help other women sharing this struggle? I can let them know through my knowledge what I've gone through and my challenges. I can't keep this information to myself. I find that so selfish."

Most storytellers say that while it can be challenging to share a personal story, they felt it was truly important to do so. And it *is* important. To own your story is to take back the power—and challenge dominant and sometimes false (or even deadly) narratives.

In "Go Back and Tell," writer, poet, and activist Hannah Drake shared a sweeping story about racial tensions in America, framed by her eye-opening trip to the Door of No Return in Senegal and a heartbreaking visit to a plantation in Mississippi. It's a powerful story, and a difficult one to hear—and sometimes to tell—but Hannah was up for the challenge.

We asked her what the experience was like, and she talked about the subject of her most requested poem, "Spaces." She said, "Many of us are called to be space makers. We're there for a reason. That's why I stand in these spaces, even when it makes me uncomfortable. I know I'm making space for people that will come behind me."

SISONKE MSIMANG, MOTH HOST AND STORYTELLER: Bearing witness is a form of action. It's sometimes the single most important thing that we can do in order to fix everything within us that is broken.

Stories are told in courtrooms, and in protests, and to shine a light on inequities. Over the years, we've taught storytelling workshops with communities of all sorts: the Innocence Project, LGBTQ alliances, and veterans' groups, just to name a few. The Innocence Project, which works to exonerate the wrongfully imprisoned, is our longest-standing workshop partner. The Legal Aid Society, Trial Lawyers College, and other legal groups use tools of storytelling in legal proceedings.

Stories can be used to influence policy—nationally, locally, and globally—and can show us that what we *think* we see is not all there is to be seen. Stories take you and your audience from binary thinking into something more complex. Hearing one person's lived experience has the power to dismantle a previously held belief.

We've read studies on the devastating effects of climate change, but when Hannah Morris shared her story "Counting Down the Tides," about working on an archeological site at Mission Santa Catalina de Guale, on an island off the coast of Georgia, we *felt* the impact. Hannah described doing what she called "archeological triage." They were trying to protect the sixteenth-century Spanish mission, where 2,432 people were buried, from the rising tide.

I found myself knee-deep in water, covered in sand, holding a floodlight. And we were working into the night, because we didn't know what would be left of this site in the morning when the tide went out. Like any research project, we only have so much time and money, and we had been counting down not the days we had left on this dig, but the tides. We have three tides left. We have two tides left. And this night we had no tides left. This was it. The monster was in the water with me that night. It was coming

*in with this tide and swimming around my feet. And it was telling
me exactly what the consequences of climate change would be.*

How different would the conversation about a global issue be if
you could hear from someone who actually lived it?

Studying infectious disease? Listen to a story from a person who
had to keep vaccines cold while delivering them to rural communities in the summer.

Discussing natural resources? Hear from a young scientist who,
against all odds, helped marine life thrive in Bali by designing a
"fish bank" with local fishermen.

Considering the factors of economic mobility? Hear a woman's
story of choosing to leave paid work in order to care for her ailing
husband.

Recognizing gender inequities? Listen to a story in which a
woman in Cameroon attempts to publish her first novel.

Debating the American justice system? Go on a journey with a
just-paroled man, navigating the subway for the first time, alone, on
his first day out of prison, trying to get home before curfew.

If you are using a story as a tool for advocacy, you generally
don't have five full minutes of uninterrupted attention. You probably have only a minute or two, so what can you do in that time?

- **FIND THE MAIN EVENT.** What is the *big* scene that your whole
  story is leading up to? Shrink-wrap it. Can you tell this
  scene in one minute? Now what are the two or three things
  your audience *must* know for this event to make sense?
- **TO WHOM WILL YOU TELL THIS?** Are you telling your story to
  teenagers? Fathers? Nurses? A broad audience? Point out the
  details and context that will help *them* relate. Remember,
  the same basic plot and arc can be told from many angles.
- **ADD THOSE DATA POINTS!** Well-placed story-related facts
  and figures help to paint a picture. "One hundred percent
  of Chicago's Urban Prep Academy graduates—all Black
  males—have been admitted to college." Too much data may

weigh the story down, but a well-placed point or two can raise awareness of the greater situation at hand.

- **ADD A CALL TO ACTION AT THE END.** Your story is your platform! Point people in the direction you want them to go. Sign this petition; vote for gender equality; invest in small businesses. The sense of community will motivate the audience to learn more. Make the most of that.

What if one person was moved by your story? Now imagine what happens when you bring ten people together to hear it. Stories spark conversation. You begin to sow the seeds of a community, forging lasting bonds and mutual understanding.

Now envision telling it to a thousand people. What will they do with the story? Who will they tell it to? Imagine the ripple effect.

Pamela Yates told a Moth story about the making of her documentary about the civil war in Guatemala, *When the Mountains Tremble*. As she filmed, she was struck by the bravery she witnessed. At the end of her story, she says, "I always remember what the Guatemalan Mayans said to me. When I asked them why they risked their lives for a just society, they'd answered, *'Quiero poner mi granito de arena.'* I just want to add my tiny grain of sand."

By finding the courage to tell your own story, you're adding your own grain of sand to the world. Sometimes that grain of sand can start a movement.

CHAPTER 12

LISTENING

Our philosophy at The Moth is that communities can be made better if we listen.

—JAY ALLISON, PRODUCER, *THE MOTH RADIO HOUR*

On a hot morning in Naivasha, Kenya, twelve people pulled up to a hotel in a bus. It was the day before a Moth Global Community workshop was to begin, and these twelve strangers (many of whom had just flown in from different countries) were about to spend the next three days telling personal stories together. The Moth workshop was for religious leaders who wanted to use storytelling for advocacy in their communities—and from that bus stepped twelve people wearing hijabs and habits, cassocks and other vestments. It sounds like a setup for a joke: "A nun, an imam, and a rabbi walked into a Moth workshop . . ." They were ready to craft and refine their *own* stories but also to *listen* to fellow leaders from different faiths tell theirs. There is no punchline, but these very different religious leaders found lots of common ground (and laughter!) through their personal stories of family, friendship, and love.

Our opinions, reactions, upbringing, and culture might be different, but we all know what it feels like to be filled with excitement or leveled by disappointment, to have dreams for our future and regrets from our past. As we listen to the stories of others, we may wish for the opportunity to do better, to be better. What will you discover when you take the time to listen?

Almost everyone who is great at anything learned from folks before them. Great musicians have listened to thousands of hours of music; great novelists have read great books.

You learn by listening. As you work on *your* story, immerse yourself in the stories of others. (For starters, The Moth has thousands on our website!) Note what you love. Note what works. Note what isn't for you *at all*. Some of the stories you love might stray from the suggestions we make. Some may follow them exactly but still not land right for your ears.

Great storytellers notice the turn of phrase, the beautiful wrap-up, the blistering detail that draws the picture. Follow the path of the stories that have moved you.

STORIES AS ANTIDOTE

There are multiple ways listening to stories can help others. You can "prescribe" stories to friends and family, depending on what they're going through. If someone is struggling with self-doubt, what if they listen to stories of Nobel laureates and athletes who also worried that they'd never succeed? Is your sister convinced she won't find love again after fifty? What if she listened to these stories where people find true love later in life?

There are stories for hope. Stories to bring us out of sadness. Stories to expand our idea of what is possible and to help us feel we are not alone. They can make us sit still and take it in.

JENIFER: One evening, our neighbor Patty told me that she was upset. Her twenty-year-old daughter had recently shared that she was gay and then added that she wanted to bring her girlfriend to their family Thanksgiving. Patty said, "I had absolutely no idea.

And I'm not ready. I know I have to get there, that I can't change things, but I'm finding it very hard. I don't want the girl to come to our Thanksgiving. I'm a terrible person." I had so many questions, but I tamped down what would have been an unsolicited fire hose of advice and quietly listened. I acknowledged that, yes, "you might need a little time to process." I highlighted that it was good that her daughter was finally sharing this very vital part of herself and left it there. After she left, I remembered two Moth SLAM stories about people who came out to family members who were not exactly supportive or accepting at first (Catherine Smyka's "My Grandmother's Nerve" and Tara Clancy's "Cops and Cuckoo Clocks"). I forwarded the links and casually suggested she listen. In effect, I prescribed these two stories, both of which have a lot of heart and happen to be funny.

Two days later, Patty said she loved the stories and that she thought about it, and, although she still wasn't 100 percent comfortable, she told her daughter she could extend the Thanksgiving invitation to her girlfriend. Did those two stories change everything? Definitely not—there were still many hurdles. But that Thanksgiving, the gravy was passed, the pumpkin pie was devoured, and brand-new stories were born.

We've received many emails from people asking us to thank a storyteller—and they usually include wording like "I never understood" or "I never knew." Hearing someone's experience opened a window for them and allowed them to empathize and see something from a new perspective.

Danusia Trevino shared a story about a trial in New York City and the quick assumptions she made about her fellow jurors' capacity for compassion. Ultimately their kindness toward her helped her make the right decision in the case. The story "Guilty" aired on *The Moth Radio Hour,* and she's received many fan letters. Here's one:

I work at an automotive parts store here and deliver car parts to local auto shops. Today while I was driving a route, I was flipping through the radio stations because the music started to become monotone and bland due to the overpowering depression. Anyways, I came across your lovely voice and decided to stop browsing as I heard laughter from an audience. As I listened to your jury duty story, I became so drawn to the story that I wanted to pull my truck off to the side of the road and just listen. Your story touched my heart on many different levels and I felt joy and hope. I have never been one to show emotion and I'm supposed to be a "tough guy" Marine, but I was on the verge of tears. Your story has also inspired me to have an open mind as well as an open heart. I am again, just so grateful that your story reached me out here in the middle of nowhere to lift my spirit.

STORIES EVOKE REFLECTION

The smallest details in a story can conjure specific memories, shift your perspective entirely, or help you see another person's life in a revolutionary new light. Cheech Marin told a story about moving to Canada to avoid being drafted into the Vietnam War. When describing the final scene, the moment he saw his father for the first time after the war, a high-pitched sound escaped from his throat. After the show, an audience member told us that he burst into tears upon hearing this sound. He said the sound comes out when you tighten your larynx so you won't cry. He said that crying wasn't accepted in his household—and he makes the same sound. He had tears in his eyes, because Cheech was audibly reflecting his same emotional experience growing up. One sound summed up a specific and shared childhood.

In "Making Moves," chess grandmaster Maurice Ashley tells a story about growing up in Jamaica and his expectations of what America was going to be like when he finally arrived.

> *I could see my friends were green with envy, because America was the land of promise. And the only thing we knew about America*

was what we saw on television, so it was The Partridge Family. *I was going to go to America and be like Danny Partridge, or
Arnold and Willis on* Diff'rent Strokes, *and we were going to
live in a penthouse with a pool on the roof. We got in the plane,
and we finally were over the lights of New York City. Got in the
car, and something was different about this version of America.
We thought the streets would be paved with gold.*

Marina Klutse, The Moth's director of finance and administra-
tion, interviewed Maurice for *The Moth* podcast. In the episode, she
said:

*Listening to Maurice's story made me feel so seen. When I was
two, my older siblings and I were sent to live with our grandparents
in Ghana, while our dad stayed behind in the U.S. Before the start
of the school year, we would happily open boxes from our father that
had fancy American sneakers that lit up, bedazzled clothes (before
"bedazzle" was a thing), notebooks, stickers, and other accesso-
ries. Things that would pretty much read "I have family in America." Yup, that was us, the American kids in Ghana. Just like
Maurice, these boxes filled us with joy and fostered an idealized
image of America. My dreams of living in America didn't include
a penthouse with a pool on the roof. But they did include a purple
TV, my own room with purple decor in a big fancy house. Everything would sparkle, glimmer, and we would live happily ever
after. A few months shy of my ninth birthday, I was told that we
were returning to the U.S. When the day came, I remember getting on the plane with my father and three siblings. I beamed like I
knew something sunnier was on the other side for us. My mind was
racing with visions of the American Dream. But, when I did get
here, life was not as expected. Maurice and I connected over our
stories, but we were also able to recognize some of our differences.
Which reminded me that no two journeys are alike, that our stories
are unique, complex, and nuanced, but we can often find pieces of
ourselves in the reflection of others.*

These connections are powerful for the listener but also for the teller, who, prior to sharing their story, might have thought their experience was inconsequential, only to find a community of people who may have experienced or felt something similar. Suddenly they feel validated and not so alone in the world. They feel stronger as a result.

Your audience wonders: How is my life similar to or different from the experience of this person? What else have I misunderstood about the world? How did I never consider this before?

Samuel James told his story "Jenny" to a sold-out audience at the State Theatre in Portland, Maine. In his story, he described growing up in social services—living with a series of foster parents and in shelters until a friend's parents opened their home to him.

After he told his story that evening, the cast was sitting around the table at the post-show dinner, reeling from the adrenaline of a successful night. Samuel looked at his phone and suddenly his expression changed. A woman who had been in the audience found him on the internet and emailed to say thank you. She said she had learned earlier that evening that her son's fifteen-year-old friend was being placed in the foster system. Her first instinct was that her family could take him in, but then immediately she started to question herself: her ability as a parent, whether they had the resources to care for him properly. But after hearing Samuel's story she decided that she would put herself forward for this kid. Because Samuel was brave, they felt they could be brave too. The magnitude of knowing that his story might change the course of a boy's life left everyone at the table speechless.

Being courageous enough to share a story is powerful only if there is someone brave enough to listen with an open heart and mind. The simple act of listening forges unlikely bonds. It's been our honor to witness people who should be in deep, irrevocable conflict come together once they understand each other's stories. In Hector Black's "Forgiveness," he comes to make peace with the man who murdered his daughter once he hears the story of the man's childhood.

I wanted to know who he was. I wanted to know what had hap-
pened to him that made it possible for him to do such a deed. My
first reaction was that he was a monster, he was no human being,
he deserved no compassion from me. But little by little, I learned a
bit about his life. That he was born in a mental hospital. When
he was eleven years old, his mother took him and his younger
brother and little sister to a swimming pool, saying God was ask-
ing her to drown them as enemies of God. He and his little brother
got away, and stood there while she drowned his little sister in
front of them. I couldn't help thinking that here we are, the richest
country the world has ever known, the most powerful, and there
was no one for this little boy. What would I be like if the woman
who brought me into the world had tried to destroy my life? It
wasn't that I was trying to excuse what he had done, but I felt for
him as another human being, suffering.

This man, Ivan Simpson, is eventually tried and found guilty, and Hector meets him in court.

I turned around and faced him. I said, "I wish all of us who had
been so wounded by this crime might find God's peace. And I wish
this for you also, Ivan Simpson," and our eyes met for the first time.
The tears were streaming down his cheeks. I'll never forget the
look. It was like a soul in hell. They were going to lead him away,
knowing he'd die in jail. He asked to come to the microphone, and
twice, with the tears streaming down his cheeks, he said, "I'm so
sorry for the pain I have caused, I'm so sorry for the pain I've
caused." That night I couldn't sleep. I kept thinking about this.
He had nothing, and he'd given me the only thing he had. He
could've said, "To hell with all of you, my life is over," but he
didn't. I knew then that I had forgiven him. I felt a peace that I
hadn't had in a long time. And I felt a great burden lifted from me.

At the core, stories remind us that there is always the potential for people to care and for people to change.

. . .

The Moth was conceived from one person's idea—but it was birthed and cared for and struggled with and cried over and loved and grown by many people's sweat, determination, and care. It went through growing pains and growth spurts, aced tests, and had its heart broken (more than once). It started with one story, but it is now an international community where more than fifty thousand storytellers have shared their stories.

It is no exaggeration to say that The Moth exists and thrives thanks to the contributions of millions—and many of those millions are listeners. The act of sharing a story is courageous, but the act of listening to personal stories is just as important. It is an act of generosity—a gift you give not just to the storyteller but also to your entire community.

In honor and celebration of The Moth's many decades of life, our hope is that you will take these skills and use stories to find common ground, create a dialogue, and encourage others to share their stories as well.

You are a multitude of stories, and those stories are part of our shared world.

Your stories matter. Tell them. We're listening.

AFTERWORD

The world today can sometimes seem as strange as Alice's Wonderland—where we debate even the most fundamental questions of what is fake and what is real. But in all of this confusion, there is one thing we can count on for certain, and that is the truth of our own stories and the validity of our own experiences. They are ours to know and feel and share.

Now it's your turn to share yours! This is an invitation to step into the limelight. You've got this. We know your inner storyteller is just waiting to be unleashed.

By crafting your story and examining the threads of your life through your own lens, with your full heart, you will connect more deeply to the moments and events that make you who you are today. The process will help you see how the joys, heartaches, and struggles fit into the larger arc of your life. Most of all, telling your story allows you to own it. It gives you permission to abandon the narratives others may have ascribed to you, cast off the harmful ones you may be telling yourself, and define your own. This is your story; only you can tell it.

Trust me! I've witnessed the magic of our artistic and workshop teams leading people through the vulnerable and delicate process of discovering and shaping their stories. I've seen time and again how people emerge from this experience feeling a renewed sense of self and reconnecting with their purpose and value. It is transformative. Now you have the wisdom of this team literally at your fingertips. I believe you will be transformed too.

So go forth and tell your story. Be courageous. Feel your worth. Share it wherever you can, whether it's on a road trip, in line at the post office, or on a Moth stage. The important thing is to let others see you—the real you. And once you do, we're certain your act of bravery will spark others to share their real selves. When they do, return the favor. Make space for them and truly listen. Watch them light up and inspire someone else to tell their story. It creates an avalanche of connection and human understanding. This is the magic dust of empathy, and it all starts with you and *your* story.

—*Sarah Haberman*
Executive Director, The Moth

ACKNOWLEDGMENTS

The Moth would like to thank:

Our storytellers and the millions of listeners around the world for your generosity of spirit.

Our founder, George Dawes Green.

Our board of directors: co-chairs Eric Green and Ari Handel, Serena Altschul, Deborah Dugan, Joan D. Firestone, Neil Gaiman, Gabrielle Glore, Adam Gopnik, Alice Gottesman, Dan Green, Courtney Holt, Lisa Hughes, Sonya Jackson, Chenjerai Kumanyika, Maybel Marte, Joanne Ramos, Melanie Shorin, and Denmark West for their extraordinary leadership and dedication.

The Moth StorySLAM community, and local producers who keep the flames lit all over the world, making homes for thousands of stories every year.

Our talented musicians, who light up the stage with their sound.

Our audio and video recordists and photographers, who capture and preserve our live shows.

Our volunteers, who have given us their late nights and early mornings for twenty-five years.

Our incomparable Moth hosts, who bring their nimble wit, emotional intelligence, and fiery energy to audiences night after night—you are our ultimate ambassadors.

Our community, corporate, and high school partners, storytellers, and instructors, who share themselves, listen with empathy, and demonstrate the power of storytelling every day.

Our collaborators, who challenge and inspire us: Jay Allison, Viki Merrick, and everyone at Atlantic Public Media and Transom, Ann Blanchard, Michael Carroll, Meryl Cooper, Katherine Handin, Carla Hendra, Kerri Hoffman and Jason Saldanha and everyone at PRX, Bonnie Levison, Alan Manevitz, Mark Oppenheimer and THREAD at Yale, Jordan Rodman, Roger Skelton, and Carmen Rita Wong.

Our partners at the Bill & Melinda Gates Foundation.

The hundreds of public radio stations around the country who air *The Moth Radio Hour,* and all of our national partners for both the Mainstage and StorySLAM series.

Our incredible donors and members, who make it all possible through their generous support.

Our gifted agent, Daniel Greenberg—thank you for your brilliance, vision, and wise candor. You convinced us years ago that The Moth could work in print, and pushed us to take it one step further this time.

And *also*: our extraordinary editor, Matt Inman, who has now carried us through this and three story collections. Thank you for your patient guidance, grace, steady editing hand, and for taking our calls even when you were working on a book with The Boss and 44.

The rest of the team at Crown—we are the luckiest: Gillian Blake, Annsley Rosner, Melissa Esner, Sierra Moon, Julie Cepler, Gwyneth Stansfield, Dyana Messina, and Alonzo Vereen.

Everyone on staff who, in addition to the authors, put their hearts and souls into advising, guiding and supporting the birth of this book. They are: Sarah Haberman, Jennifer Birmingham, Marina Klutse, Suzanne Rust, Brandon Grant, Inga Glodowski, Sarah Jane Johnson, Aldi Kaza, Patricia Ureña, Melissa Dognazzi, Larry Rosen, Michelle Jalowski, Jen Lue, Chloe Salmon, Jodi Powell, Ana Stern, Keighly Baron, Heather Colvin, Melissa Brown, Anna

Roberts, Juan Rodriguez, Ignacia Delgado, Marc Sollinger, Travis Coxson, Melissa Weisberg, Angelica Jacinto, Devan Sandiford, Amanda Garcia, Zora Shaw, Jo Chiang, Salma Ali, Neaco Fox, Nicole Sol Cruz, Vella Voynova.

And to Emily Couch, our fearless, creative, "document driving" queen of all things grammatical.

All the former staff at The Moth over the years, who helped make The Moth what it is today, including our former board, artistic and executive directors, and board chairs not previously mentioned: Kathleen Kerr, Anne Maffei, Alexander Roy, Judy Stone, Lea Thau, and Joey Xanders.

Extra special thanks to: Jennifer Echols, the women of Chief G18 and G275, Nicole James, Anya Kuznetsova, Madeline McIntosh, Molly Ringwald, Sharon Salzberg, and Krista Tippett.

And to our families, chosen and blood: Annabelle and Everett Hixson-Denniston, Nick and Greta Ericson, Lena Von Wachenfeldt, James Maurice Rogers, Barbara Parsons, Jean Mandel Frank Burns, Wayne Gay, Joshua and Harold Polenberg, the women of Straight on 'Till Morning, Cameron, Thornton, and Maureen Jenness, Jason, Fritz, and Iris Falchook, Paul Tellers and Adam Clark.

NOTES

11   *A study led by neuroscientist Uri Hasson* Greg J. Stephens, Lauren J. Silbert, and Uri Hasson. "Speaker-listener Neural Coupling Underlies Successful Communication." *Proceedings of the National Academy of Sciences* 107, no. 32 (2010): 14425–4430. doi:10.1073/pnas.1008662107.

115   *Their results, published in the October 2011 issue* Mikkel Wallentin, Andreas Højlund Nielsen, Peter Vuust, Anders Dohn, Andreas Roepstorff, and Torben Ellegaard Lund. "Amygdala and Heart Rate Variability Responses from Listening to Emotionally Intense Parts of a Story." *NeuroImage* 58, no. 3 (October 2011): 963–73. doi:10.1016/j.neuroimage.2011.06.077.

138   *"If you are afflicted with PTSD"* Diana Clark Gill. "Words Matter: Telling Your Story an Alternative to Medication for PTSD." AUSA (November 2017). www.ausa.org/articles/words-matter-telling-your-story-alternative-medication-ptsd.

213   *Scientists at Texas A&M* Marianela Dornhecker, Jamilia J. Blake, Mark Benden, Hongwei Zhao, and Monica Wendel. "The Effect of Stand-biased Desks on Academic Engagement: An Exploratory Study." *International Journal of Health Promotion and Education* 53, no. 5 (April 2015): 271–80. doi:10.1080/14635240.2015.1029641.

253   *According to* Forbes *magazine* Naz Beheshti. "10 Timely Statistics About the Connection Between Employee Engagement and Wellness." *Forbes* (January 16, 2019). www.forbes.com/sites/nazbeheshti/2019/01/16/10-timely-statistics-about-the-connection-between-employee-engagement-and-wellness/?sh=454a188f22a0.

THE MOTH PITCHLINE

We hope by this point you are considering putting all your new-found storytelling knowledge into action. Maybe telling better stories to your friends or at work is your sole aspiration, but maybe you're wondering if you have what it takes to tell it on stage.

Back in 2009, we established the Moth Pitchline at the suggestion of radio producer Jay Allison. We wanted to meet people who had stories they were itching to tell. Since then, thousands upon thousands of people, from all around the world, have called and left a two-minute pitch of a story they would like us to consider developing for our Mainstage. And we listen to them all!

We've met some amazing storytellers through the Pitchline: a luchador wrestler, a contestant on *Who Wants to Be a Millionaire,* a catwalking fashion model, an ER doctor who fled Vietnam as a child. We've heard tales of generous neighbors, awkward encounters with former U.S. presidents, terrifying home invasions, and epic mysteries solved by an unwitting sleuth. They all started with a two-minute pitch that caught our ear!

A good pitch uses all the elements of a good story. You need stakes, emotions, and an arc. It has to explore something deeper than just *this thing that happened.* For a pitch to work, you have to summarize your story in a way that illustrates that all those elements are in there waiting to be developed.

ADVICE FOR PITCHING FROM DIRECTOR CHLOE SALMON: A good pitch is deceptively difficult to pull off. Many people's first instinct is to tell us *about* the story they want to tell, to keep it vague and talk around it. For example:

"The story I want to tell you is about a time I laughed the hardest I've ever laughed. I won't go into it now, but it was a really funny event that I still think about to this day, and I'd love to tell a story about it. Call me back!"

What happens in this story? Couldn't tell you. How did the events of the story change this person? I don't know!

The best pitches are a two-minute version of the story you want to tell. Packing your whole story into two minutes is no easy feat. Here are some tricks:

- Know your arc! Beyond the events of the story, what was it really about for you? How were you changed? Challenge yourself to say it in one sentence. Once you have that sentence, use it as a lens through which you edit your pitch.
- Find your angle! Why is this a story only you can tell? Identify your personal stakes and make us see why this story matters to you. That's all we need to be on board.
- Finish the story! No cliffhangers, please. It might seem like a good way to entice us to give you a call, but the opposite is true.
- Be yourself! Moth stories are told without notes—bring that spirit to your pitch. Imagine you're telling it to us over a cup of coffee.

To pitch your two-minute story: Call, or visit themoth.org and pitch right on our website. Pitch away! We can't wait to meet you.

STORY PROMPTS

Need some more help finding your story? Here are some themes and prompts to get you started. Choose one prompt and see where it takes you. There are no wrong answers! The stories are yours!

FIRSTS

Tell us about a breakthrough moment.

Tell us about a first time that you regretted.

Tell us about a first time that changed your life.

NINE TO FIVE

Tell us about a time you worked hard and played hard.

Tell us about a time you were working for the weekend.

Tell us about a time you didn't see eye-to-eye with management.

Tell us about a time you definitely weren't being paid enough.

LOVE HURTS

Tell us about a time it was too little, too late.

Tell us about a time you had to follow your heart.

Tell us about a time you loved and lost.

CAUGHT

Tell us about a time you were busted.

Tell us about a time you wove a tangled web.

Tell us about a time your hand was in the cookie jar.

LOST AND FOUND

Tell us about a time you couldn't see what was right in front of you.

Tell us about a time you couldn't find a way out.

Tell us about a time you were reunited with something you treasure.

NOTES ON PROGRAMS

THE MOTH MAINSTAGE: Born in 1997, the Moth Mainstage is a live two-act show, featuring five tellers and a notable host sharing true personal stories without notes. Each unique night is curated and directed by The Moth's creative team. Moth Mainstages have been produced in nearly all fifty U.S. states and on five continents. (We're coming for you, South America and Antarctica!) There are more than forty Mainstages presented around the world every year. Many of the stories excerpted in this book were originally told on the Moth Mainstage, which features storytellers we have met through all of our Moth programs.

THE MOTH STORYSLAMS: The early success of our curated Moth Mainstage series inspired many people to contact the Moth office with pitches. We were flooded with calls: "I have a story!" But the tiny staff (just two full-time employees back then) wasn't able to screen and cultivate all the potential tellers. It was a beautiful problem: too many stories! So in 2000, we decided to experiment with opening the stage to anyone interested in sharing a story. The Moth StorySLAMs were born. The show was a competition, but moreover, a community where anyone could share a five-minute story.

We provided a host, the stage, a theme, the guiding principles, and picked judges from the audience to help choose a winner. Any and all were invited to sign up for the chance to tell a story, but just ten audience members were picked at random to get time on stage. Winners of each StorySLAM are invited to compete in the GrandSLAM, the ultimate storytelling competition. Based on the wild popularity of the show in NYC, we decided to branch out in 2006 and now present monthly StorySLAMs in cities across the United States and worldwide, providing thousands of opportunities for would-be storytellers each year.

THE MOTH COMMUNITY PROGRAM: From the very beginning, we recognized that stories have the potential to change lives and the power to build communities. Starting in 1999, The Moth's Community Program has developed partnerships with nonprofit organizations and cultural institutions to create workshops that empower participants to craft and share their stories. Some organizations came to us; others we sought out, hitting the pavement and knocking on doors. Not every door opened! But we were able to convince some veterans' organizations, hospitals, support groups, and community centers to let us in. After the workshops, we all felt the power of story and the shared experience—and vowed to continue.

Since then, we've had the honor of facilitating storytelling workshops with hundreds of organizations such as the Innocence Network, the Wounded Warrior Project, RESULTS, the Islamic Center at NYU, SAGE, Her Justice, the Museum of Jewish Heritage, and the Jed Foundation, among others.

The Community Program's goal is to connect across cultures and generations. We believe that people should take the lead in sharing their own stories. We aim to uplift the broadest array of voices possible, especially those voices that too often struggle to be heard. Through our workshops and live events, participants shape their life experiences into stories to share with members of their communities and beyond.

MOTHWORKS: In 2002, The Moth got a call from an agency asking us to lead a storytelling workshop. We said, "But we don't do corporate training," and they said, "But we don't want corporate training, we want great storytelling training." We were skeptical. We weren't sure that what we were doing in downtown theaters would translate to the corporate world. But their enthusiasm won us over and ultimately we agreed.

In those first workshops, we talked about storytelling and gave feedback in the same way we gave it to storytellers. To our delight, we found that our storytelling geekery fit right in.

Word spread quickly and soon a dedicated team from The Moth was traveling the world to lead workshops and host private events across industries, with the people at Nike, Google, the International Women's Forum, the U.S. State Department, Spotify, the W. K. Kellogg Foundation, Genentech, American Express, Lululemon, NBCUniversal, A&E Networks, LEGO, (RED), Cole Haan, Ogilvy & Mather, Wrigley, and more. We uncovered stories from marketers, creatives, medical professionals, financial experts, and great tech minds. Our work has been profiled in publications like *The Wall Street Journal, Fortune, Forbes, Crain's,* and *Inc.* magazine.

In our early days we were acutely aware that our goals as a creative organization might be at odds with our profit-driven clients. But as we developed our programming we realized that most of the time what we were teaching our clients practically had a larger impact culturally. We were helping them to become better communicators, to understand key principles of storytelling, while also connecting them as humans. Over and over, we heard one workshop participant tell another: "I've worked with you for years, but I've never known you until today."

Over the past twenty years, we've seen changes in the workplace that reflect social and cultural shifts. Sharing stories can be a way for employees on all levels to feel seen and heard at work and to move toward flatter hierarchies. Storytelling can be the social and emotional glue holding together morale and sense of purpose.

It's been proven to us time and again that storytelling belongs at work. We're glad we took the call.

THE MOTH PODCAST: While in Australia for a Moth Mainstage with the Perth International Arts Festival, Moth host and storyteller Dan Kennedy told former executive and creative director Lea Thau he would be interviewed by Apple about his newest book. He said, "Why don't you join me in conversation on stage and also . . . The Moth should announce that it's starting a podcast!" We had no plans for a podcast. The interview was in two weeks. But Dan's challenge inspired us! After fast strategic meetings, and with nervous excitement—we went for it. The podcast premiered in the spring of 2008 and was edited in the free software GarageBand by an intern. *The Moth* podcast now features original episodes as well as full episodes of *The Moth Radio Hour,* including stories from all of our programs. It is now downloaded more than ninety million times a year (per *Podtrack*, January 2021) and is regularly ranked in the top podcasts on iTunes. The podcast is nimble, allowing us to speak directly to our audience and reflect the world we're living in.

THE PEABODY AWARD-WINNING *THE MOTH RADIO HOUR*: When we first dreamed of The Moth on the radio, we were told again and again, "Ten-minute stories will *never* work on air!"—but after extensive meetings, we were championed by our now longtime producer Jay Allison and our friends and partners at the Public Radio Exchange (PRX). In 2009, we launched the show with five episodes and by 2013 listenership had swelled, and we nervously made the leap to weekly. *The Moth Radio Hour* is hosted by rotating members of The Moth staff and community, and features stories chosen from The Moth's live shows. *The Moth Radio Hour* is now heard on more than 570 public radio stations in the United States, as well as the BBC and outlets in Australia, Germany, and France, among other countries. It is produced by The Moth, Jay Allison, Viki Merrick, and Atlantic Public Media and is presented by PRX.

THE MOTH EDUCATION PROGRAM: When we first thought about teaching storytelling to teens, we wondered if young people had enough perspective to reflect upon their experiences through story. After our first few high school workshops, we discovered just how rich student stories could be. In 2012, we formalized The Moth Education Program in order to provide students and teachers with a forum to share personal stories with one another and then with the world.

Through afterschool and weekend workshops, students brainstorm ideas, learn storycraft, and have the opportunity to take the stage and share their stories with friends and family. The results are profound. Students connect with their own personal experiences, develop their voices, and through listening, get to know their peers in ways that they hadn't imagined before.

Sharing stories breaks down barriers. When young people listen to one another, they better understand each other's challenges, missteps, joys, and triumphs. What is meaningful to one becomes meaningful to many. Storytelling builds empathy for others, but also for ourselves (the young people we are or once were).

To reach as many students as possible, The Moth Education Program also works with teachers, providing the tools to bring storytelling directly into their classrooms. The Moth's high school curriculum—which helps teachers help students with brainstorming and storycrafting— is available free online, for educators around the world. We also conduct workshops for fifth-to-twelfth-grade educators from across the United States, where they experience the vulnerability of developing and sharing a story in community with their fellow teachers. Often, they'll tell stories from when they were young; it's a chance to remember what it's like to be in the shoes of their students.

Having worked with thousands of young people, we've seen how storytelling workshops give youth the skills to articulate their experience, empathize with others, and strengthen their confidence.

THE MOTH'S GLOBAL COMMUNITY PROGRAM started in 2014 thanks to a call from the Bill & Melinda Gates Foundation inviting us to work with health experts from the global south—the recipients of the Aspen Institute New Voices Fellowship. "We want to help the fellows with their advocacy work. Maybe you can adapt your Community Program model? Design workshops to strengthen the fellows' personal storytelling skills?" Brilliant! We said yes.

Since that first workshop outside of Nairobi, Kenya, we've adapted our curriculum again (and again!) to create intensive cross-cultural workshops that are taught with a core of instructors who hail from Kenya, India, and Uganda, among other countries. Instructors are graduates of Moth workshops and are ambassadors of the program, modeling ways in which stories can move the needle, or start a movement.

Over the years we've been honored to continue our partnership with the Aspen Institute and the Bill & Melinda Gates Foundation and to collaborate with the Ford Foundation and UN Women, among other organizations. The Moth's Global Community Program now has more than 500 graduates from over fifty countries, who use their personal stories to drive social change on a global scale. Graduates of the Global Community Program have told their stories on the floor of the UN, at the EU Summit in Brussels, started podcasts and grassroots movements, and used personal stories to reform laws.

Through the Global Community Program, we continue to develop and elevate true personal stories from extraordinary individuals in the global south. These stories spark conversations on world health issues including: agriculture and ending hunger, infectious disease prevention and education—and there is a strong overall focus on stories of women and girls. By honoring a broad range of individual experiences, we believe we can challenge dominant narratives, deepen connection, and create a more productive dialogue around the world.

INDEX

THE MOTH is an acclaimed nonprofit organization dedicated to the art and craft of storytelling. Since its launch in 1997, The Moth has presented more than fifty thousand stories and received the MacArthur Award for Creative and Effective Institutions and a Peabody Award for *The Moth Radio Hour*, which airs on more than 570 stations nationwide. *The Moth* podcast is downloaded more than ninety million times annually. **MEG BOWLES, CATHERINE BURNS, JENIFER HIXSON, SARAH AUSTIN JENNESS,** and **KATE TELLERS,** along with The Moth's artistic and workshop teams, have spent more than two decades helping people all around the world tell their true personal stories.

TheMoth.org
Facebook.com/TheMoth
Twitter: @TheMoth
Instagram: @mothstories

MEG BOWLES is a senior director and a host of the Peabody Award–winning *The Moth Radio Hour*. Signing on as a volunteer in 1997, she had no idea where The Moth would take her. Over the decades, she has directed Mainstage shows everywhere, from Anchorage to London. Although her background in television and film has served to sharpen her editorial sense and eye for detail, she is recognized for her ability to spot stories in the wild and to home in on what transforms a seemingly small story into something universal. For her part, Meg loves working with people one-on-one, witnessing and supporting their progress. She is especially excited to see people who never imagined themselves as having a story go on to proudly claim the moniker of storyteller.

CATHERINE BURNS is The Moth's longtime artistic director and a host of the Peabody Award–winning *The Moth Radio Hour.* As one of the lead directors on The Moth's Mainstage since 2003, she has helped many hundreds of people craft their stories, including a New York City sanitation worker, a Nobel Laureate, the Tower of London's Ravenmaster, a jaguar tracker, and an exonerated prisoner. She is the editor of the bestselling and critically acclaimed books *The Moth: 50 True Stories, All These Wonders,* and *Occasional Magic.* She is the director of the solo shows *The Gates* (written and performed by Adam Gopnik) and *Helen & Edgar* (written and performed by Edgar Oliver), which was called "utterly absorbing and unexpectedly moving" by Ben Brantley of *The New York Times,* and the feature film *A Pound of Flesh.* Prior to The Moth, she produced television and independent films, interviewing such talent as George Clinton, Chuck D, Ozzy Osbourne, Martha Stewart, and Howard Stern. She attended her first Moth back in 2000, fell in love with the show, and was, in turn, a GrandSLAM contestant and volunteer in the Moth Community Program before joining the staff full-time. Born and raised in Alabama, she now lives in Brooklyn with her husband and son.

Instagram: @thecatherineburns

SARAH HABERMAN (AFTERWORD) has been the executive director of The Moth since 2013, providing oversight of the organization's business and strategic development. She also supervises The Moth's Education, Community, and MothWorks programs, and launched The Moth's Global Community program in 2014 in partnership with the Bill & Melinda Gates Foundation. She has held senior management and development roles at the world's leading arts nonprofit and academic institutions including the New York Public Library, the Whitney Museum of American Art,

Columbia Business School, and Jazz at Lincoln Center. Prior to moving to New York, she was an acquiring editor in Paris for Éditions Robert Laffont, a major French publishing house. She is also a member of the board of directors for the Richard and Ethel Herzfeld Foundation in Milwaukee.

JENIFER HIXSON is a senior director and one of the hosts of the Peabody Award–winning *The Moth Radio Hour*. Each year she asks hundreds of people to identify the significant turning points of their lives—fumbles and triumphs, leaps of faith, darkest hours—and then helps them shape those experiences into story form for the stage. She falls a little bit in love with each storyteller, and hopes you will too. In 2000, she launched The Moth StorySLAM, which now has a full-time presence in twenty-five cities in the United States, the UK, and Australia and provides more than four thousand individual storytelling opportunities for storytelling daredevils and loquacious wallflowers alike. Jenifer's story "Where There's Smoke" has been featured on *The Moth Radio Hour* and *This American Life* and was a part of The Moth's first book: *The Moth: 50 True Stories*.

SARAH AUSTIN JENNESS has a loud and distinct laugh that will make you smile. She joined the staff at The Moth in 2005, and as the executive producer she has had the honor of working with many hundreds of people to craft and hone their unique personal stories. She is a Peabody Award–winning director, is one of the longstanding hosts of *The Moth Radio Hour*, oversees *The Moth* podcast, and launched The Moth's Global Community Program, designing and coaching storytelling workshops for participants in the United States, South Asia, and Africa to elevate conversation around gender equality and human rights. Moth stories Sarah has directed in the past fifteen-plus years have been told on the floor of the United Nations, at the Sundance Film Festival, on rickshaws and buses, and as far afield as the Kenya National Theatre. Elliot, Amelia, Evie, and Opal, her nephew and nieces, have given her the Best Aunt in the World Award. Sarah believes in challenging dominant narratives—and that stories change the world by creating connection.

Instagram: @sarahaustinjenness

CHENJERAI KUMANYIKA (INTRODUCTION) is a researcher, journalist, and organizer who works as an assistant professor in Rutgers University's Department of Journalism and Media Studies. His research and teaching focus on the intersections of social justice and emerging media in the cultural and creative industries. He has written about these issues in journals such as *Popular Music and Society, Popular Communication, The Routledge Companion to Advertising and Promotional Culture,* and *Technology, Pedagogy and Education.* Dr. Kumanyika is also a collaborator for Scene on Radio's Season 2, *Seeing White,* and Season 4, *The Land That Never Has Been Yet.* He is the co-executive producer and co-host of *Uncivil,* Gimlet Media's Peabody Award–winning podcast on the Civil War. He has also been a contributor to *The Intercept, Transom,* NPR's *Code Switch, All Things Considered, Invisibilia,* and *VICE,* and he is a news analyst for Rising Up Radio with Sonali Kolhatkar. As an organizer, Chenjerai is on the executive committee of 215 People's Alliance and a member of the Philadelphia Debt Collective and the Media, Inequality & Change Center.

PADMA LAKSHMI (FOREWORD) is an Emmy®-nominated food expert, television host, producer, and *New York Times* bestselling author. She is the creator, host, and executive producer of the critically acclaimed Hulu series *Taste the Nation,* nominated for a 2021 Gotham Award for Breakthrough Series. Lakshmi also serves as host and executive producer of Bravo's two-time Emmy®-winning series *Top Chef.* Lakshmi is co-founder of the Endometriosis Foundation of America and an American Civil Liberties Union Artist Ambassador for immigrants' rights and women's rights. Lakshmi was also appointed a Goodwill Ambassador for the United Nations Development Programme. She's a prolific author, including two *New York Times* bestsellers: the children's book *Tomatoes for Neela* and the memoir *Love, Loss, and What We Ate.* Additionally, she has written the *Encyclopedia of Spices and Herbs* and two cookbooks, *Easy Exotic* and *Tangy Tart Hot and Sweet.* She lives in New York with her daughter.

KATE TELLERS is a senior director, a host of The Moth's live storytelling series and podcast, a storyteller, and a director. Just a few stories into her first Moth event, fortuitously themed *Beginnings,* she knew she had found her home. Since then she's developed stories with heroes from her Pittsburgh childhood to the present day and helmed storytelling events around the world. She's designed and led storytelling programs with nonprofits, including the Bill & Melinda Gates Foundation, the Kellogg Foundation, and Ashoka, as well as Spotify, Nike, Google, and the U.S. State Department, that harness the power of storytelling as an empathetic communication tool. Her story "But Also Bring Cheese" can be heard on the Peabody Award–winning *The Moth Radio Hour* and is featured in The Moth's book *All These Wonders: True Stories about Facing the Unknown*. Her writing has appeared on *McSweeney's* and *The New Yorker*. Through it all, her love of storytelling runs deep because it gives her the phenomenal opportunity to laugh and cry with strangers. She was the intern that edited the podcast on GarageBand.

Instagram: @thekatetellers

Available from **THE MOTH**

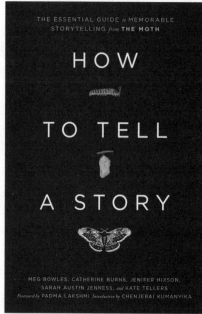

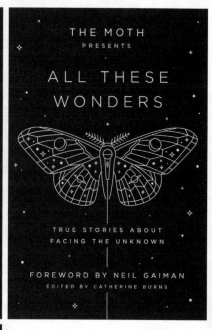

"Stories that attest to . . . the shared threads of love, loss, fear and kindness that connect us."

—MICHIKO KAKUTANI,
The New York Times

CROWN
NEW YOR